Changing Innovation in the Pharmaceutical Industry

Globalization and New Ways of Drug Development

Springer
Berlin
Heidelberg
New York
Barcelona
Hong Kong
London
Milan
Paris
Singapore
Tokyo

Andre Jungmittag · Guido Reger
Thomas Reiss (Eds.)

Changing Innovation in the Pharmaceutical Industry

Globalization and New Ways of Drug Development

With 46 Figures
and 28 Tables

 Springer

Dr. Andre Jungmittag
University of Potsdam
Economic Policy/International Economic Relations
August-Bebel-Straße 89
14482 Potsdam
Germany

Prof. Dr. Guido Reger
Fachhochschule Brandenburg
University of Applied Science
Magdeburger Straße 50
14770 Brandenburg an der Havel
Germany

Dr. Thomas Reiss
Fraunhofer Institute for Systems
and Innovation Research (ISI)
Breslauer Straße 48
76139 Karlsruhe
Germany

ISBN 3-540-67357-1 Springer-Verlag Berlin Heidelberg New York

Library of Congress Cataloging-in-Publication Data
Die Deutsche Bibliothek – CIP-Einheitsaufnahme
Changing Innovation in the Pharmaceutical Industry: Globalization and New Ways of Drug Develop-
ment; with 28 tables / Andre Jungmittag ... (ed.). – Berlin; Heidelberg; New York; Barcelona; Hong
Kong; London; Milan; Paris; Singapore; Tokyo: Springer, 2000
    ISBN 3-540-67357-1

Springer-Verlag is a company in the BertelsmannSpringer publishing group.
© Springer-Verlag Berlin · Heidelberg 2000
Printed in Germany

Hardcover-Design: Erich Kirchner, Heidelberg

SPIN 10766682   43/2202-5 4 3 2 1 0 – Printed on acid-free paper

Preface

The internationalization of research and technology is one key component of the globalization of trade and business, with potentially major impacts on patterns of economic development and public policies worldwide. Although certain aspects of this internationalization trend are well documented, and some effects can be quantified, the overall processes are extremely complex and the outcomes are highly uncertain. The existence of the phenomenon is generally accepted, but its importance and the trends are currently the topic of a lively debate.

This study on "New Ways in Drug Development in Pharmaceuticals" is part of a three year project which aims at investigating how new concepts of industrial knowledge creation are implemented in the different environments of the innovation systems of the United States and Germany. The main focus of the overall project is a series of case studies of innovation practice in different national and sectoral contexts. The following sectors and technological fields are investigated: pharmaceuticals and new ways in drug development by the Fraunhofer Institute for Systems and Innovation Research (ISI), advanced materials by the University Hohenheim, Institute of International Management and Innovation (Alexander Gerybadze), financial services and home banking by the Massachusetts Institute of Technology (MIT), Center for Industrial Performance (Richard Lester) and the Sloan School of Management (Edward Roberts). Financially the project was supported by the German-American Academic Council, the German Federal Minstry of Education, Science Research and Technology and the Fraunhofer Society. The project is linked to research in Japan (University of Tokyo and NISTEP, Ryo Hirasawa) and Australia (Australian National University, Canberra, Mark Dodgson), where case studies with overlapping questions are being conducted.

This case study impressively shows the far-reaching consequences of new ways in drug development on the research system as well as the industrial system and market structures. A new emerging modular interactive framework for innovation challenges R&D-performing actors and government policy.

Karlsruhe, February 2000   Frieder Meyer-Krahmer
                                              Director, Fraunhofer Institute for
                                              Systems and Innovation Research

Contents

List of Tables

List of Figures

1

Introduction

Andre Jungmittag, Guido Reger, Thomas Reiss

This study pays particular attention to the driving forces which are motivating changes in the innovation process, including the globalization of markets, production and technology, the accelerating pace of innovation, and the increasing need to link new innovations and technology to end-user markets. We also explored the restructuring of companies' R&D organization, as well as the division of labor between large companies and external actors, including young start-ups, public R&D institutions and universities.

1.1 New Ways in Drug Development: Changes of the Locus of Innovation

Our case study on "New Ways in Drug Development in Pharmaceuticals" followed these intentions and concentrated - in line with the overall project - on the following goals:

1. To study the processes that companies in pharmaceuticals in the United States and Germany are using to acquire technical knowledge and apply it to the development of new drugs, services or processes.

2. To understand what accounts for leadership in pharmaceuticals against the background of the changes in the innovation process, to examine whether or how this has changed over time, and to understand the causes of these changes.

3. To analyze the implications of these changes for enterprises and for the national system of innovation, especially in Germany and the US, and to develop recommendations for industrial managers, science and technology policy-makers, universities and public research institutions.

Our research on new ways in drug development started from the assumption that the innovation process in pharmaceuticals has dramatically changed since the late 1960s. The "old" way of drug development was largely based on knowledge in chemistry, and was mainly conducted in the large pharma companies. Cooperation was limited to some research projects with universities and close contacts to universities, in order to attract the best researchers/scientists. New discoveries and findings about the building blocks of life (e.g. molecular biology, biotechnology, genetics), about chemical synthesis (combinatorial chemistry), but also in information technologies or automation/robotics have resulted in a "new" way of drug development.

At the beginning of our research we assumed that many of the large pharma companies were unable to fully recognize the large potentials of these new discoveries and findings (which is expressed by "organizational inertia") or tried to "make their risks safe" by monitoring technological trends and young biotech firms (and acquiring the successful ones). New scientific findings, the innovation ideas, came out of public research institutes, universities or science-related spin-off companies and were further developed and applied for certain diseases or disease groups by young biotech start-up companies. These organizations seem to be the institutionalized "technological gatekeepers" for innovation in pharmaceuticals. Organizational inertia of the large pharma companies made the market entry of young start-up firms possible and left room for innovator strategies.

The "new" ways of drug development can be characterized not only by new findings and new technological knowledge. Important additional characteristics comprise:

- the growing significance of science for drug discovery

- inter-/multidisciplinarity and growing importance of technological knowledge outside the "traditional" sector

- the industrialization of the drug discovery process (research) itself

- occurrence of small biotech firms and a "supplier industry", e.g. in robotics/ automation, information technologies, genomics, combinatorial chemistry

- in line with the occurrence of new actors a growing "decomposition of the innovation process" and division of labor between different organizations

- the generation of new drugs abroad and far away from the headquarters.

The reason we have chosen the innovation process in pharmaceuticals for our case study was - among others - that this industry is highly internationalized. This is true for the exploitation of innovations generated in the home country (export of new drugs), the application of a global product to specific regulations in national markets (application of new drugs to national drug application procedures), cross-border technology-related cooperations/alliances and the generation of innovations in countries outside the home base. Based on other empirical research on the internationalization strategies of large companies, our assumption here was that the mode of the internationalization of R&D has changed since the 1980s.[1] If this is also true for pharmaceuticals, large pharma companies no longer just establish development units abroad to apply and introduce new drugs (developed in the home country R&D labs) into a nationally regulated market or just to scan and monitor new scientific findings. Based on our research on large companies, we assumed that large pharma companies try to tap into the worldwide leading centers where leading-edge research is done and where new drugs can be introduced best and first to the market. New here is that the innovation (new drug) is generated outside the home country and, after having learnt much from the innovative and "leading" market, is diffused - from the company's foreign "center of excellence" - to other markets. Against the background of a stronger division of labor in the drug development process, this would mean that the institutional as well as the geographical locus of the generation and implementation of the innovation is changing.

It is very interesting from a regional viewpoint to become one of the world leading centers in a certain technology or product area. R&D investment, leading researchers and companies are attracted to the region, which leads to an increase in economic wealth and improvements of social conditions in this region. Further, researchers from academia and industry are sought worldwide for R&D cooperation and partnership. Examples for such highly attractive, world leading centers in bio-pharmaceuticals are the Greater Boston area, San Diego/San Francisco or the so-called Mid-Atlantic corridor (Philadelphia-Baltimore-New York) in the United States.

R&D investments from foreign companies may not initiate, but positively reinforce the development of such a world leading center. Obviously, other institutions are necessary in a certain region, among them leading universities and teaching hospitals, excellent researchers/scientists, "entrepreneurial spirit" and the willingness to take risks, young start-up biotech and "supplier" firms and venture capital companies. The simple existence of these "players" may not be sufficient; it is necessary that these organizations have the ability to learn and cooperate and stay flexible. If a trend towards the development of a few leading centers in pharmaceuticals can be observed, the regional innovation system will be of growing importance against the background of the internationalization process.

From the viewpoint of a national innovation system or economy, this trend can be regarded from two sides. On the one hand, it is very interesting to become such a world leading center or "junction" in bio-pharmaceuticals where excellent knowledge is generated and implemented in new drugs, ser-

---

[1] See Gerybadze/Meyer-Krahmer/Reger (1997), and main results summarized in Gerybadze/Reger (1998), pp. 183-217.

vices or processes. On the other hand, a country can become less attractive, less innovative and less competitive in pharmaceuticals. R&D investment abroad may not be compensated for by R&D investment from foreign companies in the country. This would raise serious questions on the strengths of the location and the environment for innovation. Following this line of argument, we tried to describe the economic and technological position of the United States and Germany in the pharmaceutical sector in comparison with other OECD countries, and how this position has changed since the beginning of the 1980s.

1.2 Research Approach

If these arguments and linkages are to be studied - from a methodological point of view - an analysis on various levels is necessary. Therefore, we started our research at four different levels of investigation:

1. *Sector level*: we analyzed the national innovation system as well as the economic and technological development in pharmaceuticals in the US and Germany; these developments were compared with the pharmaceutical sector in other OECD countries.

2. *Level of the company*: we looked at changes of the innovation strategies of large pharma companies and young start-up bio-pharma firms with their home base in the US, Germany and other parts of western Europe; our special interest lay in the international generation of innovation and the extent and forms of cooperation between different organizations.

3. *Innovation process*: we identified the characteristics of the innovation process in pharmaceuticals and analyzed the changes of this innovation process towards a new way of drug development.

4. *Therapeutic area/disease group*: finally, we tried to track some of our findings in more detail in a specific therapeutic area/disease group and chose autoimmune diseases as an example.

We used different instruments of investigation in our research approach. While interviews can lead to deep insights in decision-making processes, strategies, intentions, and linkages between intra- and inter-organizational units, it is very difficult to show quantitative significance or trends. Therefore we complemented interview based approaches by statistics- and data-base-type analyses. Further, we implemented "learning loops" and discussed preliminary results with external researchers and experts from companies, universities, public institutions and venture capital companies. The set of the following methods for our investigation were applied in our study:

1. Review of relevant literature.

2. Development of different structured interview guidelines.

3. Conducting interviews in large pharma companies, young start-up firms, venture capital companies, public R&D institutions and universities.

4. Analysis of patent data from the European Patent Office.

5. Bibliometric analysis by using online databases.

6. Analysis of databases on the Internet.

7. Analysis of secondary statistics, especially from the OECD.

8. Visiting various conferences and discussing our preliminary results with other researchers in this field.

In the following chapter we analyze the national innovation system of the United States and Germany in the pharmaceutical sector and describe the main actors in each system. Chapter 3 shows the economic and technological trends of the US and German pharma sector since the 1980s and compares these developments with other OECD countries. The characteristics of the innovation process and the techno-scientific changes which influence the changes of the "old" innovation process are described in chapter 4. Chapter 5 deals with the generation, transfer and exploitation of new knowledge and the occurrence of new actors and a new distribution of roles. Internationalization strategies in the generation of innovation and the driving forces are analyzed in chapter 6. A detailed case study on new therapies for selected autoimmune diseases as an example of a specific therapeutic area is presented in chapter 7. In chapter 8 we draw conclusions from our observations for companies' managers, policy-makers in the area of science and technology, public R&D institutes and universities.

2

The National System of Innovation in the United States and Germany

Andre Jungmittag

2.1 The Concept of the "Systems of Innovation" Approach

One key insight of modern innovation theory is that innovations, which are defined here as novelties of economic value, are created systematically. The creation of new knowledge and new technologies occur as an interactive and collective process involving interdependent agents as well as institutions. The processes on which innovations are based are still exceedingly complex and encompass not only the generation, diffusion and combination of elements of knowledge, but also their transformation into new products and production processes.[1] This supersedes the traditional linear model of innovation, in which a sequential transmission of new knowledge, from basic research via applied research up to development and introduction of new products and processes is assumed. Rather, innovation processes are characterized by various feedback mechanisms and interactive relationships, in which science, technology, learning processes, production, demand, organizations, institutions and politics act together. This perspective forms the conceptual basis which underlies the "systems of innovation" approach.

One variety of the "systems of innovation" approach, the concept of the national systems of innovation, was introduced almost concurrently by Freeman (1988) and Nelson (1987). Whilst these studies were highly empirical in character, Lundvall (1992) provided a theoretically oriented foundation for this concept. His aim was to show that it is necessary to create an alternative to the economic theory in the neoclassical tradition, in which interactive learning and innovations occupy centre stage (Lundvall, 1992, p. 1).[2] The tailoring of the approach to the national state is justified in that even in times of increasing globalization, national systems play an important role in the promotion and controlling of innovation and learning processes because of the character or types of knowledge. Knowledge has in many cases the character of a quasi-public good. Innovation pro-

---

[1] Cf. Edquist et al. (1998), p. 18.

[2] A historical overview of the concept of the national innovation system can be found in Edquist (1997).

cesses are often very complex, formed by experiences or "tacit" and only very slightly codified knowledge.[3] Under these conditions the common national environment of the actors facilitates interactive learning and innovation processes, because of shared norms and cultural background/customs (Lundvall, 1992, pp. 3-4). However, a number of alternative approaches were suggested, which either take observed regionalization tendencies into account and favorize a regional limitation of innovation systems (e.g. Saxenian, 1994)), or place the global character in the generic technologies (such as e.g. pharmaceuticals, biotechnology, microelectronics, but also aircraft) in the forefront and attach greater importance to technological or sectoral innovation systems (e.g. Carlsson, 1997).[4] As regionalization and globalization are two sides of one and the same coin, the transitions between the various approaches to limit the innovation systems are not clearly cut. Thus the term "regional" can refer to a region within a state or to parts of different states (then they are usually bound up with one technology), or to supranational entities, such as the European Union. Along the same lines, Carlsson/Stankiewicz (1995, p. 49) established for the concept of technological innovation systems that these systems are often limited by the boundaries of national states, or can be regarded as regional or local technological systems. Other technological systems on the other hand are international or even global. The setting of geographical boundaries depends finally on the technological and market requirements, the capabilities of the various actors and the degree of dependencies between them.[5] But the representatives of the concept of national innovation systems also perceive the challenges which increasing internationalization poses for the traditionally rather nation-oriented innovation systems. But it is even more urgent to understand the functioning of these national systems (Lundvall, 1992, p. 4). At the same time the concept must be kept as open as possible and it must take the heterogeneity of various innovation systems into consideration, in order to be able to take up these developments. For most empirical studies it may be a useful starting point to adapt the argument in Gregersen/Johnson (1997), that the concepts of territorially and technologically based innovation systems should be regarded as complements rather than substitutes.

---

[3] A knowledge classification oriented to the public good theory of science and technology can be found in Grupp (1997), pp. 319-320.

[4] In the approach to technological innovation systems which has been essentially influenced by Carlsson, the generic technologies are the focus of attention. They can, but must not, be limited to one industrial branch. On the other hand, Breschi/Malerba (1996), as well as Malerba/Orsenigo (1990), (1993) and (1995) explicitly take sectoral innovation systems as their starting point. With this approach it is assumed that the individual industrial branches work under different technological regimes which are characterized by specific combinations of possibilities, by appropriation capabilities, degrees of accumulation of technological knowledge and features of the relevant knowledge base.

[5] A very similar argumentation can be found in Nelson/Rosenberg (1993), p. 5.

In principle, either a narrow or a broader viewpoint can be chosen for the definition of innovation systems. In a definition in the narrower sense, an innovation system encompasses those organizations and institutions which participate directly in the search and research process (R&D departments of enterprises, research institutes and universities), or which have direct influence on this process (for example, rules for research promotion). In a definition in the wider sense which does justice to the theoretically based fact that the creation of new knowledge is an interactive and collective process, all those areas and aspects of the economic and institutional structure are to be considered, which affect not only learning but also search and research processes. Accordingly, production, marketing and the financial system are sub-systems in which learning processes take place (Lundvall, 1992, p. 12). The differentiation between organizations and institutions is common to all definitions of innovation systems. Organizations are the actors (or in more modern terms: the players) in innovation processes. They are deliberately created, formal structures with an explicit task (Edquist et al., 1998, p. 18). Besides innovative enterprises, this means all facilities with which these enterprises interact in order to gain, develop and exchange knowledge, information and other resources. These can be other enterprises (customers, suppliers as well as competitors), but also other organizations, like universities, research institutes, financing agencies, schools, government bodies, etc. There is contact between enterprises not only via the market place, but also through longer-term cooperative alliances, because in innovation processes strong linkages between the users and producers of new technologies are often necessary. Questions about the organizations which are raised when analyzing innovations systems are:

- As regards innovations, how is the performance of enterprises and other organizations concerned?

- Is the support from public facilities appropriate?

- Do the organizations responsible for technical support function adequately?

- Do the organizations react adequately to structural changes, respectively do they re-group successfully to cope with such challenges?[6]

Institutions, on the other hand, are the rules of the game the actors have to play by. In other words, the organizations interact within an institutional structure of laws, social and cultural rules and norms, practices, customs and routines, as well as technical standards. A number of institutions have been deliberately created, whereas others have developed, more or less spontaneously, over longer periods of time. The social and cultural

---

[6] Cf. Edquist et al. (1998), pp. 18-19 on these questions.

context also belongs to the institutions which influence the behavior of enterprises. These environmental conditions are often seen as specific to local, regional or national geographical entities. On the other hand, they also alter under new political conditions, changed technological situations, or for example, through economic integration processes.[7]

The central question which arises concerning the institutions (or institutional structures) when analyzing innovation systems, is, whether they are adequate to the task of promoting innovations. In a dynamic perspective the question is how institutions must be altered or newly created in order to encourage innovations. In particular, it must be examined whether the incentives for innovations are sufficiently strong. The fact must also be taken into consideration, that through the change or new creation of institutional rules, changes in the entire innovation system can be triggered off.[8] Among the great variety of institutions, those that have been set up by public agencies are the ones that can be deliberately used as policy instruments. Other institutions which have evolved spontaneously over longer periods of time often cannot be directly influenced by policy actors.

Fundamental to all analyses of innovation systems, however, is the consideration of interactive and collective (learning) processes on which they are based. Only if organizations and institutions are considered as a whole, the mode of functioning and the efficiency of different innovation systems can be judged. An overview of these interactions and the feedbacks on the collective learning processes and the innovative performance is depicted in figure 2.1. This systemic character also implies that innovation systems with very differently designed organizations and institutions can lead to similar innovation successes or to similar economic welfare. Conversely, it also implies that the transfer of individual elements from successfully operating innovation systems must not lead inevitably to improvements in the performance of less successfully operating innovation systems, because the ability to adapt can be missing from the configuration of the latter system. An efficient innovation policy must also regard the system as a whole and not tend towards the optimization of single elements. Especially if the definition of innovation systems in the wider sense is being used, then innovation policy can no longer be limited to one department, but must be an integral component at least of general economic policy, but also of other policy areas, such as e.g. education policy.

---

[7] The question of how European integration will affect the national innovation systems is discussed by Gregerson/Johnson (1997). Using the concept of the "learning economy" as an analytical framework, the hypothesis is derived that European integration will not abolish the national innovation systems in Europe, and that in the near future only a very limited European innovation system in the narrower sense will evolve.

[8] A detailed discussion of the nature and mode of operation of institutions can be found in Edquist (1997), pp. 24-25, and Edquist et al. (1998), p. 19.

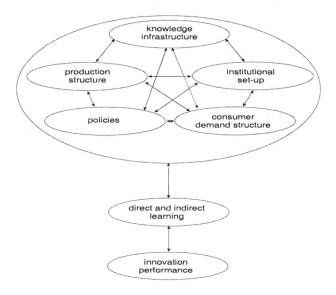

Source: Gregerson/Johnson (1997), p. 484

FIGURE 2.1. Systemic structure of innovation systems

The differentiation between the elements of innovation systems in Lundvall (1992), p. 13, derived from the theoretical definitions, is a good starting point for empirical studies of innovation systems. According to this, the significant elements, besides the general production system and institutional structure, in which national historic differences and specific characteristics are reflected, are:

- the internal organization of the enterprises,

- the relations between the enterprises,

- the role of the public sector,

- the institutional structure of the financing sector,

- the R&D intensity and the R&D organization.

Even if the national innovation systems as a whole have not been compared in the present case study, but taking the pharmaceutical industry and its new ways of developing medicines as an example, the consequences of international changes in industrial innovations for the research system - especially in the comparison between Germany and the US - should be analyzed, in an empirical survey the sequential working through the elements of innovation systems suggests itself, which correspond more or less to those mentioned above. As the pharmaceutical industry is internationalized to a high degree, it remains open at the beginning of the survey, whether the concept of the national innovation system is acceptable for this branch of industry, or whether, freed from national roots and specific characteristics, the concept of technological or sectoral innovation systems will increasingly prevail. Inasmuch, the survey is lead by an eclectic innovation system approach. All the same, this cannot be interpreted as a lack of theoretical foundations, as, on the one hand, the firm upholders of the concept of national innovation systems admit that the definition of an innovation system must be kept open up to a certain degree and flexible as regards the subsystems to be included and the processes to be examined, so that one single approach to the national innovation system cannot be the only legitimate one (Lundvall, 1992, p. 13). On the other hand, the supporters of the technological systems approach realize that this too can have regional or national boundaries (Carlsson/Stankiewicz, 1995, p. 49).

2.2   Systems of Innovation in the German and US Pharmaceutical Sector

Although in the framework of this case study a comparison of the sector-specific characteristics of the innovation systems in Germany and the US is the main focus of interest, it is helpful to sketch out some general differences which characterize the German and the US innovation systems before entering into the more disaggregated analysis. As far as possible, the direct, if only exemplary relevance for the pharmaceutical sector, especially for the sector pharmaceutical biotechnology, which is gaining increasingly in significance for the development of new active substances, will be shown. Directly following, the innovation systems in the narrower sense of the pharmaceutical sectors of both countries will be outlined very roughly. Many of the aspects mentioned here will be taken up again in the following chapters in depth.

2.2.1   Some General Characteristics of the National Innovation Systems of Germany and the US

If one wants to roughly characterize the different economic constitutions of the US and Germany, then the US can be described as a liberal market economy, while for Germany the label "coordinated market economy" (Soskice, 1994) or "consensus-oriented market economy" apply. These two market systems exhibit a number of fundamental differences in their institutional framework conditions. These differences in individual subsystems are shortly outlined in the following.[9]

In the area of *industrial relations*, we deal first with wage negotiations and the relations between employers and employees. In Germany, employers' associations and trade unions play an important role in the formal and informal coordination at the sector level. A relatively low mobility of skilled workers and a low flexibility of wages and wage structures can be observed here. On the other hand, in the liberal market economy of the US, for the most part the negotiations take place at the company level, and are uncoordinated. At the same time, there is a high mobility of skilled workers and a high flexibility of wages and wage structures. This low (or rather high) mobility of qualified personnel in Germany (or rather in the US) is regarded as a problem (or rather opportunity) for risky start-ups. This applies also for young, therapeutics-oriented biotechnology enterprises. Most of these start-ups do not succeed, so the career risk of a failure must be low. Simultaneously, innovations by the start-ups would be promoted ideally by a knowledge transfer via networks of scientists who move between the start-up companies, universities and pharmaceutical enterprises. Conditions in the US are more conducive to this because of the labor market structures and because non-competition clauses are illegal. Both factors allow extensive head-hunting and the creation of career paths within the company even though frequent job changes take place. On the other hand, non-competition clauses and the orientation towards long-term careers in one large enterprise hamper the creation of an active labor market for scientists and managers at the middle level in Germany. The risk of starting work in a start-up company is too high.[10]

In industrial relations within enterprises, the institutions elected by the employees play an important role in the company's decision-making process. These bodies also have connections to extra-industrial associations and are also represented in supervisory bodies. Otherwise in the US: employees' representatives hardly appear in collective negotiatons. Their influence on the structuring of work contracts in the private sector is small. On the whole, the role of the trade unions is relatively insignificant.

In the *educational system*, on the one hand, the occupational training system and on the other the university system, especially the engineering sciences, are important. In Germany, occupational training enjoys a high standing, with the industrial associations and the trade unions greatly involved. The picture is similar for academic education: there is a close connection of engineering faculties to industrial technologies, with the strong involvement of the professional associations. Further, in the basic sciences

---

[9] The following leans heavily on Soskice (1997) as well as the modifications thereof in ZEW/NIW/DIW/ISI/WSV/WZB (1999).

[10] See Casper (1998) on this line of argument.

and also in engineering, there are programs for doctoral candidates (post-grad) with relatively close contacts to large enterprises. In the US, the further qualification of workers at the lowest levels is seldom. A supplementary, obligatory general education is important. Again, a mirror image; the study of engineering is not closely bound to specific technologies and programs for doctoral candidates exist, not only in the basic sciences, but also in engineering without close connections to enterprises.

In the *financing system and enterprise controlling*, there are also fundamental differences to be found in the institutional framework conditions of the two countries. In Germany, there are stable shareholder systems in the enterprises dealt with on the stock exchanges. The banks play an important supervisory role. Opinions from various quarters are sought for, as a monitoring process. Hostile takeovers are difficult to engineer. Otherwise in the US: here there are legal framework conditions which allow such takeovers of companies on the stock exchange. At the same time, there is sufficient venture capital available for high risk projects in the form of a large venture capital market. It is acknowledged that Germany was lacking in venture capital funds a few years ago, due to its bank-centered financing system. But the situation changed recently. The availability of venture capital is no longer a problem. Venture capitalists are rather looking for better ideas in which they can invest. This last named point naturally directly affects the financing possibilities for start-up companies, which are in great need of this venture capital, for example, especially in the area of biotechnology, to develop therapeutics because of the long-term nature of the discovery and development process, and the risk of losing the innovation race (cf. Casper, 1998).

The *system of relations between enterprises* deals on the one hand with the establishing of standards and on the other hand with competitive policy. In Germany the setting of standards is based on consensus, whereas in the US standard setting is market-based. As regards competitive policy, in Germany a high competitive intensity can be found in foreign trade, but at the same time direct competition is avoided by product differentiation. Also, business connections play a role in conflicts over contractual relationships and when setting up framework rules. In the US, on the other hand, competitive policy tries to prevent collusive or consultative behavior. Moreover, there is only a limited framework for problems with contractual relations.

The last group of differences in institutional framework conditions relevant here refer to the *role of the state*, or here more specifically, *innovation policy*. If one considers the public R&D infrastructure policy and technology transfer, then German universities and research institutes are distinguished by close links to certain enterprises in established technology fields. Experience is important for cooperations. In addition, a high regional variety of the R&D institutions with a low regional concentration can be observed. In the US, on the other hand, there is only a limited institutional framework for technology diffusion. Simultaneously, a high regional concentration of public R&D institutions can be found. The innovation and technology policy is characterized in Germany on the whole by a comparatively speaking high technology-oriented promotion and "broadly based" support. In the US, however, we find a concentration on individual technologies and an emphasis on (military) large-scale projects. It is true to say that there is a strong tendency in Germany to establish detailed framework conditions, with a great number of regulatory restrictions as a result. In the US, on the other hand, the preference is to set up general framework conditions with considerably less regulations and restrictions.

The clear differences in the institutional framework conditions in the two countries observed leads also to clearly differentiated profiles of innovation strengths.[11] Germany's strengths are high-quality products in established industrial branches, whose manufacture requires complex production processes and maintenance performance, as well as close relations to customers, a so-called diversified quality production. German strengths are accordingly in "cumulative" product and process innovations in "established" technologies, especially in mechanical engineering and road vehicle construction, in electrical engineering and the chemical industry. The manufacturing process of these products requires highly qualified and experienced personnel, who can assume a high degree of responsibility. The German innovation pattern - high-grade innovations along pre-plotted development lines with high value added in established industries - corresponds also in many cases to the above mentioned relevant institutional framework conditions.

The US institutional framework conditions are more suited to a different production and innovation strategy. The US have their particular strengths in "radical" innovations in the fields of newly emerging technologies (e.g. biotechnology, microprocessors), as well as in large-scale, complex technical systems in extraordinarily R&D-intensive sectors, which contain complex systems or the freedom for managers to decide under conditions of strict financial targets. Examples of this are the new entertainment media, military systems, large software and computer products, as well as air travel and aerospace. Conversely, the US are not particularly successful in the fields where Germany's strengths lie.

2.2.2   Innovation Systems in the Narrow Sense of the Pharmaceutical Sectors in the US and Germany

Without a doubt, the pharmaceutical sector belongs to the science-based branches of the economy, in which research and development play a decisive

---

[11] Cf. on the following conclusions and evaluations ZEW/NIW/DIW/ISI/WSV/WZB (1999). These conclusions maybe seen as the consensus within the innovation research community.

role.[12] The main reason for the high R&D expenditure are the costs of developing new pharmaceuticals. In 1995, these amounted to 350 - 500 million US$ per new pharmaceutical (see chapter 4.1.2). As a comparison, the corresponding costs for 1985 were estimated at 120 million US$ for each new medicine. The largest part of these costs, namely approx. 70 %, arise during the clinical development phase (Drews, 1995). The pharmaceutical industry has been facing some serious challenges since the beginning of the 90s. From the market side, reforms in public health systems and cost containment measures have been bringing prices down. This deterioration of the profit situation is accompanied by a parellel increase in the costs of developing new substances. There are two main consequences of this development, from the viewpoint of the pharmaceutical industry: firstly, it is necessary to shorten the development times of new substances and medicines, and secondly, the proportion of innovative medicines in the companies' product portfolios must be increased.

In addition to the economic situation, new developments in science and technology are posing new challenges for the pharmaceutical industry. In particular, the approach to discovering and developing new drugs is changing completely. The traditional procedure for the development of new drugs was based mainly on the screening and testing of thousands of chemicals which were available through huge substance libraries. As opposed to this more classical scheme, new ways of drug discovery are becoming more complex and are based on more different disciplines. Therefore, the integration of a number of different disciplines like chemistry, information science, pharmacology, molecular biology, biotechnology, and combinatorial chemistry becomes crucial for future success in drug development. This clearly demonstrates that research and development in the pharmaceutical industry is developing towards interdisciplinarity.

These challenges are being confronted by two very differently structured innovation systems in the narrower sense of the pharmaceutical sector, which are naturally influenced in many aspects by the innovation systems in the wider sense. In the following, first of all, the most important organizations in the innovation systems in the narrower sense and the mechanisms for technology transfer will be depicted for each country individually. Subsequently, a comparison will be drawn between the relevant regulations for the pharmaceutical sector. Large sections of the innovation systems, such as the production structure, the total economic development, but also the R&D expenditure, the R&D structure and the whole innovation set-up will not be dealt with in this introductory chapter. They will be dealt with in detail in separate chapters (especially in chapters 3 and 4), in order to do justice to the significance of these topics.

---

[12] See Pavitt (1984) on the term science-based enterprises in the framework of a taxonomy to explain different sectoral patterns of the technical change.

The United States

Actors in the process of innovation in the American pharmaceutical sector are academic research organizations (universities and colleges), departmental research institutes, other research institutes as well as industry.

In general, the US academic research organizations appear to be heterogeneous and decentralized in administration and management. The US research universities and colleges are a highly autonomous population of public and private organizations, each established and developed in response to some unique combination of local, regional (state), and national needs and opportunities. These organizations vary considerably in the size of their research budgets, the general research orientation, the reputation (quality and productivity) of their research activities, the scope and intensity of their technology transfer activities, and their administration and accounting practices (Abramson et al., 1997).

The US Federal Government maintains about 720 laboratories, encompassing more than 1,500 separate R&D facilities. These facilities were established and developed to support the public missions of federal agencies, such as national security, energy independence, the cure of disease, fruit production or science and engineering research. Altogether, federal laboratories and research facilities are the second largest segment of US R&D organizations. They perform roughly 18 % of all basic research, 16 % of all applied research, and 13 % of all technology development in the United States (NSB, 1996). Federal laboratories vary widely in their size, mission, organization, and management. Among these governmental research institutes the National Institute of Health (NIH) is particularly important. It is one of the main funding sources besides the National Science Foundation (NSF), the Department of Defense, the National Aeronautics and Space Administration (NASA), the Department of Energy, and the Department of Agriculture. The National Institute of Health (NIH) is the largest federal contributor to university research, accounting for almost half of these funds.

The US pharmaceutical industry is the strongest in the world. It has the highest R&D expenditure, the largest number of introductions of new chemical entities and the products from its firms dominate the Top 50 (Casper/Matraves, 1997). R&D spending by the pharmaceutical companies nearly tripled between 1985 and 1995. The most prominent trend in the drug and medicine industry has been the merging of pharmaceuticals and biotechnology research: For example, more than one third of drug companies' R&D projects are primarily biotechnology-related (NSB, 1998).

The question of how technology transfer between the various organizations in the innovation system of the pharmaceutical sector in the narrower sense takes place, is still of great relevance. In this context it must be mentioned that US technology transfer takes place to a large extent between the departments of large private companies or externally between enterprises.

Concerning the private sector, technology transfer occurs through formal measures such as mergers and acquisitions and licensing of patents, software and trade secrets, as well as via less formal mechanisms such as sharing technical know-how, exchanges of personnel, and technical and marketing assistance. According to a study by the NSF and the US Bureau of Consensus, the three most important sources of information leading to development and commercial introduction of new products are internal sources, clients and customers, and suppliers of materials and components (NSB, 1996). This study also found that the least important sources of such information were governmental laboratories, technical institutes, and consulting firms.

Three types of mechanisms can be distinguished with respect to technology transfer from academic organizations to industry in the United States: The first includes such things as faculty consulting and the transfer of university intellectual property and proto-technology embodied in graduates and faculty staff which are hired by private companies. The second type includes patent licensing, university acquisition of private-sector licenses, and various approaches to enhancing industry access, up to a sponsorship of university-based research. The third type includes activities such as technical assistance, programs and technology business, incubators, associated with commercializing research or improving university-industry relations more generally.

The about 720 laboratories, maintained by the US Federal Government, perform around 50 % of all American R&D (Abramson et al. 1997). However, less than 100 federal laboratories have the technology and resources to engage in significant technology transfer activities. Included among these are all of the large multi-program laboratories of the Department of Energy, many of the Defense Department's laboratories, most field centers of the National Aeronautics and Space Administration (NASA), as well as facilities of the USDA, and the Public Health Service, including the NIH and NIST.

Most federal labs allocate only a small percentage, if any, of their total R&D budget to technology transfer and related activities. According to a recent survey, the federal laboratories rank fourth as sources of external technologies after other firms, universities and private sector research databases (Roessner, 1993).

Germany

In Germany, industry, universities and a broad variety of public and semi-public research organizations are actors in the innovation system related to the pharmaceutical sector. According to the legal definition, there are around 1,100 pharmaceutical manufacturers in Germany. This figure covers drugstores as well as multinational companies, but small and medium-sized enterprises are prevalent (BPI, 1997). Concerning the public and semi-public research organizations, obviously the Fraunhofer Society (FhG), the Max Planck Society (MPG), the Helmholtz Centers (HGF), the Federation of Industrial Research Associations (AiF) and the government research institutes are the most important. These organizations are described below in further detail.

The *Fraunhofer Society* (FhG) presently comprises 47 institutes. It is a non-commercial organization conducting industry-orientated applied contract research on behalf of industry, the service sector, and the government. The main research fields are, among others, biochemical engineering, materials technology and components, production technology, microelectronics, microsystems technology, process engineering, environmental research and health (FhG, 1998). FhG institutes that are actors in the pharmaceutical sector are the Institute for Biomedical Engineering (IBMT), the Institute for Surface Technology and Biochemical Engineering (IGB), the Institute for Systems and Innovation Research (ISI), the Institute for Toxicology and Aerosol Research (ITA) and the Working Group for Toxicology and Environmental Medicine (ATU).

A typical organization in the area of fundamental research with a high reputation is the *Max Planck Society* (MPG) which is financed largely by public funds (50 % from the states (Laender) and 50 % from the federal government). In general, MPG's main areas of focus are the biological-medical sector, physics, and chemistry. All in all, the research is actually conducted in approximately 100 Max Planck Institutes (MPI), whereby the Institutes for Biochemistry, for Biology, for Biophysical Chemistry, for Brain Research, for Cell Biology, for Experimental Medicine, for Immune Biology, for Infection Biology, for Medical Research, for Molecular Genetics, for Molecular Physiology, for Neurological Research, for Neurophysiological Research as well as for Physiological and Clinical Research cover health-related aspects.

The *Helmholtz Centers* (HGF), were created chiefly within the framework of government-funded programs for nuclear research and nuclear technology, aerospace research, data processing and, increasingly in recent years, biomedical research, polar research, environmental research and non-nuclear energy technology. They are funded primarily by public money (90 % from the federal government and the remaining 10 % from the states). At present, there are 16 Helmholtz Centers carrying out fundamental research in their specific fields. Centers focusing on medical research are the German Cancer Research Center (DKFZ), the Gesellschaft für biotechnologische Forschung (GBF) and the Max Delbrück Center for Molecular Medicine (MDC).

The former *Blue List institutes*, which were so called because the first list of their names was printed on blue paper, are now united in the *Leibnitz Community*. The federal government and the states pay equal shares of the budget of these independent research institutes with supra-regional importance and specific scientific interests (e. g. social sciences, economics, biology or other natural sciences). In 1996, 82 Blue list institutes existed, with the following institutes covering health-related aspects: the Institutes for Neurobiology (IfN), for Molecular Biotechnology (IMB), for Molecular Pharmacology (FMP), for Food Research (DIFE) and Primate Center (DPZ).

In addition, there are several *government research organizations*, the German counterpart to the smaller and medium-sized US federal and state laboratories. They are connected directly to ministries of the states and federal government (BMBF 1996) and often carry out general research besides R&D activities in the area of the related ministry. They perform all in all 8 % of German R&D. Federal ministries with important ties to departmental research organizations include the Ministries of Health, Agriculture, Transport, and Defense. Compared with their counterparts in other countries, German government research institutes account for a relatively small share of total publicly funded R&D (Abramson et al. 1997). In the case of the Ministry of Health, health-related departmental research work is done by the Federal Institute for Consumer Protection and Veterinary Medicine (BgVV), the Robert Koch Institute (RKI) for Infectious Diseases, the Federal Institute for Pharmaceuticals and Medical Products (BfArM), the Paul Ehrlich Institute Federal Agency for Serums and Vaccines (PEI), and the German Institute for Medical Documentation and Information (DIMDI).

The following kinds of technology transfer can be observed among the mentioned actors of the innovation system in the German pharmaceutical sector. First of all, a notable fact in this context is the long demonstrated comparative strength of the German innovation system in supporting incremental innovation and rapid technology diffusion in many industries. The main reason for this might be a special characteristic of the German technology transfer system, namely that the public and semi-public research organizations including universities have a high level of direct contract research and research cooperation with industry.

Technology transfer is realized through various channels in the pharmaceutical industry. One important channel is via R&D cooperation with other companies (primarily customers of small and medium-sized enterprises), consulting engineers, universities, and other research organizations. In addition, small and medium-sized enterprises profit from a closely linked network of non-R&D-performing organizations, the result of a high level of industrial self-organization. The Chambers of Industry and Commerce, industrial associations (e. g. AiF) and other organizations effectively support the diffusion of technology and know-how through innovation-oriented consultation and by organizing knowledge exchange among firms through journals, meetings and informal networks.

Cooperative research within the framework of industrial research associations has proved to be an effective instrument for performing projects that exceed the capacity of individual small and medium-sized enterprises. The associations and their umbrella organization AiF have implemented an intensive collective evaluation procedure that guarantees effective selection of appropriate research projects. Nevertheless, technology transfer to other member companies is limited. The major restriction of cooperative industrial research is its limitation to pre-competitive problems, since several companies in the same industry have to cooperate. In some less research-intensive industries the share of cooperative research compared with the total R&D activities is quite large. However, in research-intensive industries like chemicals the role of cooperative research is negligible.

Technology transfer in public and semi-public organizations is realized in different ways and to different extents. The FhG conducts industry-oriented research. Moreover, there is a close relationship to German universities, which is institutionalized by the appointment of FhG directors as regular university professors. Thus, the FhG is a real bridging organization between academic and industrial research. In the Max Planck Society the exchange of scientific personnel is the most important channel of technology transfer. Collaborative research with industry plays a modest but increasing role in this context. In case of the Helmholtz Centers, technology transfer is realized through scientific publications. Besides this classic instrument, the major mechanisms in this direction are the participation of industry in advisory boards and committees and collaborative research, uniting industry and the centers in large projects or programs. With respect to Blue List institutes and the government research institutes, only few institutes in this group have close relations with industry and perform technology transfer.

German universities' major channels of technology transfer to industry are collaborative and contract research, consultation, informal contacts, conferences and provision of qualified personnel. In addition, scientific publications are intensively used. An effective transfer channel for German universities are external organizations like technology centers and particularly so-called Aninstitutes (institutes affiliated with a university). The temporary transfer of personnel, however, is rarely practiced in Germany.

All in all, technology transfer in Germany is primarily institutionalized rather than personalized. Its main channels are contract and cooperative research supported by other means, such as conferences and informal meetings. Bridging organizations like the Fraunhofer and university affiliated institutes play a decisive role in technology transfer. Many professors in engineering departments of universities come from industry, which implies a flow of knowledge from industry to university and, later on, close university-industry relations.

2.2.3 Regulations Concerning the Pharmaceutical Industry

The pharmaceutical industry is subject to a multiplicity of government regulations at all levels of research and development, manufacturing and sales. These are certainly characterized differently in the individual states, or recently at the European level, but common basic points of contact and operating mechanisms can however be determined. Moreover, the health system as a whole is also an object of political design, because of its funding.

Starting Points and Effects of Possible Regulations

The following opportunities and effects of regulations are possible along the value-added chain of the pharmaceutical industry.[13]

In the area of innovations, patent legislation which limits the patent-protected lifetimes of preparations, and market entry approval for new products, which lead to an increased use of resources and time, is always of great relevance. If an enterprise does not exploit its invention itself or not alone, then another enterprise needs licenses from the innovator to manufacture innovative medicaments. At the same time, the manufacturing process is subject to continuous controls. Both regulations imply also increased input of resources for the enterprises.

The marketing opportunities of the pharmaceutical industry are also limited in manifold ways. First of all, many medicaments are only available on prescription. This requires special sales efforts and marketing methods. Closely linked to this are restrictions on advertising for medicines and limits on advertising expenditure, which are in force in many countries and which restrict the possible forms of competition and the effectiveness of the advertising. Furthermore, the labelling, packaging and patient package insert of medicines need special approval, so that special knowledge is necessary and delays in market introduction are possible.

This market is moreover often characterized by price and profit controls. Such measures naturally limit the cash flow of the companies. Further regulations in this area are the limits to reimbursement for medicines, which can make price reductions necessary. Medicines can also be completely barred from reimbursement, so that sales decrease as a result. On the other hand, the sales of generics can be encouraged, i. e. of medicines which are no longer protected by patents and which can now be manufactured and sold by other pharmaceutical companies who have not had to bear the brunt of development costs. In this case price competition would increase.

Measures which affect distribution channels also directly limit competition. Here on a national level there are limits to the number of outlets for medicines as well as profit margins. In international trading these are possibly joined by quotas, customs duties and non-tariff trade barriers, which according to one's perspective either support domestic production, or from the perspective of the foreign countries involved lead at least to higher costs.

---

[13] The following is strongly oriented towards Erbsland/Mehnert (1992), as well as the literature cited therein.

A Comparison of Significant Regulations with Impacts on the Pharmaceutical Industry in the US and Germany

A central starting point for government regulating is the financing of the healthcare system. These regulations do not intervene directly in the value-added chain of the enterprises, but have not only an indirect but also a direct influence on the possible options open to the companies of the pharmaceutical sector, because the different sources of funding, which again are subject to different regulations, for their part allow various degrees of freedom of action for the companies.

The comparison of the financing structures of the healthcare systems in the US and Germany reflects basically the characterization in our introduction of the US as a liberal market economy and Germany as a coordinated or consensus-oriented market economy (cf. table 2.1). In the US the private share of financing in 1992 (i. e. self payment, private health insurance and other funding) amounted to 60.7 %, while this share in Germany came to only 19.4 %. The coordinated or consensus-oriented structures in Germany are especially apparent in the high share of social insurance funding. Similarly high shares are found in Europe only in France (66.2 %) and the Netherlands (72.1 %). Other European countries, such as the United Kingdom and Sweden with shares of 72.9 % and 76.7 % respectively, have state-financed healthcare systems. The EU as a whole has a similarly high public share of financing of 77.6 % (social insurance and state) as in Germany (80.6 %), however here 47.2 % falls on the social insurance and 30.4 % on financing by the state.

A further significant area of regulation is the sales and distribution systems for medicines. In Germany, the distribution of medicines takes place exclusively through pharmacies. Ordering by mail is not permitted and physicians are also not allowed to dispense medicine. It is also not allowed to advertise prescription medicine to the general public. On the other hand, advertising for non-prescription drugs is permitted in all media. The substitution of brand-name medicaments has been in the discussion for some time, as a viable instrument for cost cutting, as an increased price competition is hoped for from the so-called generics. In Germany, pharmacies are

TABLE 2.1. Financing of the healthcare system 1992

	State in %	Social insurance in %	Self-payment in %	Private insurance in %	Other fundings in %
US	37.5	1.9	21.1	36.1	3.5
Germany	11.5	69.4	11.3	7.1	1.0
EU	30.5	47.2	15.3	6.4	0.7

Source: Schneider et al. (1995), pp. 538-542

permitted to substitute generics or re- and parallel imports for a prescribed medicine, with the approval of the prescribing physician.

The US sales and distribution system for medicines differs in a number of points from the German one.[14] So although medicine is distributed mainly through retail pharmacies, in addition over 6,000 hospital pharmacies supply outpatients. The health centers of the Health Maintenance Organizations (HMOs) also dispense drugs. The following rules apply for the substitution of medicines. The pharmacist can choose the cheaper medicine for prescriptions. The choice of medicine is in part transferred by the doctor to the pharmacist. The substitution of generic medicines is permitted in many federal states.

In addition, a number of regulations aims at controlling the expenditure for medicine. Starting points for this are the control of the manufacturers' prices, the publication of so-called positive or negative lists for drugs, for which reimbursement can be made or not, as well as the elaboration of regulations on own contributions by the patients. In this area of regulation there are also crucial differences between Germany and the US. In Germany, for example, the manufacturers of pharmaceuticals have a free hand in pricing in principle, but de facto price restraints take place for a number of medicines through so-called fixed amount rulings.[15] On the other hand, there are no standard prices for medicines in the US. Some insurance companies negotiate the prices directly with pharmacies. The attempt was made in Germany to reduce the amounts spent by the social insurance on medicine by passing a negative list, which excludes a number of medicaments from being reimbursed by the health insurance. Presently, the opposite way is being tried; a positive list, which names the medicines admissible for reimbursement, should be the basis for reimbursement. There is neither a positive nor a negative list in the US. However, this is not a

---

[14] Cf. Schneider et al. (1995), pp. 485-486 on this point.

[15] According to § 35 paragraph 1 of the Social Security Code (SGB) V, which incorporates the rulings of the Healthcare Reform Law of 20.12.1988, the Federal Committee of Physicians and Health Insurers decide for which groups of pharmaceuticals fixed amounts can be determined. These groups should encompass medicaments with 1.) the same active substances, 2.) pharmacological-therapeutically comparable active substances, especially with chemically related substances, and 3.) pharmacological-therapeutically comparable effect, especially medicines (acc. to the Healthcare Structure Law of 21.12.1992, only with therapeutically comparable effect). The fixed amounts which will be reimbursed for the medicine groups should be oriented towards the "most reasonable (cheapest) possibility of supply" according to § 35 paragraph 5 SGB V and therefore proceed from "in principle the cheapest pharmacy sales price in the comparison group". Apart from the fixed amount ruling, medicines with "patented active substances, which have a new mode of operation and which mean an improvement in therapy, also on account of lesser side effects". The applicable time limits and waiting times after the end of patent protection have been in part newly regulated in the Healthcare Structure Law of 1992. See Erbsland/Wille (1994) for a detailed discussion of the legal basics and their economic impacts.

real question here. Firstly, as shown above, the public share of funding the healthcare system is much smaller in the US anyway and secondly, the patients' own contributions for medical services are very much higher. For example, with Medicare (the health insurance for the over 65s), the own contribution for medicine amounts to 100 %. Patients' own contribution towards medicine is much lower in Germany. The patients' contribution for medicine not on the fixed amount list are charged according to the package size and "fixed amount medicines" are reimbursed up to the limit of the fixed amount.

Besides these regulations which primarily affect the financing of the health insurance system, the distribution systems for pharmaceuticals and the control of medicine costs, there are a number of regulations within the framework of research and development, and above all, in the certification of medicines. These will be dealt with in the next chapters, as necessary. In the case of Germany, however, it must be said that national regulations in this area are being increasingly replaced by regulations applicable for the whole of the European Union. The significant catalyst for this development was, besides the general European integration process, also the rapid technological development in the field of biotechnology, which again had repercussions on the entire pharmaceutical industry.

According to the interdisciplinarity of the pharmaceutical industry, the policies for R&D, patenting and regulation are strongly connected with the present stage of development in the new field biotechnology which raises issues where there is a great deal of uncertainty. The European policies for R&D, patenting and regulation affect company decisions about their biotechnology activities. Concerning patents and regulation of biotechnology, the EU had to seek harmonization between the various member states' approaches to these issues. A unified European regulatory system for approving medicinal products has been developing in the course of time. In the period until 1992, the UK and France were the preferred regulatory authorities for handling applications with an EU-wide interest. Preference was based on their ability to process applications expeditiously, and on having a high level of international credibility with regulatory authorities in other major markets. Since 1995, the EU approval process has come under the aegis of the European Medicine Evaluation Agency (EMEA). Procedures differ for non-biotechnology and biotechnology medicines. There are decentralized procedures for non-biotechnology medicine, under which approval in one member state is recognized by all the others. Any disputes are solved by the EMEA. Centralized procedures are mandatory for biotechnology products, and optional for other high-tech products. Application from manufacturers for approval are made directly to the EMEA. Product approvals by the EMEA are valid in all other member states.

3
Dynamics of the Markets and Market Structure

Andre Jungmittag, Guido Reger

3.1 Introduction: Market Categories and Structure

The pharmaceutical industry is based on global products sold in nationally segmented markets. This segmentation is a result of divergent national regulations in the areas of public health and new product approval. Due to this national segmentation, a direct presence in the markets for end products is often necessary. Generally, foreign trade in the pharmaceutical industry is not so intensive as in other sectors of the manufacturing industry. Intra-industrial trade in intermediate products, direct investments, as well as take-overs and mergers for the purpose of acquiring new technologies, play a substantially greater role than in other sectors.

Conveniently, pharmaceuticals are divided into three categories (OECD, 1996):

1. In-patent pharmaceuticals,

2. out-of-patent pharmaceuticals or generic pharmaceuticals,

3. over-the-counter (OTC) pharmaceuticals.

In-patent pharmaceuticals are only sold on prescription. They are also the basis for activities in the generic sector. Generic pharmaceuticals are out-of-patent products sold on prescription under their original brand name, other brand names or generic names. On the other hand, OTC pharmaceuticals are sold directly to consumers without prescription.

Estimates of the volume of the global pharmaceutical market necessarily have to remain relatively vague and depend, among other things, on whether only prescribed (ethical) medicines are included or also "over-the-counter" (OTC) products. Thus the OECD estimate of the world market volume for prescription-only products in 1995 was approximately 225 bn US $ (1992: 188 bn US $). The European Federation of Pharmaceutical Industries' Associations (EFPIA, 1996) puts its estimate for the 1995 market higher, at 282 bn US $ (215.8 bn ECU). The differing estimates are quite compatible if the 16 % market share of OTC products in the six largest OECD countries is taken into account. THe most important market in quantitative terms is North America, with a 32.6% share of the world

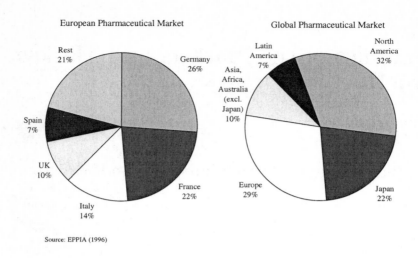

FIGURE 3.1. Shares of pharmaceutical markets

market, followed by Europe with 28.9% and Japan with 21.6% (cf. figure 3.1). In the European pharmaceuticals market, Germany comes first with a share of 26.2%, followed by France (22.4%), Italy (13.7%) and Great Britain (9.5%).

Due to a lack of consistent data it is also difficult to estimate the shares of the different categories of pharmaceuticals in the world market. So, the OECD secretariat yields the following estimates for the period from 1985 to 1987: in-patent pharmaceuticals 70 %, generics 14 % and OTC pharmaceuticals 16 % of the total market. However, there are large differences among individual countries. Nevertheless, EU data for 1993 show similar patterns (cf. EU, 96): 85 % of all pharmaceutical products sold - including the hospital market - were prescription pharmaceuticals.

Cost-containment programs introduced by several governments to control spending on health-care, by reducing the reimbursement rates of medicines or putting limits on prescriptions, have increased the market shares of generics on the one hand and limited the growth in sales of prescription pharmaceuticals on the other hand. Nowadays, in Denmark, for example, the generics' share amounts to 20 % of the total market and in Germany to 15 %. Generics make up about 10 % of the total market in the United Kingdom and the Netherlands (cf. EU, 97). Especially in these countries the development of a market for generics has been encouraged by the health authorities. The market for OTC pharmaceuticals is also growing faster than the total market for pharmaceuticals. Germany, Italy and Spain showed growth rates between 10 and 11 % and the four largest markets for OTC pharmaceuticals were growing by 8.1 % in 1994, whereas the total growth rate was 6.6 % (cf. EU, 97). Thus, the self-medication market is expected to remain one of the most dynamic in the medium term (cf. EU, 96).

In 1990, the OECD countries accounted for over 70% of pharmaceuticals production and pharmaceuticals consumption world-wide. As a group, the OECD countries produce slightly more than they consume in this sector. In all the other groups of countries, pharmaceutical consumption is somewhat higher than production. This global distribution is also relatively stable in the long term. In the 15 years from 1975 to 1990, the share of the OECD countries in both production and consumption rose by approx. 6 percent, whereas the shares of the other groups of countries dropped accordingly.

World-wide, the pharmaceutical industry is led by about 20 large research-based firms. However, none of these firms has a dominant world market share. The leading positions in a ranking of these firms change frequently, but the group at all remains largely the same. In 1992, only two firms had world market shares above 4 %. No single firm had a market share above 20 % in a large national market. In 1995, three firms had world market shares above 4 %, but only one firm had a world market share above 5 %. However, the picture changes when the submarkets for single therapeutics are considered. The three top products in such a submarket account for 45 - 60 % of sales. Single top products hold 20 - 25 % of the European market.[1]

In the following section the main players - at a nationally aggregated level - are examined more closely. These are the G7 countries as well as Sweden and the Netherlands.[2] First, a comparative analysis is made of production, consumption and employment. Secondly, different aspects of foreign trade in pharmaceuticals are considered. Finally, some conclusions for the international competitiveness of the pharmaceutical industry in selected countries are drawn from the empirical findings.

3.2   Production, Consumption and Employment

Unlike many other sectors of manufacturing industry, growth in the pharmaceutical industry is relatively independent of the business cycle. This relatively even growth is seen in the development of the production of pharmaceuticals in terms of billions of US $ purchasing power parity (PPP) (cf. figure 3.2).[3] Three groups of countries can be distinguished here. The first

---

[1] See OECD (1996), pp. 82-84.

[2] Switzerland - another significant player - has to be excluded in many important areas from an investigation at a national level, since no OECD data are available.

[3] The use of purchasing power parity based in each case on the gross domestic product of the country concerned, in international comparisons at a sectoral level is certainly not without problems, however, it is the only way available where no relevant sectoral price indexes exist.

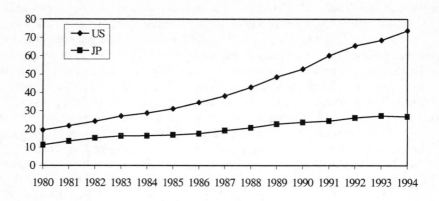

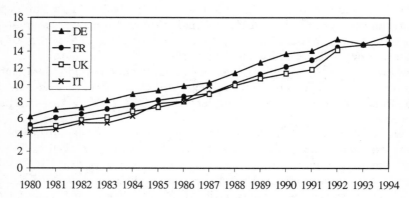

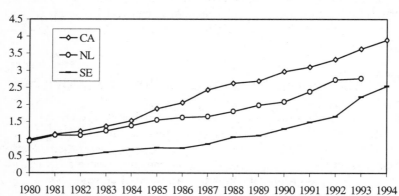

Source: OECD STAN database, own Calcution

FIGURE 3.2. Pharmaceutical production in billions PPP-$ 1980 - 1994

group consists of the US and Japan, where production was around 19.4 and 11.2 bn $ PPP respectively in 1980, rising to 73.8 and 26.8 bn $ PPP respectively by 1994. The development of the US pharmaceutical industry, with an annual average growth rate of 7.53 % within the period under review, is substantially more dynamic than Japan's, with an annual average growth rate of 5.58 %. France, Great Britain, West Germany and Italy constitute a second group of countries with a relatively homogeneous development of production. In these countries production in 1980 lay between approximately 4.5 bn $ PPP (Italy) and 6.2 bn $ PPP (West Germany). In subsequent years, too, the course of production development in these countries ran fairly parallel. Although data for Italy are only available up to 1987, it can be assumed that pharmaceuticals production in Italy continued to keep up with the group. This is also true for Great Britain with an annual average growth rate of 7.56 %, for which data are available up to 1992. In 1994 the pharmaceuticals production volume in France had gone up to 14.8 bn $ PPP and in West Germany to 15.8 bn $ PPP. This means that pharmaceutical production in France went up with an annual average growth rate of 6.36 %, whereas in Germany annual average growth was 5.89 %. The development of production in the third group of countries was distinctly lower. In 1980 the volume of pharmaceutical production in Canada amounted to 0.98 bn $ PPP and in the Netherlands to 0.93 bn $ PPP, with Sweden at 0.38 bn $ PPP bringing up the rear. However, even in these countries vigorous growth was apparent. By 1994, pharmaceutical production in Canada had increased, with an annual average growth rate of 8.48 % to 3.89 bn $ PPP, and in Sweden annual average growth rates of 9.35 % resulted in a level of 2.54 bn $ PPP. In the Netherlands production rose with an annual average growth rate of 6.56 % to c. 277 bn $ PPP in 1993. Thus, together with the US and Great Britain, the pharmaceutical producers in the smaller countries actually showed the most dynamic developments.

As a result of the massive expansion of production in the pharmaceutical industry, the percentage share of this sector in manufacturing industry as a whole also increased substantially in the individual countries (cf. figure 3.3). In relative terms, Sweden leads the field again here, with its pharmaceutical industry increasing its share from 0.75% to 2.84% of Sweden's overall manufacturing industry within the period under consideration. Pharmaceuticals also became more important in France, which increased its share from 1.50% in 1980 to 2.62% in 1994. Percentages shares in Great Britain and the US are also among the highest, at 2.56% (1992) and 2.24% (1994) respectively. In the Netherlands the share of the pharmaceuticals industry is more moderate, increasing from 1.17% in 1980 to 1.95% in 1993. In 1994, the lowest percentage volumes of the manufacturing industry as a whole are found in West Germany (1.58%), Japan (1.54%) and Canada (1.33%).

As already mentioned, the OECD countries produce altogether slightly more medical drugs than they consume. If the ratio of consumption to pro-

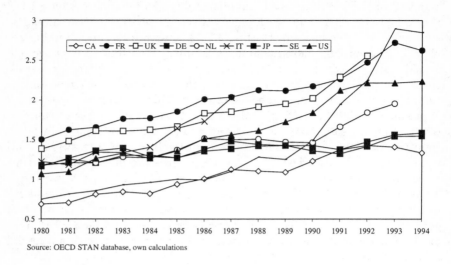

Source: OECD STAN database, own calculations

FIGURE 3.3. Percentage share of the pharmaceutical industry in the manufacturing industry as a whole (1980 to 1994)

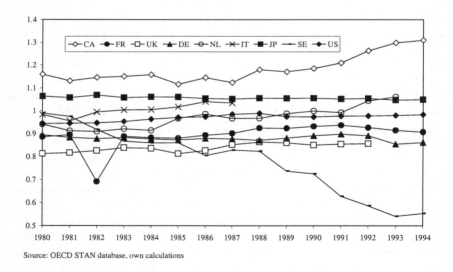

Source: OECD STAN database, own calculations

FIGURE 3.4. Consumption-to-production ratios for pharmaceutical products

duction is examined for the individual OECD countries, there are sometimes substantial variations (cf. figure 3.4). Thus throughout the observation period, consumption in Canada considerably outstripped production,
showing an upward trend: in 1980 only 1.16 times as much was consumed
there as was produced, but by 1994 consumption was 1.31 times higher
than production. In Japan the consumption of pharmaceuticals was slightly
higher than production throughout (1.06:1 in 1980, 1.05:1 in 1994). Only
two OECD countries have shown an inverse ratio of consumption to production in the past. Until 1991, the Netherlands produced slightly more
than they consumed; consumption then overtook production, with a ratio
of 1.04:1 in 1992 and 1.06:1 in 1993. Data for Italy are only available up to
1987, but a similar turnaround took place there as early as 1983 and continued up to 1987 at least. In France, Great Britain, West Germany and the
US, pharmaceutical production exceeded consumption fairly consistently,
with 1994 consumption-to-production ratios of 0.91, 0.86 (for 1992), 0.86
and 0.98 respectively. A massive shift took place in Sweden, where the
consumption-to-production ratio dropped from 0.99:1 in 1980 to 0.55:1 by
1994. Thus Sweden is the only one of the countries included in our survey
which was producing far more pharmaceutical products than it consumed
at the end of the observation period.

The growth of the pharmaceutical industry is also reflected in employment figures (cf. figure 3.5). Growth increased fairly steadily over the observation period in all the countries included in the survey. Of the countries
for which 1994 statistics are available (Canada, West Germany, Sweden
and US), a decrease in employment is found only in West Germany and
Canada. In the case of Germany, where national data are available until
1998, this decrease continued until today, however from 1997 to 1998 at
least the speed of job cuts decreased.

Over the same period, the share of pharmaceutical sector employees in
employment for the manufacturing industry as a whole went up quite substantially in most countries (cf. figure 3.6). The largest comparative share
is found in France (2.22% in 1993), followed by Great Britain with a share
of 1.79% in 1992. At the end of the observation period most other countries show medium employment shares of between 1.15% and 1.62%. Only
in Japan is the comparative share of the pharmaceutical industry in employment relatively small, at 0.91% in 1994.

When making comparisons of this kind it must be borne in mind, however, that growth of the pharmaceutical industry's share in employment
may be attributable to two different causes: firstly, employment in the
pharmaceutical industry may have risen or, secondly, there may have been
an overall decrease in the numbers of employees in the other sectors.

For this reason, in figure 3.7 the absolute growth of employment figures
in this sector of industry (GEMPPI) and in manufacturing industry as a
whole (GEMPMI) in 1980 - 1994 are compared with the relative growth
of the share of employees in the pharmaceutical industry (GEMPPItoMI)

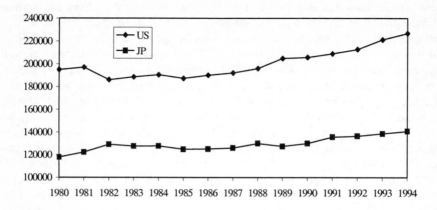

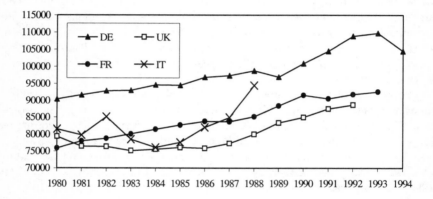

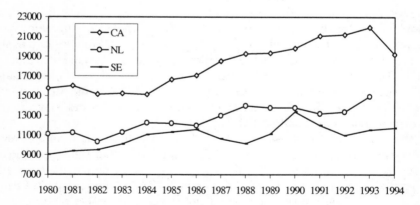

Source: OECD STAN database

FIGURE 3.5. Development of employment in the pharmaceutical industry

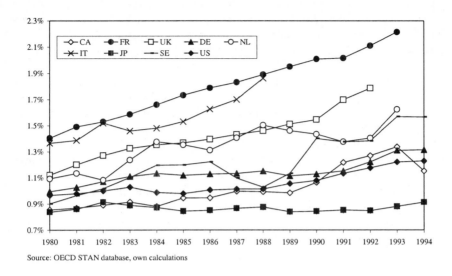

Source: OECD STAN database, own calculations

FIGURE 3.6. Development of employment in the pharmaceutical sector as a proportion of employment in the manufacturing industry as a whole

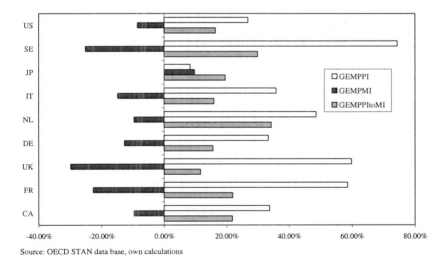

Source: OECD STAN data base, own calculations

FIGURE 3.7. Absolute growth in employment in the pharmaceutical industry and in the manufacturing industry as a whole (in %), compared with the relative share of the pharmaceutical industry in overall employment, 1980-1994

from 1980 to the end of the observation period. From this comparison, it emerges that only in Japan the increase in the relative share of employees in the pharmaceutical industry is due solely to an increase in the absolute numbers of employees in this sector - this being, in fact, the only country in which the number of employees in manufacturing industry as a whole also increased in absolute terms. In all the other countries, an increase in the numbers of employees in the pharmaceutical industry is accompanied by an employment decrease in manufacturing industry as a whole. This interrelation is weakest in the Netherlands and strongest in the case of Great Britain. In Canada, West Germany, the Netherlands, Italy, Sweden and the US, the percentage increase in employment in the pharmaceutical industry is stronger than the percentage decrease in employment over the manufacturing industry as a whole. In two countries, the percentage increase in employment in the pharmaceutical industry is exceeded by the overall percentage decrease in the manufacturing industry - in France slightly, and in Great Britain massively.

3.3   Foreign Trade and Foreign Direct Investment

Foreign trade in pharmaceutical products is strongly dynamic. Thus world exports in this product group rose from approximately 14 bn. US $ in 1980 to just under 72 bn US $ in 1995. However, it is basically true to say that due to its structure and global organization, the pharmaceutical industry is not so export-intensive as many other sectors of the manufacturing industry. Taking an export/production index of 1 for the manufacturing industry of the OECD countries overall, the equivalent index for the pharmaceutical industry would be approximately 0.66 (OECD, 1996).

Figure 3.8 and table 3.1 show the development of exports in the nine countries included in the survey. Germany, Great Britain, France and the US emerge over the whole observation period as the leading exporters of pharmaceutical products, with Germany dominating most of the time. Only in the period from 1981 to 1985 the US took over the lead position. In 1995, the US was also overtaken by both Great Britain and France, which then occupied the second and third places. If Switzerland had been included here, it would have ranked second until 1995 when, despite an export volume of 7.515 bn US $, it would have ceded its second place to Great Britain. Italy and the Netherlands occupy mid-field positions and their export development is very similar. Italy starts in 1980 with an export volume of 688 million US $, increasing to 3.630 bn. US $ in 1995. Similarly, exports from the Netherlands totaled 619 million US $ in 1980 and rose to 3.968 bn US $ by 1995. In the group of the three smallest exporters, Japan, Canada and Sweden, on the other hand, a clear differentiation takes place over time. Although the export figures for these three countries are relatively similar

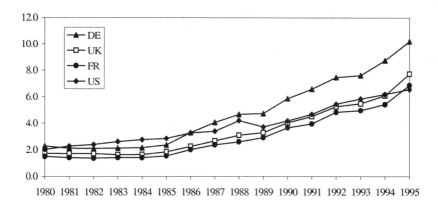

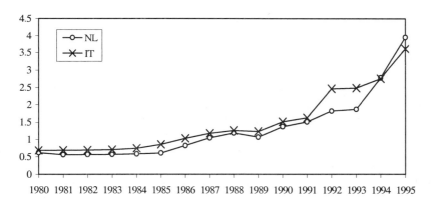

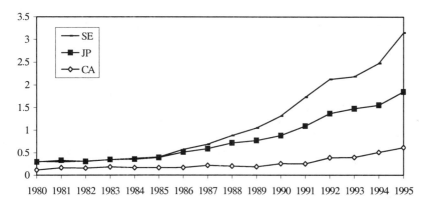

Source: United Nations

FIGURE 3.8. Exports in pharmaceutical products (billions of US $), 1980 - 1995

TABLE 3.1. Ranking of exports and imports

	Exports		Imports	
	1980	1995	1980	1995
Germany	1	1	1	1
US	2	4	3	3
Great Britain	3	2	7	5
France	4	3	4	2
Italy	5	6	5	6
Netherlands	6	5	6	7
Sweden	7	7	9	9
Japan	8	8	2	4
Canada	9	9	8	8

Source: United Nations, own calculations

in 1980, (Canada 114 million US $, Japan 295 million US $ and Sweden 305 million US $), their growth diverges. Canada's exports increased with an annual average growth rate of 13.48 % to 611 million US $ in 1995, Japanese exports with an annual average growth rate of 13.42 % to 1.844 bn US $ and Sweden's pharmaceutical exports showed an annual average growth rate of 17.41 %, increasing to 3.144 bn US $. Altogether, the nine countries considered here accounted for 62.2% of world pharmaceutical exports in 1995. This increases to 72.7% if Switzerland is also included.

When imports are considered, the countries do not split clearly into three groups as they do with regard to exports (cf. figure 3.9). Only the Federal Republic of Germany succeeds in holding an almost continuous first place in this respect, being overtaken only by the US in 1984 to 1988, and by Japan in 1988 and 1989. The import volumes of the various countries definitely lie closer together than their export volumes. Only Canada and Sweden depart from a broadly "mid-field" position.

It is also clear from table 3.1 that more frequent and more intensive ranking changes take place among imports than is the case for exports. Altogether, however, the world trade shares of the countries considered here remain relatively constant. Figure 3.10 shows the world trade shares of each country, differentiated according to exports and imports, for three points in the observation period (1980, 1990 and 1995). Only the US shows a large decrease in its share of world exports (from 14.51% in 1980, through 11.06% in 1990 to 9.15% in 1995) and a corresponding increase in its share of imports (from 5.62% in 1980, through 6.24% in 1990 to 7.61% in 1995). The other three big exporters (Germany, France and Great Britain) show only slight decreases in their shares of exports, and slight to moderate increases in their shares of global imports. Development in the smaller countries is not so homogeneous. Sweden's share of world exports shows a continuous increase (from 2.19% in 1980, through 3.47% in 1990 to 4.39% in 1995), whereas its share of global imports decreases slightly in the long

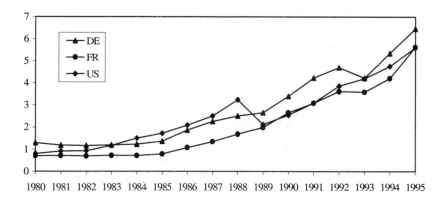

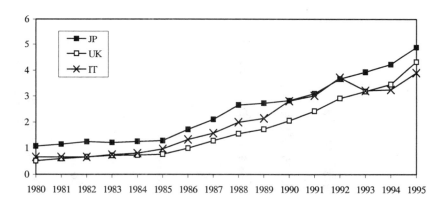

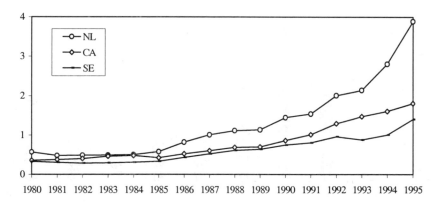

Source: United Nations

FIGURE 3.9. Imports in pharmaceutical products (billions of US $), 1980 - 1995

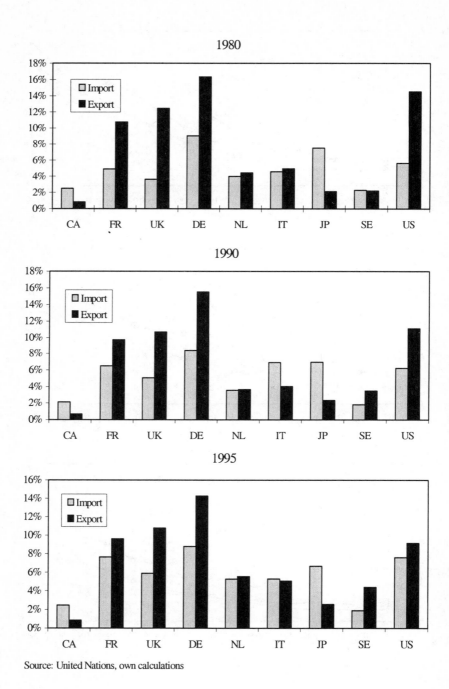

FIGURE 3.10. Development of shares in world trade

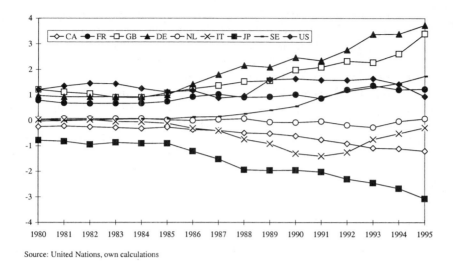

FIGURE 3.11. Foreign trade balances (billions of US $), 1980 - 1995

term (from 2.28% in 1980, through 1.84% in 1990 to 1.90% in 1995). The export shares of Canada, the Netherlands and Italy first recede slightly between 1980 and 1990, but these losses are more than made up by 1995. Japan, as a net importer, succeeds in reducing its share of world imports from 7.52% in 1980, through 6.97% in 1990 to 6.67% in 1995. At the same time its share in world exports shows a slight improvement (from 2.12% in 1980, through 2.33% in 1990 to 2.58% in 1995).

Taking a look at the foreign trade balances in figure 3.11, it is seen that Japan and Canada constantly show import surpluses. From 1983 onwards, Italy imports more pharmaceutical products than it exports. For the period from 1990 to 1994, the Netherlands also have a negative foreign trade balance. In the remaining five countries, exports exceed imports for the whole of the observation period. West Germany's export surpluses first overtake Great Britain's in 1983 and from 1986 onwards, the Federal Republic occupies a leading position in this respect, too. In 1995 Germany's export surplus reached the record figure of c. 3.731 bn US $.

Due to the specific structure of the globalization of the pharmaceutical industry, which is characterized by extensive production (particularly final production), packing and packaging - and extensive marketing - in the end consumer countries, central importance often attaches to trade in intermediate-products and to intra-industrial trade. A great part of intra-industrial trade will also be intra-company (i.e. taking place within the same enterprise or corporation). Although there are no exact data for intra-industrial and intra-company trade, the following indices for intra-industrial trade can at least be constructed for guidance.[4] These indicators, which provide another tool for analyzing trade patterns as they show the extent of international linkages for a industry, are shown in figure 3.12. In 1980, at the beginning of the observation period, the share of intra-industrial trade is very high for the Netherlands (92%), Sweden (94%) and Italy (95%). The Netherlands retain this high share for the whole period. In Italy, an initial decline down to 54% is observed. This continues until 1990/91, with the share of intra-industrial trade subsequently rising again to 93% in 1995. In Sweden, on the other hand, the share of intra-industrial trade falls fairly continuously to a final level of 45% in 1995. In another group of countries, initial 1980 values for intra-industrial trade are between 40% and 57%. This group includes the US (40%), France (47%) and Germany (57%). Whereas France and the US consistently build up their shares of intra-industrial trade to final levels of 82% and 86% respectively, the level for Germany remains almost constant throughout the observation period (63% in 1995). The third group of countries (Japan, Great Britain, Canada) have low initial values around 30% for intra-industrial trade. Japan and Canada also remain more or less at this level and have intra-industrial trade shares of 37% and 34% respectively in 1995. By contrast, Great Britain increases its share of intra-industrial trade to 56% by 1995. This might be an indicator that the British pharmaceutical industry became more global.

Further information about the structure of foreign trade can be gained from the shares of intermediates in the total exports and imports of the countries under consideration (cf. figure 3.13). The relative importance of intermediates shows also the global structure of the industry with final conversion, mixing, packaging and presentation in national final markets. Some countries that had high shares of intermediate products in their imports at the start of the observation period in 1980 reduced them over time, in some cases drastically. Canada and France should be mentioned as taking a lead here; they reduced their shares of intermediate products in imports from 69.38% and 80.01% respectively in 1980 to 33.44% and 42.93% in 1995. Italy and the US made more moderate reductions in their proportion of intermediate products in imports: from 61.41% and 61.55% respectively in 1980 to 47.13% and 49.50% in 1995. Slight reductions in the proportion of intermediate products in imports can be also be observed for Great Britain and Japan, whereas in the Federal Republic of Germany the proportion remained virtually constant (41.78% in 1980, 39.68% in 1995). Only in the Netherlands does the share of intermediate products in im-

---

[4] For product groups which are sufficiently distinct, indices for intra-industrial trade can be constructed by relating exports to imports for these product groups in bilateral trade flows, with the smaller flow forming the numerator in each case and the larger flow the denominator. In this way the index will be 100 if exports and imports are equal, and zero if either exports or imports are equal to zero. On this subject, cf. OECD (1996).

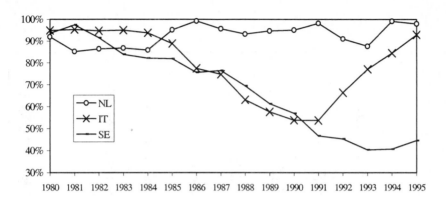

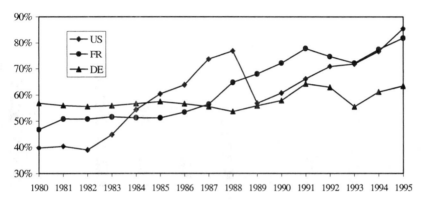

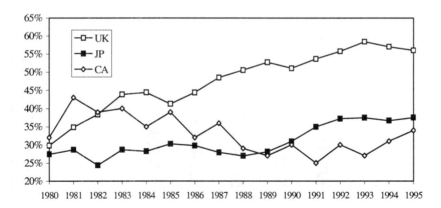

Source: United Nations, own calculations

FIGURE 3.12. Indices of the development of intra-industrial trade, 1980 - 1995

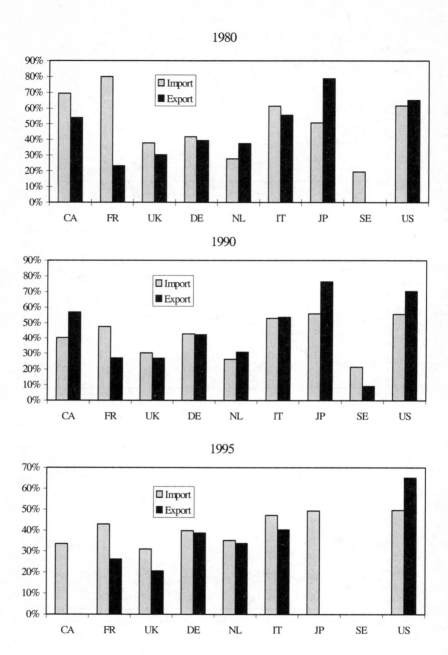

Source: United Nations, own calculations

FIGURE 3.13. Shares of intermediate products in foreign trade

ports go up, from 27.70% in 1980 to 35.06% in 1995. These declines of intermediates in imports probably may be the result of wider acceptance of common testing and inspection procedures on a regional basis fostering greater intra-regional trade in finished products and relatively reducing trade in intermediates (cf. OECD, 1996, pp. 89 - 90).

As regards the shares of intermediate products in exports, the development over time is relatively stable. The largest share of intermediate products in exports are constantly shown by Japan (78.81% in 1980, 76.36% in 1990) and the US (from 65.19% in 1980, through 70.22% in 1990 to 64.98% in 1995). Canada also has a relatively large share of intermediate products in its exports, with a level of 54.02% in 1980 and 56.83% in 1990). In the countries that occupy a mid-field position (Germany, Italy and the Netherlands), the shares of intermediate products in exports are between 33.66% and 40.19%. Intermediate products constitute a fairly small share of exports in France (developing from 23.23% in 1980, through 27.03% in 1990 to 26.21% in 1995), in Great Britain (30.31% in 1980, through 26.91% in 1990 to 20.53% in 1995) and especially in Sweden, where the share of intermediate products in exports was 9.03% in 1995. Again, reductions of the shares of intermediate exports for European countries may be the result of the wider acceptance of common testing and inspection procedures. On the other hand, increasing exports of intermediates (like for France and partly also for Germany) might be linked with the expansion of international operations including intermediate exports to affiliates (cf. OECD, 1996, p. 90).

As mentioned before, due to different governmental regulations pharmaceutical firms often must be present in the national markets for final products. Local marketing is also essential in many cases. Furthermore, there are many international cooperations to develop new technologies. As a consequence, a strong increase of foreign direct investment and of all kinds of international cooperations can be observed. In the eighties, average annual growth in foreign direct investment between the three major markets Western Europe, Japan and the US was 17.5 % compared to 12.9 % for finished products trade and 11.2 % for intermediates trade. The sources and distribution of stocks of direct investment at the end of 1988 are displayed in figure 3.14. It is obvious that the US and Western Europe are the main sources as well as destinations of foreign direct investment.

The importance of foreign direct investment is also reflected by the market shares of foreign-controlled firms in major national markets. In 1989, the major pharmaceuticals producing countries had foreign-controlled market shares between 20 % and 60 % (figure 3.15). Considering the source of ownership, European firms hold the largest foreign-controlled shares, except in the United Kingdom where pharmaceutical firms from the US were the most important.

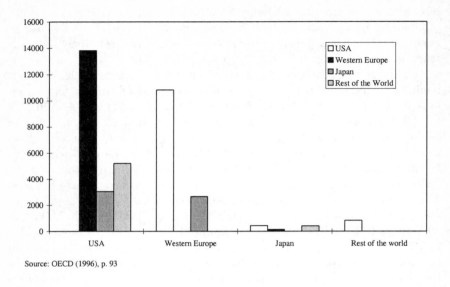

Source: OECD (1996), p. 93

FIGURE 3.14. Stocks of foreign direct investment in 1988 (millions of US $)

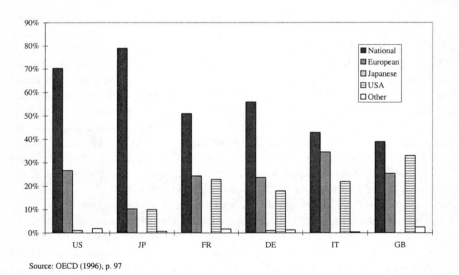

Source: OECD (1996), p. 97

FIGURE 3.15. Market shares of foreign-controlled firms in 1989

3.4 Conclusions for the International Competitiveness of Selected Countries

The term or even concept of "international competitiveness" is still to a large extent vague (Gehrke/Grupp, 1994). A picture of "international competitiveness" of countries or of a particular sector in several countries cannot be drawn on the basis of just one indicator. This task requires a number of indicators that describe how a country or an industry stands in international comparison and how its position has developed over time. Economic data on production, employment and foreign trade can help to provide a first sketch of the international competitiveness of the pharmaceutical industry in selected countries. This sketch can then be augmented by further data on R&D, patents etc. to give a clearer picture (see chapter 6). But it is unnecessary and would be probably wrong to condense the individual indicators to just one indicator or to a rank order. Researchers are still working on the aggregation problem but a solution is out of sight (Porter and Roessner 1991): There is no solution on principle. Anyhow, such compilations which are e. g. offered by the World Economic Forum/IMD show the systemic character of questions concerning "international competitiveness".

Considering international competitiveness in a careful way, the data compiled in the two former sections show the following: the US are clearly the largest producer of pharmaceuticals. Comparing the levels and growth rates of production (cf. figure 3.16), it can be seen that the level of Japanese production in 1994 is also above-average. However, Germany, France and Great Britain are still large producers of pharmaceuticals. Countries with above average annual growth rates (1981 - 1994) are Great Britain, the US, Canada and Sweden.[5]

The levels and growth rates of exports are displayed in figure 3.17. There is a clear separation between small export countries with above average annual growth rates and large export countries with below average annual growth rates. Japan belongs also to the first group with fast growing exports. High growth rates of the smaller export countries indicate that they are catching up. However, due to different country sizes, this can be only a relative catching up. The group of the large export countries remains stable over time.

The employment figures provide similar evidence (cf. figure 3.18). Small countries with small pharmaceutical industries in absolute numbers show above average annual growth rates and employment in large countries with

---

[5] Italy is now dropped from the sample because Italian data on production and employment is only available until 1987. Italy is further taken into account when the export performance is considered.

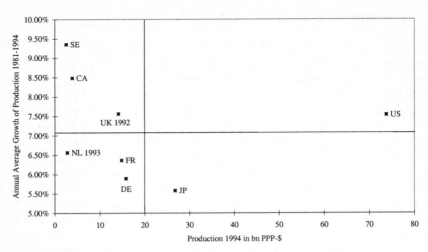

Source: OECD STAN database, own calculations

FIGURE 3.16. Levels and annual average growth rates of production of pharmaceuticals in selected countries

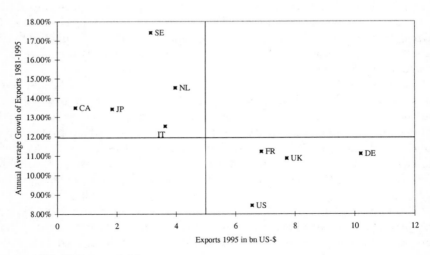

Source: United Nations, own calculations

FIGURE 3.17. Levels and annual average growth rates of exports of pharmaceuticals in selected countries

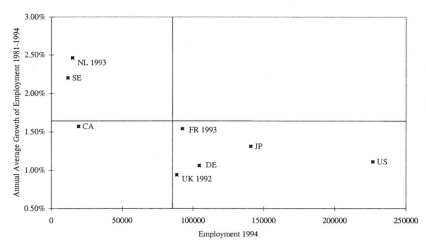

Source: OECD STAN database, own calculations

FIGURE 3.18. Levels and annual average growth rates of employment in the pharmaceutical industries of selected countries

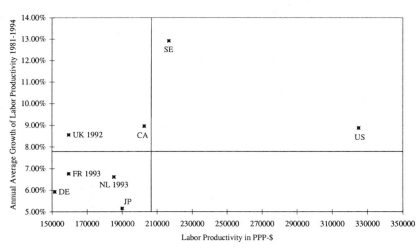

Source: OECD STAN database, own calculations

FIGURE 3.19. Levels and annual average growth rates of labor productivity in the pharmaceutical industries of selected countries

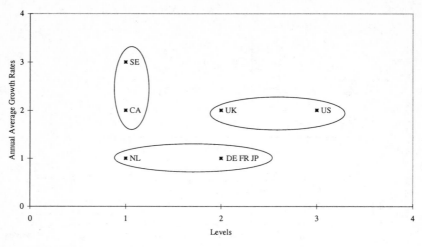

Source: Own calculations

FIGURE 3.20. Clusters of pharmaceutical industries in selected countries

large pharmaceutical sectors is growing at below average rates. The only exception here is France which shows growth rates slightly above average.

Additional insight into the market for pharmaceuticals - especially into the supply side of this market - can be gained by looking at labor productivity i. e. output per employee. The levels and annual average growth rates of labor productivity in the pharmaceutical industry of eight selected countries are displayed in figure 3.19. It is obvious that countries with high levels of labor productivity also show above average annual growth rates. The only exception is Great Britain which reached above average growth rates with only a below average level of productivity. The lowest labor productivity is in the pharmaceutical industry of Germany which shows at the same time the second lowest annual average growth rate. The lowest growth rate was realized by Japan. So, on the one hand, the country with the largest volume of production, the United States, and the two countries with the highest annual average growth rates of production, Sweden and Canada, have clear advantages on the supply side due to high levels and high growth rates of labor productivity. On the other hand, large export countries like Germany, France and partly Great Britain too, have to take care that their strong positions on the demand side will not be undermined by supply side factors.

Summing up the empirical findings related to the levels of the four indicators it can be seen that the United States are obviously the leading country in the pharmaceutical market followed by a medium cluster consisting of France, Germany, Great Britain and Japan. The third cluster is formed of the small countries Canada, the Netherlands and Sweden. If only the annual average growth rates of the four indicators (production, exports, employment and labor productivity) are considered, Sweden is definitely the leading country followed by a cluster of countries with medium growth rates containing Canada, Great Britain and the United States. A third cluster is now formed of France, Germany, Japan and the Netherlands.

The summarized findings are condensed in figure 3.20. The first cluster contains the small countries Canada and Sweden (level 1) with medium and high levels (2 and 3) of annual average growth rates, which are clearly catching up.[6] The second cluster consists of small and medium level countries (the Netherlands as well as France, Germany and Japan) with small growth rates. These countries must take care not to fall behind. The leading countries are the United States and Great Britain which show medium or high levels and medium annual average growth rates. However, the weighting problem of the individual indicators remains unsolved here too. If it is assumed that export performance is the most important indicator, Germany would yield a better position. But the results for the individual indicators seem to be so obvious that the proposed condensation into clusters might reflect reality quite well and the possible bias might be small.

---

[6] The levels as well as the annual average growth rates are now classified into three categories (1 to 3) by their similarity. This classification can be reproduced by applying a cluster analysis.

4

Innovation Process and Techno-scientific Dynamics

Thomas Reiss, Sybille Hinze

4.1 Innovation Process in Pharmaceuticals

4.1.1 Characteristics of the Innovation Process in Pharmaceuticals

The innovation process in the pharmaceutical industry is different from other innovation processes, mainly due to the regulative influence of health authorities. In order to understand this process we should first describe the different phases, the examination objects and aims, and the certification process at the health authorities.

Roughly speaking, the innovation process in the pharmaceutical industry is divided into four phases (see figure 4.1): pre-clinical research, clinical trials, certification process, and market introduction activities. The length and chronological sequence of these four phases are basically determined by legal requirements and scientific and economic necessities. In order to compare them with innovation processes in other industries, the pre-clinicals can be equated with the research phase, the clinical trials with the development phase. The division into pre-clinical research and clinical trials is basically explained by the examination of objects in human beings in clinical development and in animals and cells in pre-clinical research. So the pre-clinical phase includes all R&D activities that are carried out before the examinations with human beings take place.

The *pre-clinical research* is divided into the three stages 0, I, and II (see figure 4.1). *Pre-clinic 0* is the discovery research phase. The researchers - who are chemists and biochemists - screen a new substance for its therapeutic potential and test its pharmacological characteristics and main effects in a pharmacological model. So far, mainly classical screening approaches based on trial and error principles have been used.[1] The analytical examination (analytics) accompanies screening and includes the analysis of the results concerning target reaching and further procedures. In this phase up

---

[1] See Chapter 5.1. A good overview of possible screening methods can also be found in Herzog (1995), pp. 80-84.

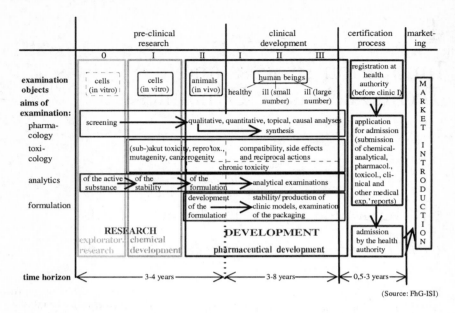

FIGURE 4.1. The innovation process in the pharmaceutical industry

to 10,000 substances are tested, but only about 20 reach the next stage.[2] The successful "hits" are also called the "New Chemical Entities" (NCEs)[3].

After screening, the NCEs are tested in *pre-clinic I* with cells. This innovation phase is called chemical development. In vitro studies are undertaken, which are defined as examinations with isolated organs, tissues, and cells. Here, and in all other following examinations, the aim is to synthesize a substance profile. This profile consists of qualitative, quantitative, topical and causal analyses of pharmacological effects, which include kinds, intensity, target, and mechanisms of therapeutic effects. The stability of a substance is especially analyzed.

In *pre-clinic II* the pharmacological and toxicological effects on bacteria and animals are tested. This research phase is the beginning of the pharmaceutical development (continued in clinical development I, II, III). Toxicological examinations cover acute and chronic phenomena. Acute toxicity examines poisoning indications after single application and includes the nature, dimension and frequency of the symptoms. This examination could

---

[2] This and the following numbers of successful substances can only give a rough average of the actual record of success. There are two reasons: the efficiency of research can differ from research unit to research unit and the innovation process is not always as linear as it is described in this chapter. Often the stages overlap and future examinations can have an influence on the number and the success of substances.

[3] Sometimes NCEs are also defined as all substances being evaluated.

already have been undertaken with cells in pre-clinic I.[4] Subacute toxicity is the determination and description of clinical, hematological, biochemical and pathologic-anatomical changes after a daily dose of the substance over one to three months. Chronic toxicity is the identification of functional and anatomic-pathological changes through long-term dosages (for therapeutical purposes) of the substance. Reproduction toxicity includes the examination of the fertility, the impact on the embryo, the deformation of newborns and the fertility of the grown-up descendants. Also the mutagenity and cancerogenity are tested. Mutagenity concerns the changes in the genetic material and cancerogenity the carcinogenic potential.

These examinations on toxicity can hardly all be done with easy to handle and cost-efficient bacterial systems, so there is a need of higher organisms. The more complicated the examinations are, the more human-like in metabolism and genetic material the examination object has to be. This examination with bacteria and then animals is a so-called in vivo study, i. e. studies with whole organisms.

For the first time formulation development is an objective of examination, this includes the examination of the quality of the drug (at this stage the substance can be called "drug") and the form of administration. This is also the main focus of the analytical examination. It must be emphasized that unlike the pharmacological examinations the described toxicological examinations must be finished in pre-clinical research (only exception: chronic toxicity to a certain degree), for obvious reasons. At the end of the pre-clinics about ten NCEs are still "in competition"; the duration of the complete pre-clinical research is between three and four years.[5]

The *clinical trials* are also divided into three phases, clinic I, II, and III (see figure 4.1). The examination objects are human beings. In *clinic I* the experimental group consists of five to eighty volunteers, who are healthy or do not suffer from the concerned illness. In *clinic II* the experimental persons are a limited number of voluntary patients suffering from the target disease. *Clinic III* is a large-scale study (100 to thousands of patients with the target disease) in different clinics with often a long period of administration. The scientists are doctors and medical assistants, in clinic I with pharmacological qualification, in clinic II with experience in testing of drugs, in clinic III clinical doctors and other local medical experts. In all three phases the pharmacological examinations are continued and become more human-specific. Chronic toxicity is tested and includes also mutagenity and cancerogenity as aims of examination. Additionally, the compatibility, side effects, and reciprocal actions of the drug are tested.

---

[4] This is not only a possibility, but also a necessity, because in this way a lot of substances can be rejected before the much more expensive pre-clinic II stage is reached.

[5] Estimates concerning the time horizon and the number of substances are adopted from Schwarzer (1994), p. 181 and supplemented by the estimates of Herzog (1995), p. 122.

The formulation examination concerns the stability of the form of administration, the production of clinic models and the packaging. The time horizon of the clinical research phase is approximately between three and eight years.

The described phases of the innovation process in the pharmaceutical industry are chronological, but they can overlap to a certain degree. All the clinical trial stages are legally required, as are most of the animal studies. The permission to undertake clinical trials is given by health authorities. This permission can be obtained through the registration before clinic I. A successful end of the clinical development phase is the finding of one or two drugs, which then have to be evaluated by the health authorities.

After clinic III the application for registration is submitted and contains all chemical-analytical, pharmacological, toxicological, clinical, and other medical experts' reports. The following certification process includes a check of the reports with a focus on quality, efficacy and harmlessness of the drug (see figure 4.1). These requirements aim to estimate risks and benefits of a drug. This is mainly justified by aspects of consumer protection and protection of the human examination objects. In the certification process it additionally could become necessary to ask the company questions concerning lack of clarity or completeness of the reports and certification papers. The certification process can last between six months and three years before the permission is granted or refused.

After the registration through the health authority, the drug can be introduced into the market. But this is not the first or single marketing activity. The pharmaceutical company can already start in an earlier phase informing consumers, doctors, sales representatives and hospital personnel about the product advantages of the drug. In the clinical development phases contacts can be established with clinics and the public can be informed about the existence of a new drug. Thus, the clinical trials are themselves considered as marketing activities (according to our interviews) to give a new drug publicity to doctors, clinics etc. Parallel to the phase of development the first production plants have to be (re)built so that after registration the drug can immediately be produced and distributed.

In addition to the described phases of the innovation process in the pharmaceutical industry, post-marketing surveillance must be mentioned. It includes scrutinizing the new drug's usage and ongoing clinical examinations concerning previously unrecognized adverse effects or abuses or changes in efficacy and side effects. This is especially necessary in the case of a widespread usage of the drug and for the discovery of new therapeutical areas of application. So these later clinical examinations provide a good source of information for further drug development.

4.1.2 The Importance of R&D for the Generation of Innovation

Conducting their own research and development (R&D) is decisively important for pharmaceutical enterprises in maintaining and extending their innovativeness and competitiveness. Accordingly the pharmaceutical industry is among the industrial subsectors with the highest R&D intensity. Throughout the OECD countries, the pharmaceutical sector is constantly among the top four R&D-intensive industries and at present it ranks second, after the space industry and before the computer and electronics industry (cf. OECD, 1996). The reason for this high level of R&D activity is that innovations are strongly based on the results of basic research. This notion is supported empirically by non-patent citations in patent applications which can be transformed into an indicator for the science-base of technologies (Grupp/Schmoch 1992): The respective NPL (non-patent-literature) indicator for pharmaceutical patent-applications is about 2,5 times the average NPL-value for all technologies (Hinze et al., 1997).

The R&D costs of bringing a new drug to the market are estimated at between 350-500 million US $ (cf. Reiss/Hüsing/Hinze, 1997; Drews/Ryser, 1997).[6] About 10 % of these costs are required for research (ending with a new lead and patent application), 90 % for development (Drews/Ryser, 1997). Development itself can be divided into manufacturing and process innovation (15 % of development costs), pre-clinical (15 % of development costs), and clinical (70 % of development costs) development. These ratios clearly indicate that clinical development is by far the most cost-intensive phase of drug development extending to about 300 million US $. The average research costs of a project per year are estimated to amount to about 6 million US $, in addition to which there are also about 14 million US $ of development costs. In the literature, a span of seven to 15 years is given as the average time it takes to perform the research and development for a new medicine (see 4.1.1): about three to four years for pre-clinical research and development, about eight years to perform the various clinical studies (clinical development) and about one to three years for the approval process. However, in order to remain competitive in practice, overall times have to be considerably shorter (about seven to eight years).

4.2 Techno-Scientific Changes

4.2.1 Introduction

The technological roots of the modern pharmaceutical industry can be traced back to the late 19th and early 20th century (Bogner, 1996). A

---

[6] This estimate does, however, include the costs of unsuccessful R&D projects.

first technological trajectory comprises the emergence of synthetic organic chemistry in the 19th century in central Europe. This technology developed alongside color-dye chemistry which was one of the foundations of the chemical industry in Europe. Synthetic organic chemistry provided a variety of new small molecules which could also be tested for biological activity. The rationale behind this type of early drug research was that the chemical agent was likely to have an impact on a certain illness. In principle, this approach is based on trial and error and deductive reasoning.

A second trajectory was research on anti-infectant compounds which emerged during the first quarter of the 20th century. The goal of this research was the development of drugs against external infectious agents like, for example, bacteria. As a result, first natural substances became available as anti-infectious or antibiotic agents. As a new tool fermentation technology was introduced into pharmaceutical research. Later, synthetic anti-infectious agents could also be synthesized.

A third line of technologies influencing the pharmaceutical industry was the utilization of natural substances which complemented synthetic organic chemistry. Vitamins, hormones, and also alkaloids were the main groups of natural compounds which attained a pharmaceutical value.

Since about 1950 biochemistry gained an increasing influence on pharmaceutical research (Drews, 1995). During that time some of the main metabolic pathways with the corresponding enzymatic activities could be elucidated. This created a large potential of new possible targets for pharmaceuticals. In consequence, between 1945 and 1965 the therapeutic spectrum of pharmaceuticals expanded considerably - a process which is sometimes referred to as the first pharmaceutical revolution.

The core principles of discovering and developing new drugs remained basically the same during the different stages: The procedure was based mainly on the screening and testing of thousands of chemical and natural substances which were available through huge substance libraries (cf. Drews, 1996). For example, major pharmaceutical companies have available chemical libraries upwards of 500,000 compounds (Bevan et. al., 1995). Natural substances on the other side add a unique diversity and functionality to the spectrum of synthetic compounds.

The screening procedures were time-consuming and more or less random because drug targets and drug functions were in most cases not known. On average, about 10,000 substances being screened led to about one new drug. Not surprisingly, the variety of different drug targets is rather small. Only about 420 different drug targets are covered by all presently available drugs (Drews, 1996).[7] This number of drug targets corresponds to the total number of receptors, enzymes, ion-channels and other targets in the human

---

[7]It should be noted that anti-infective targets in viruses, bacteria or parasites are excluded.

body for which drug molecules have been developed during the last one hundred years.

The necessary skills for developing drugs according to this scheme are mainly related to chemistry and pharmacology. Even if considering the growing contributions of biochemistry and medical research to a more rational approach to the understanding of diseases, and in consequence the foundations of drug research, the disciplinary spectrum of "classical" pharmaceutical research can be considered as rather narrow. As will be described in the following chapters, this situation has been changing dramatically since the beginning of the 90s, leading to a new picture of the future development of the pharmaceutical industry.

4.2.2   New Ways of Drug Discovery and Development

Mainly three fundamental technological developments and achievements contributed to the changing methods of drug discovery and development which emerged during the last decade. First, a whole set of new approaches (such as genomics or functional disease models) led to an increase of the number of potential drug targets. Second, new systems for High Throughput Screening (HTS) were developed. Third, the number of chemicals with potential pharmaceutical activity could be raised by orders of magnitude. All in all, these changes are leading to a new scheme of drug discovery and development (Drews/Ryser, 1997; Jean, 1997; Bellot et al., 1997; Hogan, 1997) which is characterized by higher complexity and necessitates the interaction and integration of more different disciplines (see figure 4.2).

In summary the new paradigm of drug development can be described as follows: The world-wide human genome sequencing efforts combined with the development of functional models for diseases provide an increasing number of new drug targets for known diseases. The number of these targets is estimated to rank between 3,000 and 10,000 (Drews 1996), which is at least an order of magnitude more compared to the present situation with about 420 drug targets. These new drug targets can be used in HTS systems which already today are able to screen about 10,000 substances per day. This increased screening capacity requires in turn the availability of a sufficient number of chemicals to be tested. Novel approaches in chemistry, namely combinatorial chemistry, enter the scene at this stage.

This new method of synthetic chemistry is able to provide almost indefinite numbers of different molecules within a very short time. Combinatorial chemistry and HTS systems are only possible if automation, robotics, and bioinformatics are used.

In the following sections the critical technologies and stages of this new schema are discussed in more detail.

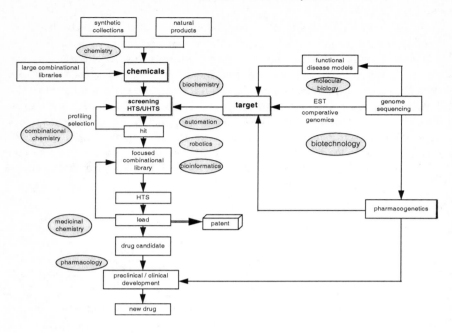

FIGURE 4.2. New ways of drug discovery and development

Target identification

The basis for the development of new targets for potential pharmaceuticals is laid by genome sequencing activities which sometimes also are described as "genomics" (Gelbert/Gregg, 1997; Christofferson, 1997; Drews/Ryser, 1997). These include the human genome sequencing program which started in 1990, but also sequencing of other organisms of prokaryotic or eukaryotic origin. The number of human genes is estimated to range between 50,000 and 100,000. Using the so-called Expressed Sequence Tagging method (EST) the expression of about 40,000 human genes has been mapped already. Until recently, forecasts estimated a completion of the sequencing of the human genome by the year 2003 to 2005. During 1998 the pace of the different private and public sequencing projects has accelerated, promising to produce a "working draft" of the human genome by 2001 (Marshall, 1998). Related to drug discovery, the challenge of human genome sequencing is to assign functions to genes, which is a prerequisite for the identification of potential drug targets. Several approaches have been developed for that purpose:

1. Comparative genomics starts with the identification of essential pathways and functions in living organisms. Common genes of such pathways between different species suggest regulatory checkpoints which are potential targets for therapeutics, because misfunctions of such checkpoints may occur in disease situations. As of April 1998 10

genome sequences have been completed. These include those of Escherichia coli, Helicobacta and bakers yeast. Fifty more sequences are expected to be completed until the year 2000. Publicly accessible databanks with lists of genome sequencing projects and sequence data have been created, thereby making this knowledge available worldwide.

2. Genes from pathogenic organisms (total sequences of some of those are already available) allow the identification of targets for drugs against virulence and pathogenicity.

3. New model systems for genomic analysis are developed. These include for example the bakers yeast system. Inactivated yeast genes can be complemented through human genes, thereby providing information about the function of the respective human gene. This complementation analysis has been done for most positionally cloned disease genes. Expression products of these genes are obvious candidates for drug action. Another approach is based on the interactions between proteins or between DNA and proteins. This provides information on regulatory events which again can be developed further into drug targets. All those new model systems should meet certain criteria, the most important being their adaptability to HTS systems, cost effectiveness, and the utilization of well defined genomes.

4. Genetic variation provides another opportunity for identifying new targets. In this case, known gene sequences are re-sequenced in a large population with the aim of identifying mutations which may probably be associated with diseases. Gene products of such mutations are potential drug targets.

An important tool during this target identification procedures is bioinformatics. This new discipline which emerged at the interface between biology and informatics uses biological data and knowledge stored in computer databases complemented by computational methods to derive new biological knowledge (Andrade/Sander, 1997). In particular, the identification of genes from DNA sequences, the assignment of genes to biological pathways, comparative genomics, and the efforts of predicting protein function from sequence information rely heavily on bioinformatic tools. Even though bioinformatics has made considerable progress during the last years, the so-called protein-folding problem (the calculation of the three-dimensional structure of a protein from protein sequence data alone) has still not been solved (Hubbard, 1997). This means that the rational design of new drugs is still limited because of the inability to predict the binding energy between two interacting molecules.

Before entering screening programs a validation of the new drug target is necessary (Lyall, 1996). Bioinformatics plays a central role in this process through the modeling of biological pathways, the simulation of biological processes, differential gene expression, and functional genomics.

Screening systems

Drug discovery remains largely a numbers game. Screening large numbers of chemicals is essential. Traditional screening procedures managed to analyze 100 to 1,000 compounds per day. New high throughput and ultra-high throughput systems (HTS, UHTS) are orders of magnitude more efficient. As a first step for developing such a system, suitable bioassays need to be elaborated. These can be based on ligand-receptor interaction or cellular systems. For the detection of the interaction between the drug target and chemicals, signal detection has to be implemented. Signals could be electrical responses, scintillation, luminescence, fluorescence and others. Robotics and automation are essential tools for developing such HTS or UHTS systems (Houston/Banks, 1997). Workstations or stand-alone systems which allow 24 hours unmanned operation comprise the present state of the art.

HTS systems which are semi- or fully automated using 96 reaction well plates are widely used today. The following figures illustrate the progress in the development of screening systems during the last decade. In the early 90s the standard performance of a lead discovery organization allowed the screening of about 75,000 samples through 20 targets within one year. This corresponds to about 1.2 million assays per year or 4,109 assays per day. UHTS systems which are being introduced by the pharmaceutical industry today are able to screen about 100,000 substances per day in a fully automated way using plates of up to 3,456 wells. The challenge is to test about one million compounds against one hundred targets per year which corresponds to 100 million assays per year or 273,000 assays per day.

Many of those HTS or UHTS systems are based on one-to-one binding assays between different molecules. In consequence, the system will identify chemicals which are good binders. However, it is not that proven that good binders are also good compounds working in the clinic, i. e. good candidate drugs. Therefore, the validation of lead compounds during screening procedures is essential.

The problem today is no more the generation of leads but rather the question how many new compounds can be validated as potential therapeutics (Persidis, 1998). The challenge for developing suitable targets for drug screening is to obtain clinically relevant information from HTS programs. The problem is located between two poles. At the one end the one-to-one interaction between molecules can be placed. Such reactions are very suitable for HTS or UHTS systems, but the clinical relevance of interactions is questionable. A currently applied approach is the refinement of the interactions signals in order to deduct disease-related information from more sophisticated signals. At the other end of screening opportunities cell-based systems are located. These are highly relevant for the disease problem under consideration, however, they are difficult to integrate into HTS or UHTS systems. An example for cellular approaches are mouse-cell-based systems (Friedrich, 1996), which are applied according to the following rationale: after the identification of human gene sequences the homologous mouse-sequence is mutated. The physiological response in the mouse-cell system is identified allowing conclusions about the respective response in the human system. This information can be incorporated into the development of a suitable clinically relevant target.

Chemicals

The improvement of the screening potential allowed for more different chemicals to be screened. Combinatorial chemistry offers a new tool for providing these (Hogan, 1997; Persidis, 1997; Gold/Alper, 1997; Myers, 1997; Whitehead, 1998). Combinatorial chemistry as a new synthetic chemistry tool emerged during 1989 and 1990 from independent discoveries in US laboratories. Combinatorial chemistry starts with a set of different chemical building blocks. These building blocks are connected in a systematic way during several repetitive chemical synthesis rounds. In principle, the synthesis circles continue until all possible combinations of the building blocks have been synthesized. The different synthetic reactions are performed in a highly parallel mode. As a result, a combinatorial library of the maximal number of different molecules made up of a given set of building blocks is prepared.

For example, libraries of tetra peptides using 20 amino acids will contain 160,000 distinct compounds. Such peptide libraries can be synthesized within a few days. The potential of combinatorial chemistry for synthesizing large varieties of different molecules is enormous. It seems to be feasible to synthesize all possible small molecular ligands, a number which is estimated to range between 1,030 and 1,050. Since the efficient and repetitive handling of large numbers of items is crucial for combinatorial chemistry, this new method relies heavily on robotics and automation.

Combinatorial chemistry is important at different stages of the drug discovery and development process (see figure 4.2). The first stage is during lead identification. For this purpose, large libraries are needed which are made up of more than 10,000 different substances. The second stage is lead optimization which requires smaller but focused combinatorial libraries. These usually comprise less than 1,000 different compounds which are synthesized starting from lead structures which had been identified during the first screening rounds. Lead optimization is increasingly used by pharmaceutical companies during drug discovery. However, due to confidentiality reasons only few reports are published. Among those are Pfizer and Eli Lilly which are able to achieve lead optimization in six to twelve month time frames. For example, an anti-arteriosclerotic lead could be increased in potency by a factor of 100 during the synthesis of about 1,000 lead derivatives.

Patent protection for the new lead is applied for after the completion of lead optimization and the lead will enter drug development, i. e. the pre-clinical and clinical stages as a new drug candidate (see chapter 4.1).

At present, there are no drugs on the market that were discovered using combinatorial chemistry. However, just recently Eli Lilly brought a new combinatorial chemistry based candidate drug into clinical trials which took less than two years from identification to entering into the trials (Persidis, 1997). This clearly demonstrates the potential of combinatorial chemistry to speed up the drug discovery process. More generally, it is estimated that using targeted combinatorial libraries will be able to increase the success rate of lead discovery by a factor of 100 to 1,000 (Hogan, 1997).

As summarized in figure 4.2, chemicals for screening systems could also be provided by natural products. This has been a preferred source of drug candidates in the past. Even though synthetic combinatorial approaches are being widely used today, natural products as chemicals for drug screening are still important. The reason for this notion is that these natural products libraries are different from chemical libraries mainly in two ways: first, they exhibit a huge molecular diversity, second, they are characterized by a superior biological functionality (Nisbeth/Moore, 1997).

Recent trends include the application of HTS approaches for the screening of natural products. Currently, a screening rate of about 1 million substances per year is achieved (Bevan et. al., 1995). Other new developments focus on the integration of combinatorial chemical approaches with natural product syntheses. Recent examples include peptide-based natural products. Finally, the development of combinatorial bio-synthesis is another option for the improvement of natural products for screening purposes. All in all, there seems to be an interesting perspective for natural products in the new frame of drug discovery and development.

Pharmacogenetics

The emerging discipline of pharmacogenetics is a consequence of the international genome sequencing efforts (see above). Pharmacogenetics means the study of polymorphism in genes that affect the response of an individual to drugs (Lichter/Kurth, 1997). This approach is significant for drug development in several ways:

1. Since genetic variants differ in response to drug treatment, pharmacogenetic studies bear a potential for optimizing drug development: using stratified patient groups for a more customized drug therapy, regime clinical testing could be speeded up. For example, genetic variants exist for many drug metabolizing enzymegenes. One gene has been identified which is supposed to be involved in the metabolism of more than 20 % of prescription drugs. This drug metabolism can be

related to diverse side reactions. Using this information for selecting patient populations for clinical studies, may help to avoid adverse reactions during clinical testing, thereby speeding up the whole process.

2. Pharmacogenetics could also be important during the discovery phase. Knowledge of genetic variations in potential drug targets could help to identify compounds with larger therapeutic markets, because of low population variability in the chosen target.

4.2.3   Implications for the Industry

The new way of drug discovery and development requires new types of knowledge. In particular, sequencing genomes, deriving information from genome sequences, parallel handling of large numbers of samples and large pieces of information, computation of an increasing wealth of information, high-speed screening, new synthetic chemical approaches like combinatorial chemistry, and pharmacogenomics are becoming increasingly important. Likewise, the number of different scientific disciplines which are forming the basis for the development of these new types of knowledge is increasing. In addition to chemistry, pharmacology and medical research which are the traditional disciplines of drug development, molecular biology, biotechnology, bioinformatics, robotics, and combinatorial chemistry are gaining importance. These new disciplines are emerging not only in an evolutionary manner within a broader disciplinary frame. Rather, new disciplines at the borderlines of traditional disciplines are becoming important. Bioinformatics is an example of such a new interdisciplinary field.

High throughput screening (table 4.1) and combinatorial chemistry (table 4.2) are other business opportunities for specialized high-tech firms (Persidis, 1997; Schneider, 1998). These firms again are mainly established in the US. HTS robotic systems specialists are located in various federal states, while combinatorial chemistry companies seem to be concentrated in California (San Diego) and Massachusetts (Boston), a view which could also be confirmed during company interviews.

The new types of knowledge and the related disciplines go beyond the experience and traditional R&D capabilities of pharmaceutical firms. Therefore, strategies, scopes, and organization of pharmaceutical R&D need rethinking. In principle, two strategies are obvious: firstly, the in-house establishment of the new technologies which could be achieved, for example, through mergers and acquisitions. Secondly, the utilization of special scientific and technological expertise from external sources which would include mainly high-tech firms, research organizations or universities. Strategic cooperations would be the way of implementation. Both approaches need to take into account how the arena of the new way of drug discovery is de-

TABLE 4.1. Examples of HTS robotic systems companies

Company	Location
The Automation Partnership	Melbourne, Hertfordshire (UK)
Beckman Instruments Inc.	Fullerton, CA (US)
Bohdan Automation Inc.	Mundelein, IL (US)
Carl Creative Systems Inc.	Bellevue, WA (US)
Corning Costar	Cambridge, MA (US)
Costar UK Ltd.	High Wycombe (UK)
CRS Robotics	Burlington Ontario (CA)
Cyberlab	Brookfield, CT (US)
Gilson Inc.	Middleton, WI (US)
Gilson Medical Electronics SA	Villiers Le Bel (FR)
Hamilton Co.	Reno, NV (US)
LJL Biosystems	Sunnyvale, CA (US)
Oyster Bay Pump Works Inc.	Oyster Bay, NY (US)
Richard Scientific	Novato, CA (US)
Robbins Scientific Corp.	Sunnyvale, CA (US)
ROBOCON	Vienna (AT)
Robo Synthon Inc.	San Francisco, CA (US)
Rosys Anthos	Madrid (ES)
Semat Technical (UK) Ltd.	St. Albans (UK)
TECAN	Research Triangle Park, NC (US)
Titertek Instruments Inc.	Huntsville, AL (US)
Tomtec	Gaithersburg , MD (US)
Wallac OY	Turku (FL)
Zinsser Analytic GmbH	Frankfurt (DE)
Zymark	Hopkinton, MA (US)

Source: Schneider (1998)

veloping. In particular, it is important to spot the new key players in the different fields.

The changing paradigm of drug discovery offers new opportunities for innovative specialized biotech firms. Nearly all of the critical technologies which are summarized in figure 4.2 are being developed by such small and medium-sized enterprises (SMEs). For example, there is a group of firms focusing on sequencing genes and assigning functions to gene sequences. Some of those genomics companies are listed in table 4.3 (Sedlak 1998, Hodgson 1998). This (and tables 4.1 and 4.2) is not a complete or representative list. However, the emerging picture of regional clusters around Boston MA, San Francisco and San Diego CA, was also confirmed during interviews with companies in the US and Europe.

The trend among pharmaceutical companies to outsource some of the key technologies of the drug discovery process such as combinatorial chemistry, however also bears a certain danger for high-tech SMEs (Whitehead,

TABLE 4.2. Examples of combinatorial chemistry companies

Company	Location
Afferent Systems Inc.	San Francisco, CA (US)
Affymax Research Institute	Palo Alto, CA (US)
Alanex Corporation	San Diego, CA (US)
Aptein Corp.	Seattle, WA (US)
Argonaut Technologies	San Carlo, CA (US)
ArQule	Medford, MA (US)
Arris Pharmaceuticals	San Francisco, CA (US)
BioFocus	Settingbourne (UK)
Cambridge Combinatorial	Cambridge (UK)
Charybidis Technologies	Carlsbad, CA (US)
Chemical Design Inc.	Mahwah, NJ (US)
CombiChem Inc.	San Diego, CA (US)
Cytogen Corporation	Princeton, NJ (US)
Gilhead Sciences	Foster City, CA (US)
Houghton Pharmaceuticals	San Diego, CA (US)
Integrated PharmaQuest Technologies	San Diego, CA (US)
IRORI Quantum Mycrochemistry	La Jolla, CA (US)
ISIS Pharmaceuticals	Carlsbad, CA (US)
Ixsys	San Diego, CA (US)
MDL Information Systems Inc.	San Leandro, CA (US)
Molecular Simulations	San Diego, CA (US)
Multiple Peptide Systems Inc.	San Diego, CA (US)
Myriad Genetics Inc.	Salt Lake City, UT (US)
NeXstar Pharmaceuticals Inc.	Boulder, CO (US)
Ontogen	Carlsbad, CA (US)
Organon Laboratories	Motherwell (UK)
Pharm-Eco Laboratories Inc.	Lexington, MA (US)
Pharmacopeia Inc.	Princeton, NJ (US)
Procept	Cambridge, MA (US)
Solid Phase Science Corp.	Watertown, MA (US)
The Technology Partnership	Royston, Hertfordshire (UK)
Trega Biosciences Inc.	San Diego, CA (US)
Tripos Inc.	St. Louis, MO (US)
Vertex Pharmaceuticals	Cambridge, MA (US)
Warner Lambert Diversome Technologies	Ann Arbor, MI (US)

Source: Persidis (1997)

TABLE 4.3. Examples of genomics companies

Company	Location
Affymetrics	Palo Alto, CA (US)
Alphagene	Woburn, MA (US)
Aurora Biosciences Corp.	La Jolla, CA (US)
Curagen Corp.	New Haven, CT (US)
Digital Gene Technologies	La Jolla, CA (US)
Exelixis Pharmaceuticals	Cambridge, MA (US)
Gene Logic	Columbia, MD (US)
Gene Trace Systems Inc.	Menlo Park, CA (US)
Gene/Networks	Alameda, CA (US)
Genezyme Molecular Oncology	Framingham, MA (US)
Genome Therapeutics	Waltham, MA (US)
Genset	*Paris (FR)*
Hexagen Ltd.*	*Cambridge (UK)*
Hyseq	Palo Alto, CA (US)
Incyte Pharmaceuticals Inc.	Palo Alto, CA (US)
Lexicon Genetics Inc.	The Woodlands, TX (US)
Lion Bioscience	*Heidelberg (DE)*
Lynx Therapeutics Inc.	Hayward, CA (US)
Morphosys GmbH	*Martinsried (DE)*
Nemapharm	Cambridge, MA (US)
Onyx Pharmaceuticals	Richmond, CA (US)
Oxagen Ltd.	*Abingdon (UK)*
Pharmagene	*Roysten (UK)*
Progenitor	Menlo Park, CA (US)
Sequana Therapeutics	San Diego, CA (US)
Sequenom	*Hamburg (DE)*
Spectra Biomedical Inc.	Menlo Park, CA (US)
SRA Technologies	Falls Church, V. A. (US)
Synteni*	Fremont, CA (US)
T Cell Sciences	Needham , MA (US)
Tularik S.	San Francisco, CA (US)
Variagenetics	Cambridge, MA (US)
Visible Genetics	*Toronto (CA)*
Vyrex Corp.	La Jolla, CA (US)

Source: Sedlak (1998), Hodgson (1998)

Note: * Acquired by Incyte Pharmaceuticals in 1998

1998). From the point of view of the big pharmaceutical firms, combinatorial libraries are turning more and more from a special innovative unique technology base into a commodity which is essential for the drug development process. In consequence, the biotech SME is at the risk of becoming a commodity supplier who must depend on delivering highest quality at lowest price to stay competitive. This will lead to lower margins in this business and in conclusion to slower re-investment, which could pose a serious danger to the technological potential. One way out of this trap could be "horizontal integration" meaning that the technology provider would need to enrich its product with properties and information. In the case of combinatorial chemistry, genomics and high throughput screening would be integrated with combinatorial chemistry in a way which allows lead development. In this scenario the biotech SME of the future would no longer offer a unique technology (which is turning more and more into a commodity), but rather a new lead compound which could be licensed to the pharmaceutical company for further clinical development and marketing.

The challenge for the large pharmaceutical companies is to monitor technological change and the emergence of new players in the arena which are candidates for technology acquisition. In general, strategies need to be developed which allow the integration of the new knowledge and technology into the drug development process. This is a rather difficult task which ranges from re-organizing internal R&D to the question of future skills, education, and vocational training of human resources.

5

Generation, Transfer and Exploitation of New Knowledge

Angela Hullmann

5.1 Changes in the Division of Labor

The pharmaceutical industry has changed fundamentally in the last few years: the technological paradigms have changed (see chapter 4.2), and so has the organization of R&D. It is not so long ago that one pharmaceutical company did all the research in own departments and basically also the development activities. The tested and registered drug was marketed by the same company via a big network of sales personnel and clinical contacts. Often one best-selling drug made the greatest contribution to the company's profits and economic power. Even companies with a more diversified product portfolio have specialized in fields with firm's traditional competencies.

A closer look at the developments in pharmaceutical research up to the 1980s helps to understand the technological background. In the early beginnings of pharmaceutical research, in the 1930s, large chemical firms specialized in extensive chemical modification of basic compounds and so discovered a large number of drugs.[1] The research was limited to the finding of new compounds in chemical screening processes and testing them under experimental conditions. This trial and error process seemed economically to be the most efficient method because of the lack of basic knowledge and of course the enormous complexity of the system concerned, the human body, which was still not completely understood. This opinion is still valid. But over the decades the methods and techniques of screening compounds, the scientific knowledge about their effects and the instruments and tools have been developed further.

In the 1960s and 1970s, the basic knowledge about the properties of the compounds expanded and so "discovery by design" started. The simple techniques of organic chemistry, with the recovery of a large number of new chemical entities, were improved and led to more rational methods with

---

[1] The actual initiation of pharmaceutical research can be dated even earlier, namely, at the turn of the century, when the German bacteriologist Paul Ehrlich discovered special bonds on the surface of bacteria with chemical agents (Ehrlich's affinity theory). But industrial pharmaceutical research by chemical companies started later, on a large scale in the 1930s (see Gambardella, 1995, p. 21).

systematization of information flows. The information stems from basic research as well as from experimental observations. In the 1980s the advanced instruments (e. g. X-ray crystallography and nuclear magnetic resonance) and the improved computer technology (e. g. three-dimensional visualization, computer drug design, geometrical configuration, chemical databases) enabled the researchers to understand better complicated molecular structures and their chemical reactions, inclusively predicting side effects. One of the most important developments took place in the field of cell receptors which activate and inhibit cells.

It must be emphasized that animal testing and clinical trials remained essential because of the complexity of the human body that still causes theoretically unpredictable reactions and effects. The progress can be found in the better sorting out of critical compounds and the more effective selection of most promising drugs.

The described development then required a profound knowledge of chemical and biological dependencies in the fields of organic chemistry, microbiology, biochemistry, physiology, and pharmacology and an effective systematization of experimental observations and theoretical findings. This theoretical knowledge base was often incorporated in the large pharmaceutical companies in specialized departments. There are several reasons for this in-house research strategy.

At the beginning of pharmaceutical research it was sufficient to test the pharmacological and toxicological effects on cells and bacteria and to transmit the positives to the preclinics and clinical trials. The key of success was the large scale research in big laboratories and the optimizing of the screening procedure in terms of time and costs. The knowledge was embedded even more in laboratories than in human capital (which also played an outstanding role, but was dependent on the equipment and experience in the company).[2] Learning and scale were two sides of the same coin. Generated knowledge was not easy to transfer because of its largely tacit nature.

Tacit knowledge includes all embedded skills and knowledge of human beings (and organizations) which are generated by personal experiences in the past. Tacit knowledge is hard to communicate, the best way is via personal contact and learning by observing, interacting, and training. The prerequisite to communicating tacit knowledge to the public is to find a kind of codification to transfer tacit knowledge into explicit knowledge and to make it publicly available.[3] The openness of this codified knowledge then depends on the availability of the code (e. g. language, technical terms, basic theories), but not on the personal contact with the owner of the tacit knowledge. Publicly accessible (scientific) theories about the properties of a compound have been rare and in an infant stage. So the strategy to

---

[2] See Gambardella (1995), p.78.

[3] For a more detailed explanation of tacit and explicit knowledge, see Polanyi (1967).

undertake all research and development and the marketing of a drug in the own large company with the direct contact between researchers and developers was economically and technologically rational.

Up to the 1980s the knowledge about properties of compounds has increased, as have the technical possibilities. These circumstances forced the companies to employ more researchers with an academic background. Two benefits have arisen from this strategy: on the one hand academic researchers are more able to cope with the new screening and information technologies, on the other hand they are part of the scientific community and capable of acquiring external knowledge and information. New theories about properties of compounds have made it possible to codify the knowledge, to transfer it and to make it publicly available. A great amount of the knowledge about drugs has become explicit.

In-house research was still the dominant strategy of the large pharmaceutical companies, but the cooperation with the outside, especially with universities, has become more attractive. Scientific research in universities has built a rich source of new findings and inventions with low costs and risks for the pharmaceutical company. In many cases (e. g. when public funds are cut back), it has been even possible to influence the scientific activities of the universities in a desired way, e. g. directing of the therapeutical area as a focus of investigation.[4]

However, external knowledge has been always seen by the big pharmaceutical firms as a supplement (not substitute) to own research. Moreover, internal research has been considered indispensable to understand the external information. This process of internal learning helps the scientists to keep up to date with recent developments, to extract the relevant information and to transfer it into applied knowledge for drug innovation. Because of the growing complexity of basic theories and therapeutic applications, the necessity of specialization in closely defined areas as core competencies has expanded dramatically.

The new technologies of the late 1980s, such as molecular biology and genetic engineering, reveal the scientific limits of pharmaceutical firms. The successful pharmaceutical companies have a long (scientific) tradition in chemical and biochemical knowledge, which now must be classified as "sunk costs" , i. e. costs that no more adduce monetary returns.[5] In new sciences like biotechnology they cannot fall back on any incorporated knowledge. Most advances in molecular biology and genetic engineering have been made by scientific institutions (and also specialized biotechnology firms - and not by pharmaceutical companies' in-house scientists.[6] The fact that biotechnological knowledge is more accessible than any other knowledge

---

[4] The question of academic freedom is not a matter of concern in this paper. But the discussion exists and can be referred to in Kenney (1986).

[5] See Gambardella (1995), p. 61.

[6] See Senker (1996), p. 221.

concerning drugs does not help the pharmaceutical firms to build up their own exclusive competencies. One other fact is important to understand the shrinking competitive advantage of large firms in research activities: successful research is no longer a question of scale - as it is with development.

The vast differences between research and development concerning organizational requirements and incentives are notorious.[7] Researchers are doing basic research and can hardly be obliged to act within the confines of therapeutic potential and economic success. To improve the success rate of new findings, new methods of screening can be developed (e. g. computer-aided molecular modeling, which enables the systematic combination of chemical molecules), but nowadays the scientific and computer scientific capabilities of the researchers are the most important factors of success. Additionally, cooperation and leadership skills have become more important. The critical mass problem of the past (scale advantages) does not play the decisive role any more, it has been solved by automation techniques.[8]

By comparison with research, the development process requires a strong hierarchy and exact instructions. The functions and side effects of pharmaceuticals have to be proved in order to fulfill the requirements of the health authorities and to make estimations of the medical success of the drug possible. The cost-intensive development procedure can only be undertaken with a strong financial background. The clinical trials (especially clinic III) are the most expensive part of the innovation process in the pharmaceutical industry (see chapter 4.1.2). Therefore and because of the human examination objects a very effective and intelligent organization in optimized work steps in optimized time, without unnecessary and double investigations is needed. Mostly, only large companies can provide the finances and infrastructure to exceed the critical mass of most efficient managing of the clinical development process.

The organizational structures in many large pharmaceutical companies reflect this dichotomy of research and development: they are almost independent of each other, in organization as well as in space. The only connections are the (applied) research-relevant aspects of the clinical trials: findings of pharmaceutical and unexpected toxicological effects and side effects. These results are very important for the researchers to get to know more information about the substances - and for the developers to adjust or even abandon further developments of the substance. But furthermore, research and development can easily be separated organizationally, even in various firms with different size and distinct scientific background.

---

[7] See Drews (1995a), p. 779.

[8] James Niedel, R&D manager of Glaxo Wellcome emphasizes that nowadays up to 10,000 new molecules can be synthesized from a computer during one week, a single chemist without computer aid would manage one in the same time. See Die Woche (1997).

There are several reasons for division of labor in innovation between companies. Arrow (1983), p. 26-27 has already pointed out that there is no economic justification for both research and development in one and the same company. Arrow argues that the division of labor in R&D is economically much more advantageous according to comparative advantages in scientific, financial, and organizational prerequisites.

This statement is based on the existence of markets for research inputs in the development process, which reduce the incentives for in-house research in large firms and extend the incentives for scientific institutions to undertake commercializable inventions. Markets for research outcomes do exist, when the outcomes are communicable and protectable from exploitation by others. As already mentioned above, the knowledge concerning drugs has become explicit and available, and therefore also patentable. After being patented, the new knowledge about chemical compounds and genetic entities can be sold in form of licenses, even if no developed product exists. Therefore, communication and protection have become technically and legally conceivable.

Scientific institutions and companies can easily patent their innovations even after the pre-clinical research phases when the compounds have taken a well-defined form. Moreover, early patenting enables to gain lead-time advantages as first-to-market drugs can secure high customer loyalty. The early and rapid commercialization of innovations requires a stable financial background, which can be supplied by large firms with experience in the pharmaceutical market and broader and experienced knowledge of legal requirements. Additionally, good connections with physicians and hospitals and a well-developed distribution system support a fast and widespread market introduction.

Another motive for the outsourcing of research activities is the bureaucratic stolidity of large pharmaceutical companies. Some companies can be compared with supertankers, inflexible and hard to control. The key for success is considered to be the specialization in selected fields with flexible organizational and scientific structures and the reliance on several partners who supply ideas, product opportunities, and new technologies. Smaller firms are considered to be more flexible and form a basis for scientific creativeness.[9] The financial flexibility of the larger firms increases also, because a big share of financial and scientific risk can also be outsourced.

At this point we should emphasize one special fact: cooperation between firms depends on a long-term exchange, not only of explicit information, but also of tacit knowledge. This process of mutual learning demands a

---

[9] Jürgen Drews of Hoffmann-LaRoche insists that all "huge research organizations should be broken down into smaller semi-autonomous units, each comprising a few topically related therapeutic areas and being staffed by a few hundred people - enough to generate new ideas, discover new drugs and provide a credible proof of concept within a given area of research" (Drews, 1995, p. 24).

high level of mutual trust and close interactions.[10] An alliance over and above simple licensing or financial support always causes an exchange of internal knowledge. Internal knowledge is firm-specific, and often the most significant comparative advantage of a firm. A hire-and-fire mentality will not be as successful as a cooperative atmosphere of trust. And secrecy, as a form of protection, is important to prevent industrial espionage, but it also abandons external and internal learning and is not the suitable method to cooperate with partners.

This short introduction on the subject of creation, transfer and exploitation of new knowledge shows the growing importance of the division of labor in the pharmaceutical industry due to technical development and economic changes. Different innovation strategies can be derived from the necessities of dislocating basic (biotechnological) research, incorporating missing competencies and/or heading for the critical mass in development. The most common and visible elements of innovation strategies are alliances between different companies. In the following chapters different kinds of alliances and partners are analyzed in a more detailed way by describing and exploiting contractual alliances of the worlds' twenty largest pharmaceutical companies with biotechnological firms, universities, and other pharmaceutical companies.

5.2   Alliances of Pharmaceutical Firms

5.2.1   Theoretical Background

In the economic theory of cooperation and strategic alliances, creation and transfer of technological knowledge is only one aim of alliances with other companies and institutions, others are the increase of efficiency and the reduction of cost, risk and uncertainty.[11] The reasons for choosing alliances as an element of the innovation strategy are the growing linkages in the innovation process, the high costs of technological development, technological complexity and novelty, technological risks, the tacit and cumulative nature of technological knowledge, the increasing speed to market, the pervasiveness of information technologies and the creation of technical standards.[12] Corporate prerequisites for the decision to choose alliances are the company's position in the market, the economic and technical objectives of the firm and its management, the core competencies and the company's structure in organization, management and culture.

The different strategies which aim at the generation, exploitation and transfer of knowledge can be systemized by different characteristics. The

---

[10] See Davenport/Prusak (1998), pp. 34-36.
[11] See for example Dodgson (1993) or Kaltwasser (1994).
[12] See Dodgson (1993), p. 10-11 and p. 25-29.

first distinction is the availability of the knowledge which is transferred; it distinguishes between knowledge which is newly created or already existing and just recycled. Another criterion is the origin of the transferred knowledge, the creation inside or outside the regarded company. The last distinctive feature is the degree of formalization which distinguishes between formalized interactions through official contracts or informal interactions which are based on contacts between scientists and other persons from different companies without any contractual agreement. Examples of formal, external alliances concerning new knowledge are R&D contracts, R&D cooperations and joint ventures; external alliances concerning already existing knowledge are technology and license purchases; in acquisitions and mergers both new and existing knowledge are transferred. Internal interactions are in-house R&D, in-house cooperations and staff training; informal strategies are espionage, piracy, reverse engineering, informal contacts and analyses of (patent) literature.[13] In the following analyses only formal contracted external alliances are discussed; the large group of in-house research cooperations and informal knowledge transfer activities are left out.

In order to understand the objectives and realization of different alliances in a better way, some of the contractual alliances are now shortly described.[14] Licenses transfer the right of disposal of a newly developed technology from one company or R&D institution to another. They can refer to patented knowledge or non-patented know-how, that means knowledge which is not protected for different reasons (not patentable, secrecy). They can be transferred unilaterally or bilaterally (swap of licenses, cross licenses). Unlike licenses through technology purchase the property rights of a new technology are also transferred. It refers to the transfer of material and immaterial technologies, that means the purchase of products or equipment, respectively of codified knowledge. In R&D contracts the principal decides about the content, the duration and the financial extent of the ordered R&D activities of a research institute or other companies (suppliers, poachers) in charge.

R&D collaborations are co-operations concerning R&D activities which are undertaken by different companies of the same or different branches. The content, the financing and the created knowledge are chosen, performed and utilized by both companies. In some cases a special R&D joint venture is founded; this joint venture is an organizational relocation of R&D in a joint company with juridical independence. Purchases of participation in form of equities of other companies are one alternative to gain influence over another company i. e. which undertakes R&D in a relevant technological field. Acquisitions are the purchase of parts of other companies or the

---

[13] See Kaltwasser (1994), p. 69-74.

[14] A good survey of the described forms of alliances with a discussion of advantages and disadvantages can be found in Kaltwasser (1994), p. 74-98.

whole company; mergers the fusion of two different companies into a new company with quasi equal rights of both founding companies. Acquisitions and mergers can also be realized through equities which are purchased or swapped.

Another important distinctive feature is the kind of knowledge which is created and transferred. Two main types of knowledge can be distinguished. First, there is the explicit or codified knowledge, which can easily be transferred through written mediums like instructions, publications, patents and standard documents. This kind of knowledge is transferred in licenses and technologies, but also in results of R&D contracts. In contrast to licensing, the transferred knowledge is new, it is generated through R&D activities referred to in the contract.

The other type of knowledge is embodied in products or persons, the latter has very often a large tacit share. This tacit knowledge is not as easily transferable as the codified knowledge and it depends on personal interaction or assignment of products and equipment. The easiest way of transferring person embodied tacit and explicit knowledge is the transfer of the persons themselves, which can be undertaken by employing them or even acquiring the whole company. Mergers and acquisitions are possible strategies. The transfer of knowledge embodied in persons is also possible through closer interactions between researchers and engineers of different companies. Joint ventures and collaborations are alliances with the aim of transferring the tacit elements of this knowledge and creating new knowledge.

5.2.2   Research Approach

In order to undertake analyses of alliances of big pharmaceutical companies with other pharmaceutical companies, but even more important with biotechnological companies, it is necessary to rely on an almost complete database of existing alliances. Such a database can be found in the databank of Recombinant Capital ("ReCap") submitted via Internet.[15] ReCap is a financial consulting firm located in California in the US. The analysts of ReCap have built up this databank in order to give an overview of existing alliances to interested pharmaceutical and biotechnological companies and investors. This information is free of charge, additional information especially concerning financial consults can be purchased. The information in the ReCap databank is generated out of publicly available information about companies, technologies, and finances. The sources are mainly press releases, home pages and business reports of companies and the SEC's

---

[15] See ReCap homepage: www.recap.com.

TABLE 5.1. Top-twenty pharmaceutical companies in 1997

Company	Country	Turnover 1997 in billion US $
Merck & Co	US	11.296
Glaxo Wellcome	UK	10.870
Novartis	CH	10.537
Bristol Myer Squibb	US	9.048
Johnson & Johnson	US	8.557
Pfizer	US	8.333
American Home Products Corp.	US	8.117
Smith-Kline Beecham	UK	7.227
Hoechst Marion Roussel	DE	6.861
Eli Lilly	US	6.363
Hoffmann-LaRoche	CH	6.232
Abbott	US	5.988
Schering-Plough	US	5.524
Bayer	DE	5.278
Astra A.B.	SE	5.163
Warner Lambert	US	4.503
Rhône-Poulenc Rorer	FR	4.393
Pharmacia & Upjohn	SE	4.391
Boehringer Ingelheim	DE	3.553
Zeneca	UK	
additionally:		
Schering AG	DE	
BASF-Knoll AG	DE	

EDGAR[16] database. For the following analyses, mainly the alliances between pharmaceutical and biotechnological companies are interesting, but consulting and device companies, R&D institutions and clinics are also included.

The analyses are undertaken in the following way: first of all the twenty largest pharmaceutical companies of the United States and Europe are identified.[17] "Large" in this context is defined by the amount of the companies' turnover. It must be emphasized that only the pharmaceutical departments of the companies are relevant. Taking the companies' turnover as the criterion of choice is based on the assumption, that the larger companies are the most likely to diversify their research and development, as described

---

[16] The U.S. Securities and Exchange Commission (SEC) regulates companies engaged in the purchase or sale of securities. The database EDGAR offers a collection of biotechnology and biomedical SEC filings.

[17] This list almost corresponds to the Top Twenty list of the world, because only one company from outside Europe and the US appears in this list (Takeda from Japan).

in chapter 5.1. Furthermore, large companies are generally more internationally orientated and therefore also alliances across national borders can be expected. Finally, turnover can be seen as one (not the only) criterion of market power and success. In addition to these 20 companies two more German companies are considered (Schering AG and BASF-Knoll AG) to expand the database for a special US-German comparison. According to this, table 5.1 presents a list of the 22 pharmaceutical companies which are the base for further examinations.

This list contains 9 US companies and 13 from Europe. The European companies are from Germany (3+2), United Kingdom (3), Switzerland (2), Sweden (2) and France (1). This list is based on the turnovers of the year 1997 and the company structures at the deadline of 31st of October 1998, so that actual mergers (e. g. between the Swedish Astra and the British Zeneca in December 1998) are not taken into account. The nationalities of the companies are derived from the location of company headquarters. In our analyses we concentrate on the innovation strategies of the top twenty companies and expand the examinations by a US-Europe comparison (includes the nine largest US and European companies) and a US-German comparison (includes the five largest German and US companies).

The pharmaceutical companies are involved in diverse alliances and other kinds of interactions with other companies, research facilities and universities. As already mentioned at the beginning of this chapter, we concentrate in our analyses on those interactions which are based on contracts in different subjects. The alliances which are analyzed in the ReCap databank are financial alliances, like loans, credits, equities or securities, alliances concerning marketing activities like distribution, commercialization, co-market, co-promotion, supply or warrants and more general or strategic alliances like collaborations, joint ventures or mergers. The most interesting alliances for the innovation process and the connected knowledge-creation process are alliances in research and development. Those alliances can also be classified by the degree of proximity, i. e. time horizon or commitment and the relevant kind of knowledge.

In order to make these alliances operable for alliance-specific analyses, it is necessary to create groups of alliances according to the criteria mentioned. Possible groups are mergers (including also acquisitions and equities), cooperations (like joint ventures, collaborations and co-development), R&D contracts (research and development) and technology-purchase (including licenses). Although other types of alliances can also be very important for knowledge creation and distribution in the innovation process in the pharmaceutical industry, they are put together in the fifth group as "others" without any further division. It must be emphasized that alliances can also consist of two or more different elements. They are classified by any of the first four groups with the higher degree of proximity, i.e. if one alliance consists of licenses, equities and research contract, it is grouped into mergers, if it consists of loans, technology and collaboration, it is grouped into

TABLE 5.2. Groups of alliances

Group	ReCap's wording	Degree of proxomity	Kind of knowledge
Mergers	Mergers, acquisitions, equity	high ↑ ↑	Embodied (explicit and tacit), existing
Cooperations	Joint venture, collaboration, co-development	↑ ↑	Embodied (esp. tacit), new
R&D contracts	Research, development	↑ ↑	Explicit (disembodied), new
Technology purchases	Technology, licence, sub-licence, cross-licence	↑ low	Explicit (disembodied), existing
Others	Asset purchase, assignment, co-market, co-promotion, commercialization, credit, distribution, loan, letter of intent, manufacturing, marketing, option, supply, security, settlement, swap, termination, warrant		

R&D cooperations. Table 5.2 shows the five groups of alliances, to which the following analyses of alliances between pharmaceutical and biotechnological companies refer.

After having identified and classified the alliances of the twenty largest pharmaceutical companies, in the next step we concentrate on the partners in these alliances. As already mentioned, there are different types of partners who play a role in knowledge generation in the innovation process. In the pharmaceutical industry six main types of partners can be identified: pharmaceutical companies (competitors in the pharmaceutical market, suppliers and users of products), biotechnological firms (mainly suppliers of biotechnological knowledge), universities (suppliers of embodied knowledge in researchers, scientists and other qualified persons), clinics (partners in development), R&D institutions (suppliers of knowledge in different technological disciplines) and finally, consulting and device firms (supplier of primary economic and financial knowledge).

The distinction between biotechnological and pharmaceutical companies is in many cases not evident because of the different functions of the pharmaceutical and the biotechnological elements. Biotechnology relies on the technological basis, pharmacy on the product. A company which produces drugs with biotechnological techniques can be classified as pharmaceutical as well as biotechnological. In our analyses, a pharmaceutical company produces drugs (the techniques are irrelevant), a biotechnological firm mainly produces (bio)technological knowledge; in cases of doubt we rely on the self-rating of the companies. The alliances with universities very often are not fixed in contracts between the institutions and companies (informal contacts of scientists, employment of staff) and so they cannot be taken into consideration in our analyses.[18]

Other characteristics of the partner companies which are included in our analyses are nationality, size and age. The criteria size is divided in small (less than 500 employees) and big (more than 500 employees); the age refers to the age of the company at the time of the relevant alliance. A company which is younger than five years is defined as a start-up company. Size and age are important distinctive features of pharmaceutical and biotechnological firms, but they are less important for universities, clinics, R&D institutions and device/consulting firms. Many experts claim that small size and young age are the crucial characteristics of biotechnological firms and take both as criteria of distinction from pharmaceutical companies. In our analyses the above mentioned (product/technology) separation seems to be more reliable and evident and will be preferred. The nationality refers to the location of the headquarter of the company, in large (multinational) pharmaceutical companies this does not necessarily conform with the main R&D locations or plants. In this context it must be emphasized that the partners can be subsidiaries of those large (multinational) companies. The attributed characteristics refer to the particular subsidiary's properties.

5.3 Results of the Empirical Analyses

5.3.1 Aggregated Analyses

The database of alliances of the twenty largest pharmaceutical companies in Europe and the US consists of 2,163 different alliances. Almost one half of the alliances are set up exclusively between US companies, one third between European and US companies, the rest is divided into European alliances and alliances with companies from other countries in the world. 1,480 alliances are between small and big companies, about 500 between big companies. About 400 alliances are between pharmaceutical companies, 1450 alliances with biotechnological firms, 150 between biotechnological companies and 50 with universities. The most frequent types of alliances are licenses (1,265), development contracts (715), research contracts (c. 500), equities (c. 400) and collaborations (c. 300). The oldest alliance in our database is from the year 1973, the most actual ones are from October

---

[18]It is of course possible to generate information about university - company collaborations, e. g. via bibliometric analyses of co-publications (see chapter 7). But in our following analyses, we confine ourselves to the contracted alliances in the ReCap databank.

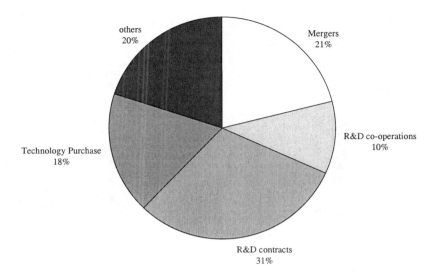

FIGURE 5.1. Shares of the groups of alliances

1998. Most alliances are from the year 1996, fifty percent of all alliances started between 1994 and 1997. The alliances with a start and end date have an average duration of three years; the average age of the biotechnological companies is about seven and a half years. About 650 out of 1,100 biotechnological companies can be defined as start-ups (five years or younger).

These key data give a short overview of the alliances which are examined in our analyses. But the "raw material" itself can also give some good clues to the structure of alliances in the pharmaceutical industry. On comparing the types of alliances and the types of the partners considered, we find some remarkable differences. First of all, figure 5.1 shows the shares of the different groups of alliances. R&D contracts have the largest share with 31 %, followed by the almost equally frequented groups mergers, technology purchase and others, whereas R&D cooperations show a share of 10 %.

In figure 5.2 we show a differentiation of types of alliances for pharmaceutical firms or biotechnology firms or other partners. It can be seen that alliances of pharmaceutical companies with other pharmaceutical companies refer - relative to alliances with biotechnological companies - mostly to other types of activities than direct R&D alliances. Among these marketing and distribution arrangements play a major role. The tendencies to technology purchase and R&D cooperations are almost similar; mergers and R&D contracts are more usual in alliances between pharmaceutical and biotechnological firms. Alliances with others (universities, R&D institutes, clinics and device or consulting firms) have an emphasis on R&D cooperations and R&D contracts.

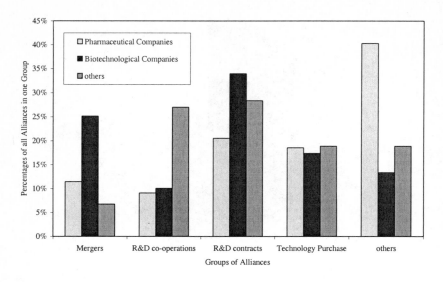

FIGURE 5.2. Profiles of alliances

Based on these data we can draw the conclusion - with all necessary reservations - that the top twenty pharmaceutical companies prefer to undertake alliances with biotechnological firms with an emphasis on acquiring the whole firm or parts of it (equities) with all embodied (tacit and explicit) existing knowledge or narrowly defined contracted R&D activities concerning new knowledge. Both types of alliances stress the necessity to acquire knowledge from the outside, which cannot be generated inside the pharmaceutical company and which specifically serves the needs of the particular pharmaceutical research entities. Technology purchase and licenses are perhaps not as important as contracts because of the particular interests of the pharmaceutical companies which cannot always be served by already existing patented knowledge and know-how. These interpretations will have to be confirmed by further empirical research, which cannot be undertaken here.

In order to investigate the dynamics of different types of alliances we analyzed their development over time since 1978 (figures 5.3 and 5.4). We can see that all groups of alliances have a nearly similar development on different levels and fluctuations. The number of alliances is increasing during almost the whole period. The peak of the number of mergers was in 1995, the peak of the other alliances one year before. In the last two years we can observe a decrease of technology purchase, mergers and others, while R&D cooperations and R&D contracts have been increasing steadily. An interpretation of these different developments is difficult, because the time horizon is not long enough to draw any conclusions about basic changes in the knowledge acquisition strategies. However, the data point to the notion

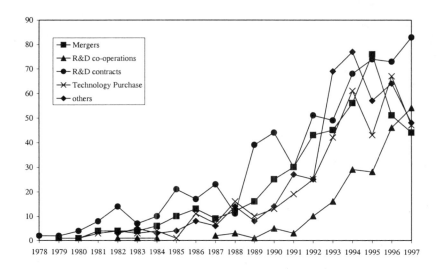

FIGURE 5.3. Number of different types of alliances in a time scale (1978-1997)

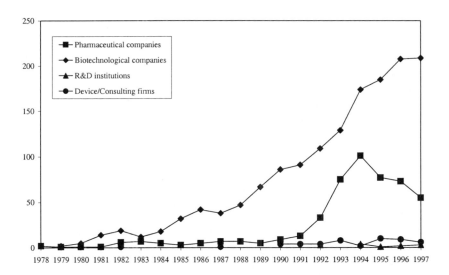

FIGURE 5.4. Number of alliances with pharmaceutical and biotechnological companies and others

that R&D co-operations and contracts are becoming more important for pharmaceutical companies.

Another interesting development can be seen in the number of alliances with different types of partners. Figure 5.4 shows the total number of alliances in the years 1978 up to 1997, with a remarkable decline of alliances with pharmaceutical companies in the years 1994 up to 1997. During the same period the alliances with biotechnology companies continued to grow. Obviously biotechnology firms suceeded in becoming preferred R&D-partners of the pharmaceutical industry.

These results give a good impression of the aggregated database concerning the top twenty pharmaceutical companies. In a next step we are going to examine the structures and number of alliances of single companies.

5.3.2 Analyses of the Alliances of the Top Twenty Pharmaceutical Companies

In our analyses we include all alliances of the twenty largest pharmaceutical companies and their subsidiaries; table 5.3 shows the absolute numbers of alliances of the different companies, in order to get a first impression about proportions and the partners of the alliances considered. The companies are listed in the order of the total number of alliances. In this table we see some differences in the number and structure of alliances. Hoffmann LaRoche is - by far - the company with the most alliances, followed by AHP, Novartis and Smith Kline Beecham. The companies with less activities in alliances are Johnson & Johnson, Boehringer Ingelheim, Zeneca and Astra. On average 28 % of the alliances are with pharmaceutical companies and 68 % with biotechnological companies. Abbott, Pfizer and Schering Plough are the companies with a stronger emphasis on alliances with biotechnological firms; AHP, Novartis, Hoechst Marion Roussel and Rhône Poulenc Rorer have a higher than average number of alliances with other pharmaceutical companies. The large number of other alliances of Zeneca (mostly with universities) and Hoffmann LaRoche (mostly with clinics and universities) is conspicuous.

These data give a good overview of the distribution of alliances among the companies, but they do not give any clues about the types of alliances, possible strategies and the geographical distribution. These analyses will be undertaken in the following sections, beginning with some more information about the structures of the analyzed companies.

In order to understand the structure of the top twenty pharmaceutical companies it is necessary to have a look at the composition of the companies. Table 5.4 shows the companies, divided according to the criteria number and region of origin of their subsidiaries. The complete list of subsidiaries can be found in appendix A, and is based on the associations in the ReCap databank. The list gives some good impressions about the degree of

TABLE 5.3. Number of alliances of top-twenty pharmaceutical companies

Company	Number	With			Share
		pharma- ceutical	biotech- nological	others	
		firms			
Hoffmann LaRoche	333	68	235	30	15.44
AHP Corp.	220	74	120	14	10.20
Novartis	188	71	106	11	8.72
Smith Kline Beecham	170	39	120	11	7.88
Hoechst M. Roussel	132	44	80	8	6.12
Bristol Myer Squibb	125	28	85	12	5.80
Glaxo Wellcome	115	39	73	3	5.33
Eli Lilly	112	30	76	6	5.19
Rhone Poulenc Rorer	112	37	56	19	5.19
Merck	101	25	72	4	4.68
Pharmacia & Upjohn	101	28	68	5	4.68
Abbott	94	15	73	6	4.36
Pfizer	82	13	59	10	3.80
Warner Lambert	80	25	51	4	3.71
Schering Plough	67	10	55	2	3.11
Bayer AG	59	17	37	5	2.74
Johnson & Johnson	46	16	30	0	2.13
Boehringer Ingelheim	43	11	28	4	2.00
Zeneca	43	11	12	20	2.00
Astra AB	34	8	23	3	1.58

internationalization of the analyzed top twenty pharmaceutical companies and their growth and R&D strategies. We have seven companies with no, or less than two, subsidiaries and five with ten or more subsidiaries. In our analyses subsidiaries are related to their multinational companies during the whole time period, even when the fusion has taken place later. The relevant mergers and acquisitions are all included in the analyzed alliances.

Regarding tables 5.4 and 5.A1, one aspect is conspicuous. Although the list of the Top Twenty pharmaceutical companies consists of an almost balanced number of US and European firms, a tendency towards subsidiaries in the United States and Canada is obvious. Most European companies have subsidiaries in the United States; in the cases of Glaxo Wellcome and Hoffmann LaRoche the overwhelming majority (respectively all) of the subsidiaries are located overseas. On the contrary, US companies on the whole do not have any subsidiaries in Europe; they are outright American. This shows different knowledge acquisition strategies: whereas the US firms stay in the US the pharma companies from Europe expanded in the US and tapped into the US system of innovation. If a company like Hoffmann LaRoche with most of its subsidiaries and R&D activities in the US

TABLE 5.4. Locations of subsidiaries of top-twenty companies

Locations	Number of subsidiaries		
	< 2	2 − 9	≥ 10
Mainly in North America	Abbott, Bayer, Pfizer, Schering Plough, Warner Lambert	BMS, Glaxo Wellcome, Eli Lilly, Johnson & Johnson, Merck	AHP, Hoffmann LaRoche
Diversified		Boehringer Ingelheim Pharmacia & Upjohn	Hoechst M. Roussel, Novartis, Rhône Poulenc Rorer
Mainly in Europe	Astra, Zeneca	Smith Kline Beecham	

(see also chapter 6) is still a Swiss (or European) company is an issue for further investigation.

Nevertheless, it is possible to draw some conclusions concerning the growth and innovation strategies of the top twenty companies. Abbott, Astra, Bayer, Pfizer, Schering Plough, Warner Lambert and Zeneca are examples of a more internally orientated growth strategy, that means, they concentrate on growth through expansion of production and marketing, diversification by means of internally derived and externally purchased knowledge and technology.[19] According to this strategy the companies can easily be associated with their country of origin - keeping in mind that the locations of R&D and production still can be found abroad. In addition to the companies' structures, the low number of alliances (table 5.3) of these companies confirm the assumption that alliances with other companies are not a central aspect of their internally orientated innovation and growth strategy.

The opposite strategy can be observed at AHP, Hoechst Marion Roussel, Hoffmann LaRoche, Novartis and Rhône Poulenc Rorer; these companies are good examples for a strategy of growth through acquisitions and mergers and an externally orientated innovation strategy (high number of alliances - see table 5.3). A very interesting aspect of the mergers and acquisitions studied are the properties of the subsidiaries. More than two thirds of the subsidiaries are classified as pharmaceutical companies, although our database includes more than 1,400 alliances with biotechnological firms (and about 400 with pharmaceutical companies). This disproportionate low share of biotechnological firms in mergers and acquisitions leads to the as-

---

[19] The merger between Astra A.B. and Zeneca in December 1998 implies a change in the growth strategy of both companies.

sumption that biotechnological firms are not often taken over; the more common strategy to acquire biotechnological knowledge and influence on the R&D of biotechnological firms are R&D contracts and equities (see once again figure 5.2).

These interpretations of tables 5.3, 5.4 and 5.A1 can be refined with a closer look at the alliances analyzed in the ReCap databank. We have to remember that the category "mergers" also includes equities, which do not lead to acquisition or merger and therefore cannot be treated the same ways as the mergers and acquisitions of subsidiaries. In figure 5.5 and 5.6, it can be seen that some profiles are similar and some are absolutely different. The group of companies with almost the same profile of alliances is the group of Abbott, AHP, Bayer, Boehringer Ingelheim, BMS and Novartis. This group represents the average of the top twenty companies (see figure 5.1) and forms a cluster of companies concerning the types of alliances. A cluster analysis also shows that Hoffmann LaRoche and Hoechst Marion Roussel are the most similar companies, another cluster is formed by Smith Kline Beecham and Eli Lilly.[20] A fourth cluster is formed by Pharmacia Upjohn, Rhône Poulenc Rorer and Glaxo Wellcome. The other companies have too different profiles of alliances, so that it is not possible to build any homogeneous clusters.

Companies with an emphasis on mergers are Johnson & Johnson, Eli Lilly, Pfizer and Smith Kline Beecham, although their profiles differ significantly. Conversely, Astra, Bayer, Merck, Rhône Poulenc Rorer and Zeneca undertake mergers below the average of 21 %. In comparison with table 5.4, the mergers of Pfizer can be explained mostly by a high number of equities, the low share of mergers of RPR by a small number of equities. R&D cooperations are not as often chosen for alliances as the other forms and their share is far below 20 % in each company. BMS, Glaxo Wellcome, Merck, Pfizer and Pharmacia-Upjohn are easily above the average of 10 %; Johnson & Johnson have almost no R&D cooperations. On the contrary, most of the companies have a stress on R&D contracts, as indicated in figure 5.1 a share of 31 % of the alliances are R&D contracts. Bayer, BMS, Novartis, Zeneca and especially Astra and Schering Plough are much higher than the average; Johnson & Johnson, Eli Lilly and Warner Lambert are much lower. Technology purchase is a preferred form of alliance of Rhône Poulenc Rorer and Warner Lambert; Astra, Boehringer Ingelheim, Merck, Pfizer, Schering Plough and Smith Kline Beecham are below the average of 18 %.

Putting this together with the results of tables 5.3, 5.4 and 5.A1, we can arrive at some further conclusions concerning the cooperation strategies.

---

[20] The cluster analysis was undertaken in order to corroborate the similarities which are obvious, regarding the figures in figure 5.5. We do not think that any further interpretations are sensible, so that the cluster analysis will not be mentioned further.

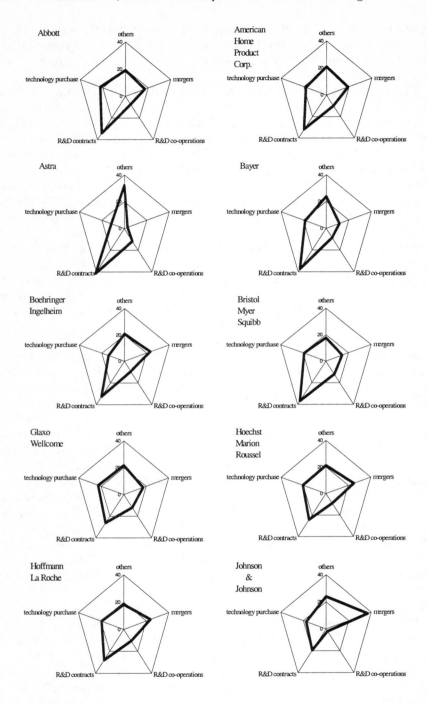

FIGURE 5.5. Profiles of alliances of the top twenty pharmaceutical companies

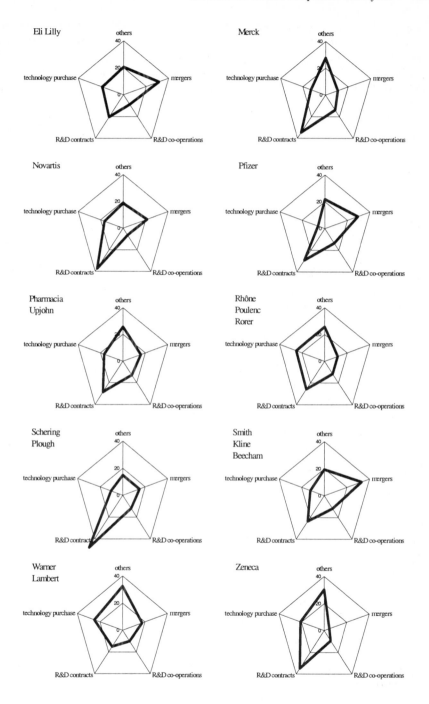

FIGURE 5.6. Profiles of alliances (continuation)

It is obvious that the different companies also have more or less different emphasis on different types of alliances. We cannot draw the conclusion, that an internal growth strategy is necessarily connected with a stress on special knowledge acquisition strategies. But it is possible to interpret similar and different profiles in connection with the kind of knowledge which is generated and to derive some assumptions on the knowledge acquisition strategies of the companies. We can find different profiles concerning the degree of tacitness and explicitness of the generated knowledge and the degree of originality with regard to the definition in 5.2.1 and grouping in table 5.2. What we cannot find, however, is a positive correlation between the knowledge acquisition strategies and growth strategies of the firms.

It is obvious that Merck is extremely oriented towards the generation of original new knowledge, both in R&D contracts and R&D cooperations. The same emphasis can be observed at Bristol Myers Squibb and with some reservations (because of the smaller number of alliances) at Astra, Bayer, Pharmacia-Upjohn, Schering Plough and Zeneca. On the other hand, we can find an acquisition strategy of existing knowledge through technology purchases and mergers at Eli Lilly, Rhône Poulenc Rorer, Hoechst Marion Roussel and - with the same reservations as above - Johnson & Johnson and Warner Lambert. To draw the conclusion that the latter are the less innovative firms is not reliable - but we can conclude that their in-house research activities are supplemented by externally generated existing knowledge more than the average of the regarded companies. To re-combine this knowledge into new inventions but also into market-oriented products is one challenge these firms have to face.

Generating explicit knowledge is a preferred strategy of Novartis, Rhône Poulenc Rorer and Abbott, Bayer and Zeneca, while the tacit component has a stronger emphasis in the alliances (esp. R&D cooperations, but also mergers) of Hoechst Marion Roussel, SmithKline Beecham and Pfizer and Warner Lambert. This emphasis on tacit elements of new knowledge has two implications: on the one hand, it shows a tendency towards the learning strategy of learning-by-interacting. An important prerequisite is the trust of the companies in their partners and vice versa. On the other hand, it is also possible to conclude that the absorptive capacity for explicit knowledge does not seem to be as highly developed as in other companies, which can easily integrate externally generated knowledge. Which alternative fits better depends on the special aims and structure of the considered companies.

5.3.3 Country Analyses

As already mentioned above, the multinational character of the most of the companies with their headquarters in a European country examined is a central problem of country-specific analyses. Therefore, it is not sensible to include the whole conglomerates in the analyses; in the following part

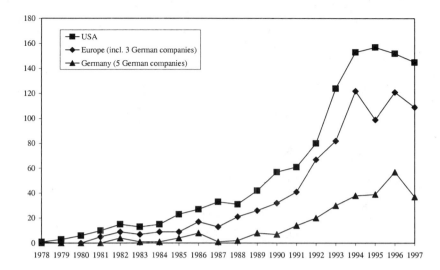

FIGURE 5.7. Number of alliances of US, European and German pharmaceutical companies in a time scale

the region of origin of the subsidiaries and the mother company will be the crucial criterion for the analyses of country-specific knowledge acquisition strategies. It has to be emphasized that, although the top twenty companies are the starting-point for these analyses, it will not be possible to derive any company-specific perceptions. Nevertheless, the database will be supplemented by alliances of the two German companies Schering AG and BASF-Knoll AG (fourth and fifth largest pharmaceutical companies in Germany) in order to extend the German database for a particular US-German comparison.

First of all, we start with a comparison of the development of alliances of the US, the European and the German pharmaceutical companies. Figure 5.7 shows the time course of the alliances. We can see that the total number of alliances is increasing during the whole time until the middle of the 1990s reaching a plateau in 1995 and 1996 in all countries, respectively country groups. The decrease of the last year can be explained by the incomplete database in 1997 (and 1998 - is left out in the figure), but the stagnation of the number of alliances during the mid 90s must have other reasons. In comparison with figure 5.2 we can draw the conclusion, that the decrease is caused by a reduction of mergers, technology purchases and other alliances. Possible explanations can be the trend towards more informal alliances and different cooperation strategies, which have taken place in the last few years in all pharmaceutical companies in all countries, but with slight time lags.

Figure 5.8 shows the proportions of the alliances in the different countries respectively country groups. It is obvious that no crucial differences exist

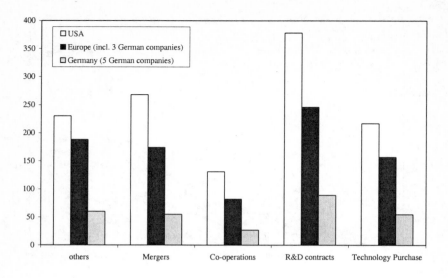

FIGURE 5.8. Number of different types of alliances of US, European and German pharmaceutical companies

between the countries. Therefore, it is not possible to conclude that the different developments of the numbers of alliances are caused by different profiles of alliances. Furthermore, we have to admit that country-specific distinctions between structures of alliances are not significant and therefore do not permit any statements concerning different innovation and knowledge acquisition strategies in the countries considered.

These results are supported by further comparative analyses of alliances (types, duration) and partners (types, ages) of pharmaceutical companies in the US, Europe and Germany. These analyses are not shown here, because of the lack of significant differences. The analysis based on the ReCap databank shows that European and US pharmaceutical companies do not differ because of their nationality, but because of their particular strategies concerning growth, innovation and knowledge acquisition of single firms and conglomerates. For these reasons we have to conclude that nationality is not a differentiating factor regarding the alliances strategies of the firms investigated.

5.4 Conclusions

The empirical analysis of alliances of the top twenty pharmaceutical companies has to deal with a number of difficulties. First of all, we have to consider the missing information about alliances between companies and universities because of the very often informal character of these contacts. Additionally, it is difficult to classify biotechnological and pharmaceutical companies - when both biotechnological research and pharmaceutical development and production are undertaken in these firms. So the distinction which is described in chapter 5.2.1 is in some cases not evident and doubtful. But it is still the best of all possible distinctions, so we rely on it. Another aspect is the difficulty to make statements concerning the direction of the alliances. In the logical order of ReCap it is not possible to distinguish between - for example - a license which is purchased and a license which is offered. In our analyses we have not made any distinctions concerning this problem and have assumed implicitly that biotechnological firms always give licenses - and always get acquired, undertake contracted R&D, get loans etc. The pharmaceutical companies are the partners who purchase licenses, acquire companies, give orders for R&D, give loans etc. With these assumptions we still have a problem with an evident association of alliances between pharmaceutical companies and between biotechnological companies. This problem has not been solved in our analyses and therefore conclusions on the deeper content of alliances have not been possible.

Another very important problem of our analyses is the lack of evident national associations. The top twenty pharmaceutical companies are multinationals and therefore cannot be associated to distinct countries. This problem was solved by an aggregated analysis of the different subsidiaries and mother companies, which can be related to different countries. But a comparison of the top twenty pharmaceutical companies in connection with their nationality was not possible - and therefore distinct analyses of country-specific knowledge acquisition strategies of particular companies were not possible. But this problem is not a statistical one, it is the result of a remarkable internationalization strategy of most of the regarded pharmaceutical companies. We have company-specific strategies of knowledge acquisition, but no country-specific strategies. Any comparisons between countries and country groups can rely on different systems of innovation (see chapter 2), including antitrust laws and consumer protection, but not on company-specific strategies of internationalization, growth and innovation strategies. So one important clue of the empirical analyses is the existence of a global character of the companies studied and the vanishing national differences. Regarding their alliances strategies, the largest pharmaceutical companies of the world do not have national particularities.

Nevertheless, it was possible to derive the preferred alliances in the pharmaceutical industry and to outline differences between the structures of groups of alliances. In connection with the particular companies' structures concerning subsidiaries, it was possible to draw conclusions about the growth and innovation strategies of single companies and to highlight differences and similarities (most important results of knowledge acquisition strategies will be supplemented soon).

Furthermore, it was possible to arrive at conclusions about different strategies of alliances in connection with different types of partners. We have to consider that most alliances of pharmaceutical companies with other pharmaceutical companies are alliances between competitors. The alliances are very often strategic ones and are motivated by reasons which are different from the pure knowledge acquisition motives. Very often these alliances are initiated in order to minimize risks of costly R&D and the often more cost-intensive marketing. As we have seen in figure 5.2, the bias towards other than direct R&D alliances can be explained by financial and market-orientated reflections concerning the market introduction and diffusion of new drugs; new knowledge is mainly acquired by alliances with biotechnological companies. It is not surprising that more than half of the analyzed biotechnological companies can be defined as start-ups; this big share is a strong expression of the big importance of basic scientific knowledge of biotechnology in the pharmaceutical industry - and the alliances are very often a consequence of (bio) industry-university contacts (which unfortunately could not be considered in our empirical analyses).

The empirical analyses could prove only a few of the assumptions of chapter 5.1. The whole complex of reasons for the division of research and development (in order to consider the different characters of both) was not analyzed. As already mentioned above, the alliances in the databank seem not to be sufficiently specialized to allow any conclusions about the division of work in research and development between companies. Another aspect which is not taken into consideration in our empirical analyses is the important role of informal contacts between university scientists, industrial researchers, and clinical pharmacologists and the employment strategies of pharmaceutical companies. We have concentrated on formal contracted alliances between companies and R&D institutions and therefore cannot draw any further conclusions about strategies of generation, acquisition and exploitation of knowledge beyond these alliances. But the great and still growing importance of alliances between pharmaceutical and biotechnological companies is obvious and has given a good insight into the cooperation strategies and knowledge-acquisition strategies in the pharmaceutical industry.

6

Internationalization of Research and Development in Pharmaceuticals

Guido Reger

6.1 Introduction

In the 1970s, investment of research and development (R&D) in foreign countries was noted only by a few academics (e.g. Ronstadt, 1977; Mansfield/Teece/ Romeo, 1979; Behrmann/Fischer, 1980). Today the internationalization of R&D is a major topic within the business community as well as for academic researchers and policymakers. Since then the international generation of innovation has increased. Large multinational firms play a key role in this process (see e.g. Cantwell, 1994; Nonaka/Takeuchi, 1995; Patel/Pavitt, 1994). During earlier periods of international expansion (the 1960s and 1970s), multinational corporations first built up their sales, distribution and asssembly operations in foreign countries. In later phases (late 1970s/early 1980s), efforts were then directed towards supporting foreign subsidiaries with corresponding capacities in application engineering and applied R&D. Although initially the tasks of development departments abroad were limited to adapting product and process technologies from the home country to local production and market requirements, there was a recognizable trend, since the late 1980s, towards strengthening R&D in foreign countries and extending the international competence portfolio. Increasingly, research became established at a high level in foreign locations. This development is strikingly described by Nosi (1999) as a process 'from technology transfer to the learning organization'.

There are mainly three reasons why we included the topic of the internationalization of R&D activities, especially the issue of the generation of innovation in foreign countries, in our study. Firstly, pharmaceuticals (including biotechnology) is - among chemicals/ materials and electrical/ electronics - a sector in which companies have already highly internationalized their research and technological activities abroad (see CEC, 1998; Odagiri/Yasuda, 1996; Patel/Vega, 1999; Reger/Beise/Belitz, 1999; Serapio/Dalton, 1999).

Secondly, based on our own research on large companies and other studies (see Chiesa, 1996; Florida, 1997; Gerybadze/Meyer-Krahmer/Reger, 1997; Kuemmerle, 1997), we wanted to learn more about the qualitative changes in the internationalization process in this sector. We assumed that large pharma companies try to tap into the worldwide leading center where leading-edge research is done and where new drugs can be introduced best and first to the market. New here is that the innovation - the new drug - is generated outside the home country and, after having learnt much from excellent research and a sophisticated market, is internationalized to other markets. Since the degree of R&D internationalization varies from country to country (see e.g. Roberts, 1995; 1995a) we expected differences between corporations with their headquarters in Germany/ Europe, Japan and the US.

Thirdly, this chapter was driven by the concern that the technological performance of pharmaceuticals in Germany has been disappointing for many years. What role does the ongoing process of the R&D internationalization play herein? For instance, if German pharma companies invest in R&D abroad this has not to be negative from the view of the national system of innovation if foreign-based companies invest more in R&D in Germany and if outflows are compensated by inflows of R&D investment. If outflows are higher than inflows, industrial R&D and the long-term technological base for innnovation is decreasing in a country.

This chapter will start with an analysis of R&D input and R&D output indicators and changes in the technological specialization of selected countries since the 1980s. Further, the internationalization strategies of selected pharmaceutical companies are investigated. It will be shown how these firms establish 'centers of excellence' at different locations, what factors influence the location decisions and what role the attractiveness of regional innovation clusters plays. The understanding what a center of excellence differs from company to company. 'Centers of excellence' may focus on a distinctive technology like biotechnology or integrate the whole value chain for a specific therapeutic area. However, the corporate-wide responsibility for a certain research field, technology or therapeutic area, talented researchers, own resources, a high degree of self-guidance as well as corporate-wide co-ordination tasks are included in many cases. Regarding regional innovation clusters we will borrow from the of other authors and define clusters as geographically proximate groups of interconnected companies, related and supporting industries, research and education institutes, and associated institutions in a particular field (i.e. pharmaceuticals, biotechnology) which are linked by commonalities and complementarities (see Porter/Stern, 1999, p. 17). Since proximity plays an important role, the focus of innovation in clusters is often at the regional level in larger countries such as the US or Germany.

Methodologically, this chapter is based on an analysis of the R&D expenditure (input indicator) and of patents (output indicator) on country level for selected countries as well as on interviews and a patent analysis for 16 selected pharmaceuticals companies.

6.2   R&D and Technological Specialization on Country Level

When collecting data on research and development (R&D), it is not possible to do so by making straightforward measurements. Nor is it possible, therefore, to analyze R&D directly. For this reason, representative parameters, known as indicators, are brought in. These may be used to measure either R&D input or output. Input in R&D is frequently measured via statistics on the R&D budget or on R&D personnel. However, the relevant information is in most cases only available in a highly aggregated form at a sectoral level. When measuring output, patents in particular are used as indicators. Patents provide a finely differentiated breakdown, both from an institutional viewpoint and with regard to areas of technology.

In the following sub-chapters the trends in input in R&D, measured in R&D expenditure, are analyzed for the US, Germany and selected OECD countries since the 1980s. Output of R&D and technological specialization, measured in patent application, are presented for the US, Germany and further countries in the time periods 1983-86, 1987-90 and 1991-94.

6.2.1   Trends in R&D Expenditure for Selected OECD Countries

Regarding their absolute levels of R&D expenditure in pharmaceuticals (in billions of US$ PPP), the nine countries investigated here fall into three groups, as they did with regard to their production and employment data (cf. figure 6.1 and chapter 3). Top of the list once more is the US, where expenditure on R&D rose from 1.777 billion US$ in 1980 to 9.633 billion US$ in 1994. This represents an increase of 444 %. Although some way behind the US, Japan is also in the leading group: here R&D expenditure grew from 0.757 billion US$ PPP in 1980 to 3.494 billion US$ PPP in 1994, representing growth of 362 %.

France, Great Britain, West Germany and Italy occupy mid-field positions. At the start of the observation period the volumes of their R&D expenditure are fairly similar. Subsequently, a strongly marked, consistent development takes place up to 1987. From 1988 onwards, R&D expenditure in the pharmaceuticals industry in Great Britain shows much more rapid growth than in the other countries in this group. Towards the end of the 15 year period, from 1992 onwards, a slight decrease in R&D expenditure in billion US$ PPP is observed in this sector in West Germany, and a stronger decrease in Italy. The overall growth of R&D expenditure between 1980 and 1994 for these four countries is as follows: France 299 %, Great Britain 447 %, West Germany 141 % and Italy 231 %. Canada, the Netherlands and Sweden have the lowest absolute expenditure on R&D. Unlike the production and employment figures, where Sweden lagged, Swe-

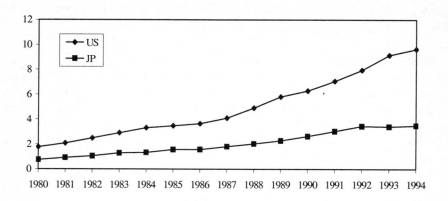

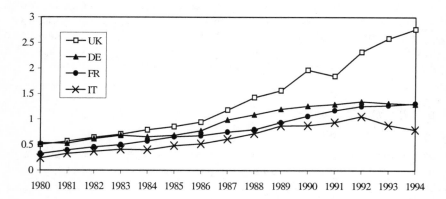

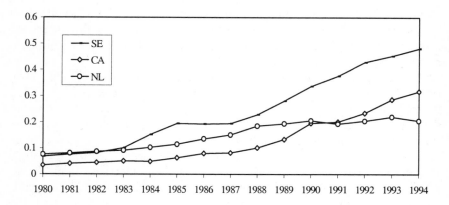

Source: OECD ANBERD database, own calculations

FIGURE 6.1. R&D expenditure in billion US$ PPP 1980-1994

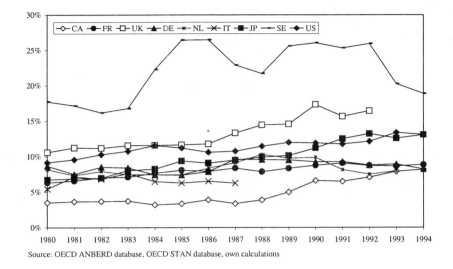

Source: OECD ANBERD database, OECD STAN database, own calculations

FIGURE 6.2. R&D intensity (in percent), 1980-1994

den is first among these three from 1983 onwards. Sweden in fact also shows
the second fastest growth rate of the nine countries in its absolute expenditure on R&D, which went up by about 600 % between 1980 and 1995.
This was only surpassed by Canada, where absolute R&D expenditure rose
by approximately 820 %. By contrast, the growth rate in the Netherlands
was pretty moderate, amounting to only 170 % over the whole observation
period.

As well as absolute R&D expenditure, particular interest attaches to
R&D intensity, i. e. the relationship of R&D expenditure to production.
This is an input indicator for the comparative analysis of the innovative
strength of sectors of the national economy. Figure 6.2 shows the R&D
intensities for the pharmaceutical sector in the nine countries considered in
this survey. In this parameter the "ceiling" is more or less set by the R&D
intensity of Sweden, which starts in 1980 at the very high level of 17.7 %
and reaches an absolute peak in 1986 at 26.5 %. There is a second peak,
almost as strongly marked, in 1990 with a value of 26.1 %, followed by a
drop to 18.9 % in 1994. Whereas the first drop in R&D intensity in Sweden
does in fact correspond to a real stagnation in absolute R&D expenditure
between 1985 and 1987, the second drop is solely attributable to the very
strong growth of production, since R&D expenditure also continues to rise
massively during this time.

The R&D intensity of the pharmaceutical industry in Canada can be
regarded as forming the "floor" in this parameter, first catching up with the
mid-field values at the end of the observation period, when it reaches 8.2 %.
Among the countries with medium R&D intensities, three groups can again

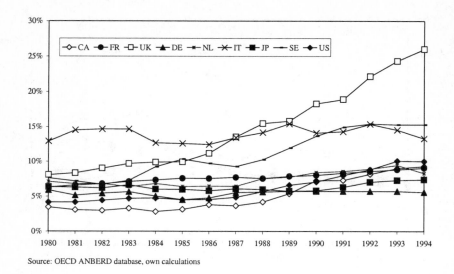

Source: OECD ANBERD database, own calculations

FIGURE 6.3. R&D expenditure within the pharmaceutical industry as a proportion of R&D expenditure in manufacturing

be distinguished. Great Britain occupies an upper middle position with an R&D intensity of 10.6 % in 1980, rising to 16.4 % in 1992. A middle position is occupied by Japan and the US, whose pharmaceutical R&D intensities are dissimilar at the start of the observation period (Japan 1980: 6.7 % and the US 1980: 9.2 %), but converge in 1994 (Japan 13.1 %, US 13.1 %). The lower mid-field comprises France (1994: 8.8 %), West Germany (1994: 8.2 %) and the Netherlands (1993: 7.9 %). No recent estimate can be made for Italy, since the calculable R&D intensities come to an end in 1987, when the level was 6.3 %.

R&D expenditure in the pharmaceutical industry as a proportion of total expenditure on R&D in manufacturing industry also goes up in almost all the nine countries within the observation period (cf. figure 6.3). The only exception here is the Federal Republic of Germany, where this proportion dropped from 5.9 % in 1980, with slight fluctuations, to 5.6 % in 1994. The lead position in this respect is occupied by Great Britain, where R&D in the pharmaceutical industry increased its share of total R&D in the manufacturing industry from 8.1 % in 1980 to 26 % in 1994. If the most recent values for each country are taken, Sweden and Italy follow with 15.3 % and 13.3 % respectively in 1994. The other countries, starting from quite divergent levels in 1980 (ranging from 3.5 % for Canada to 7.1 % for the Netherlands) later all reach levels between 7.4 % (Japan) and 10 % (US).

The findings outlined here are reproduced, albeit in a less drastic form and with slight shifts in emphasis, if R&D expenditure within the pharmaceutical industry is considered as a proportion of all industrial R&D, not

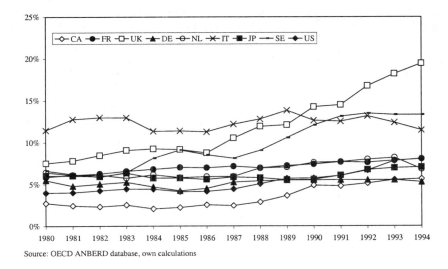

Source: OECD ANBERD database, own calculations

FIGURE 6.4. R&D expenditure in the pharmaceutical industry as a proportion of R&D expenditure in industry as a whole

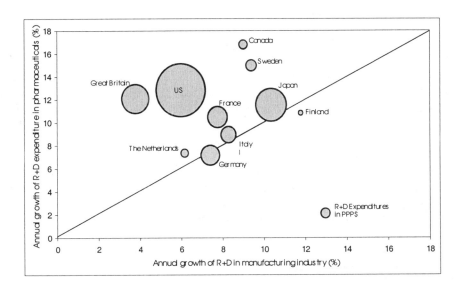

FIGURE 6.5. Annual growth of R&D expenditure in pharmaceuticals and in the manufacturing industry of the OECD countries,1980-1995

just in the manufacturing sector (cf. figure 6.4). Once more, the Federal
Republic of Germany is the only country evidencing a slight decrease in
the share of the pharmaceutical industry. Throughout nearly all the observation period - up to 1992, in fact - Canada is at the lower limit of this
parameter, starting with a share of 2.7 % in 1980 and rising to 5.6 % in
1994. Only in 1993 and 1994 does Canada's pharmaceutical industry have
a higher share of R&D expenditure than in Germany, where its share goes
down over the 15 year period from 5.5 % to 5.3 %. Great Britain, Sweden,
and Italy are well placed in this respect, too, with shares of 19.4 %, 13.3 %
and 11.5 % for pharmaceutical R&D expenditure as a proportion of total
industrial R&D expenditure in 1994. However, it should again be pointed
out here that although the proportional rise or fall in expenditure on R&D
derives on the one hand from an increase or decrease in R&D expenditure within the pharmaceutical sector, it may also result from a lesser or
stronger rise in R&D expenditure in the other sectors.

Pharmaceuticals is among the sectors of industry that are classified as
cutting edge technology.[1] It is expected that structural change in the highly
industrialized economies will move in the direction of the R&D-intensive
industries, since high-wage countries can still gain comparative advantages
in these sectors in competition with the expanding, newly industrialized
countries. For several years now growth rates have been highest in the
"science-intensive" industries. In fact, the growth rate observed in the pharmaceuticals industry in the nine countries overall is above average even for
the science-intensive industries.

In most countries, expenditure on R&D in pharmaceuticals shows higher
growth rates than R&D expenditure in manufacturing industry (see figure
6.5). This implies that in these countries structural change in R&D activities is shifting towards pharmaceuticals. In Germany, by contrast, growth
in the field of pharmaceuticals is only average, i. e. the share of pharmaceuticals in industrial R&D expenditure is not increasing. Pharmaceutical
R&D investment shows particularly strong growth in Great Britain, the
US, Sweden, and Canada, with Great Britain showing the greatest differ-
ence between the (low) growth of its overall expenditure on R&D and the
rapid growth of its pharmaceutical research. This implies that structural
change is taking place most rapidly there. In Germany, compared to the
other countries, structural change regarding the growing importance of the
science-intensive pharmaceutical sector appears to have come to a standstill.

---

[1] A sector with an R&D intensity of over 8.5 %, measured as R&D expenditure to
production, can be classified as a cutting edge technology sector (see Gehrke/Grupp
1994, p. 45).

6.2.2   R&D Output and Technological Specialization of Selected Countries

Preliminary Methodological Remarks on Patent Statistics

The use of patents as indicators is subject to certain limitations, which have to be borne in mind when collecting information in the field of applied technological research and industrial development (on this aspect, see also Schmoch, 1990 and Grupp, 1997). It should be remembered that patents cannot be used as indicators in all areas equally well, since for example user software and also medical treatment procedures, as opposed to drugs, cannot be protected by patents. There are also sectoral differences in patenting tendencies. Moreover, enterprises may use other instruments apart from patents to secure their revenue from innovations - for instance secrecy or a rapid market entry. Nevertheless, specialist analytical procedures can minimize the influence of undesirable analytical effects of this kind. Over the last few years, so much positive experience has been gained with patent analyses world-wide that now even the OECD recommends patent indicators in one of their manuals as an important instrument in the analysis of research and development (OECD, 1994).

In the present investigation only European patent applications from the European Patent Office (EPO) were used. It has been demonstrated that in comparisons between countries, distortions can be caused by the so-called "home advantage"; this occurs when patent analyses are based on national patent data, e. g. data from the US or the German Patent Office, leading to an over-high evaluation of the country concerned. Even with the European Patent Office, there is still a certain regional advantage for European applicants as compared to overseas applicants. However, this effect is much more marked in "low-tech" fields than in research-intensive fields. This observation is linked with the fact that European patent applications aim to secure protection in several different European countries and are therefore associated with considerable costs. For this reason they represent a selection of inventions that are of particular technological and economic importance. As a consequence, research-intensive inventions are particularly well-represented.

If only the absolute numbers of patents are considered, it is only the large, advanced industrialized countries that predominate. However, this approach overlooks the fact that small countries, too, can become highly internationally competitive through a high degree of specialization in clearly defined areas of technology. For this reason, the following investigation not only regards the absolute patent figures but also makes use of a specialization index, known as the Relative Patent Share (RPS). This index measures whether the patent share of a sample (enterprise or country) in a certain field of technology corresponds to the share of this field of technology in the basic set, e. g. in all applications at the European Patent Office, or whether this share is above or below the average. In precise terms, the *RPS* index is defined as

$$RPS_{ij} = 100 \tanh \ln \left[\frac{P_{ij}}{\sum_i P_{ij}} \bigg/ \frac{\sum_j P_{ij}}{\sum_i \sum_j P_{ij}} \right]$$

In this formula, P_{ij} is the number of patents of a country/enterprise i, in a technological field j. The introduction of the logarithm ensures a value zone that is symmetrical about the neutral point 0, the tangens hyperbolicus limits the value zone to ± 100. Making allowance for error tolerances, index values of more than $+15$ can be interpreted in this case as expressions of a degree of specialization in the relevant technology field that is definitely above-average; conversely, specialization is clearly below average from a negative value of -15.

Every patent application received by the Patent Office is classified according to a code, the International Patent Classification (IPC). At the lowest level of aggregation, approximately 65,000 different codes are available. For this reason, patent statistical analyses are particularly useful for a differentiation of content. On the basis of the IPC, interesting fields of technology are delimited and defined. In the present case, the area of technology to be investigated - pharmaceuticals - was subdivided into four subfields in order to perform more detailed analyses. When defining these subdivisions, the authors were able to make use of preliminary studies from other projects (Münt/Grupp, 1995).

Patent applications are generally classified under several codes in the IPC, so that in a search using all codes, overlapping of technically related subsectors may occur. In order to arrive at a clear classification without overlapping, in our project only the first classification code assigned to the patent application was taken into account in each case. This first coding reflects the most important claim of the application regarding content. In this way, the figures given in the statistics for the subdivisions can be summed up directly to the total for the relevant field. Despite its statistical clarity, one disadvantage of this solution is that codings relevant to the present investigation may be entered in the patent documents as the second classification and thus some individual documents may not have been included. However, the investigation was not concerned so much with statistical completeness as with relevant samples for the description of the main structures and trends, so that the distortions to be expected from this problem are negligible.

Despite methodological limitations, the patent analysis presented here has yielded interesting findings which complement the results of the other indicators and methods used in this study in many ways.

Absolute Figures											
Field	EU	DE	FR	GB	IT	NL	US	JP	CH	CA Others	Total
Vitamins, antibiotics, alkaloids	863	260	134	214	109	15	934	411	67	32	117	2424
Hormones	194	76	18	39	15	11	161	73	6	8	20	461
Enzymes, microorg., serums, vaccin.	2402	509	465	591	120	183	3735	726	99	183	378	7523
Other therapeutic and diagnostic aids	2273	676	328	548	240	67	3387	818	109	124	405	7115
Pharmaceuticals - total	5731	1520	946	1392	484	276	8217	2028	280	347	921	17523

Shares of Individual Countries in %											
Field	EU	DE	FR	GB	IT	NL	US	JP	CH	CA Others	Total
Vitamins, antibiotics, alkaloids	36	11	6	9	4	1	39	17	3	1	5	100
Hormones	42	16	4	8	3	2	35	16	1	2	4	100
Enzymes, microorg., serums, vaccin.	32	7	6	8	2	2	50	10	1	2	5	100
Other therapeutic and diagnostic aids	32	10	5	8	3	1	48	11	2	2	6	100
Pharmaceuticals total	33	9	5	8	3	2	47	12	2	2	5	100

FIGURE 6.6. Patent applications to the European Patent Office in the technological subfields of pharmaceuticals, 1991-94

R&D Output and Technological Spezialization of Selected Countries

In the most recent part of the observation period, from 1991 to 1994, approximately 17,500 patent applications were registered at the EPO (European Patent Office) in the area of pharmaceuticals, representing c. 6.4 % of all EPO registrations (cf. figure 6.6).

Of the four subsectors investigated, namely

- Vitamins, antibiotics, alkaloids

- Hormones

- Enzymes, microorganisms, serums, vaccines

- Other therapeutic and diagnostic aids

the third subsector - linked with biotechnology - contained by far the most applications: approximately 7,500, representing c. 43 % of all pharmaceutical applications. Most patent applications in pharmaceuticals - 47 % - come from the United States, although it must be remembered that the national

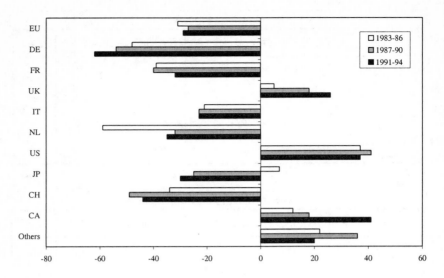

FIGURE 6.7. Specialization (by countries of origin) in the technological field pharmaceuticals in patent applications to the EPO

origin of the patent is decided by the address of the inventor. This means, for instance, that even inventions generated within corporations with a German parent company, if they have occurred in US daughter companies, are attributed to the United States.

The proportion of applications from the European Union amounts to only one third of the total. As well as considering the absolute figures, it is particularly interesting, by calculating specialization indexes, also to take the size of the nations or regions into account. It then becomes apparent that the United States occupies a clear lead position, not only in terms of absolute figures, but in terms of specialization. Index values for the US are just under 40, indicating a degree of specialization which is clearly above-average (cf. figure 6.7). The US was able to maintain this high degree of specialization from the first observation period 1983-86 onwards, despite the fact that its competitors from other countries (particularly Great Britain, Canada) substantially increased their absolute numbers of patent applications during this time. Therefore, the relative index values of the United States, which remain constant over time, imply an increase in patent activity in absolute terms. The specialization index thus proves to be a particularly relevant indicator with regard to international competitiveness, since an increase in research efforts only brings a competitive advantage if the other competitors lag behind in absolute terms.

For the countries of the European Union, specialization in pharmaceuticals is clearly below average, with negative index values around -30; the situation varies from country to country, however. In the Federal Republic

1991-94										
Field	EU	DE	FR	GB	IT	NL	US	JP	CH	CA	Others
Vitamins, antibiotics, alkaloids	-21	-48	-30	35	25	-86	19	7	7	3	12
Hormones	-5	-9	-57	32	-7	0	9	0	-62	25	0
Enzymes, microorg., serums, vaccin.	-31	-75	-19	25	-65	7	42	-46	-58	56	16
Other therapeutic and diagnostic aids	-31	-57	-45	23	-3	-70	38	-31	-47	29	28
Pharmaceuticals total	-29	-62	-32	26	-23	-35	37	-30	-44	41	20
1983-86										
Field	EU	DE	FR	GB	IT	NL	US	JP	CH	CA	Others
Vitamins, antibiotics, Alkaloids	-19	-32	-49	35	29	-86	12	29	13	-48	-12
Hormones	-9	0	-57	6	-10	-42	34	-49	-59	37	16
Enzymes, microorg., serums, vaccin.	-39	-65	-29	0	-79	-45	41	14	-32	11	22
Other therapeutic and diagnostic aids	-31	-41	-45	-8	2	-61	41	-8	-60	29	34
Pharmaceuticals total	-31	-48	-39	5	-21	-59	37	7	-34	12	22

FIGURE 6.8. Specialization in subsectors of pharmaceuticals in patent applications to the European Patent Office, 1991-94 and 1983-86

of Germany the specialization index is even more negative than the average for the European Union as a whole, and it goes down further in the course of the observation period. In Great Britain, specialization improves from an average value to a higher-than-average value.

Among the other countries, one remarkable feature is the above-average pharmaceutical specialization in Japan, which then decreases over time, whereas in Canada an opposite development occurs, with pharmaceuticals becoming a definite research focus.

When the subsectors are differentiated further (cf. figure 6.8), it becomes clear that the levels of the countries' overall indexes are largely dependent on their degree of specialization in the subsector of enzymes and microorganisms, i. e. in biotechnology. Whereas the US, Canada and Great Britain have clear positive indexes in this subsector, the index values for the European Union - the Federal Republic of Germany in particular - and Japan are strongly negative (cf. figure 6.8). Only in the subsector of hormones do inventions from Germany reach a level which at least approaches global average values; in all other areas its values are also strongly negative.

Thus from the input and output side of R&D, Germany's technological situation in pharmaceuticals is unfavorable, and it is to be feared that it will tend to follow a downward trend over time. In contrast, the US has maintained its dominant role in pharmaceuticals, especially in biotechnology.

6.3 Internationalization Strategies of Selected Pharmaceutical Companies

6.3.1 Enterprises investigated

The basis for this case study on the internationalization strategies is the analysis of a total of 16 enterprises in pharmaceuticals (cf. table 6.1), selected according to various criteria. They had to be research-performing producers of medicines, internationally active in pre-clinical or clinical research and active in Germany, or the US in research or development at least. Nine of these enterprises are from western Europe (including five firms from Germany), five have their headquarters in the US and two in Japan.

The turnover given in table 6.1 relates to the corporation, or to the relevant health or pharmaceuticals division if stated. The turnover of these 16 producers of medicines is equivalent to approximately half the world pharmaceuticals market (not including OTC - "over-the-counter"). They comprise purely pharmaceutical enterprises (e.g. Fujisawa Pharmaceutical, Glaxo Wellcome, Hoffmann-LaRoche, Eli Lilly, Pharmacia & Upjohn, Schering) and also mixed-interest corporations including chemistry, plastics, medicine, veterinary medicine(e.g. American Home Products, Bayer, Solvay, Takeda). Due to the high R&D intensity in pharmaceuticals, in some corporations the R&D of the pharmaceuticals division accounts for half - or more than half - of the corporation's total R&D budget (cf. table 6.1) (e.g. Solvay: 60 %, E. Merck: 81 %, Rhône-Poulenc: 46 %).

With an R&D intensity averaging 14 %, the enterprises included in the investigation are among the most research-intensive producers of medical drugs. Some of them have an R&D intensity which lies substantially above this average value and is very high even for pharmaceuticals/health care. These include Hoffmann-LaRoche (21.2 %), Schering (18.2 %), Hoechst Marion Roussel (17.2 %) and Pharmacia & Upjohn (17.6 %).

The following three methods were used when analyzing the enterprises:[2]

---

[2] Parts of this analysis, especially the patent analysis and conducting interviews in German firms, were financially supported by the German Ministry of Education and Research /BMBF). Without this support, such a detailed analysis would not have been possible.

TABLE 6.1. Pharmaceutical enterprises investigated

Corporation or division	Turnover 1996 in $	R&D expenditure 1996 in $	Share turnover abroad 1996	Division turnover/ corporate turnover	Pharm. turnover/ corporate turnover	Division R&D/ total R&D
Merck & Co* (Health Care)	16.7 bn. $	1.3 bn. $	n.s.	n.s.	n.s.	n.s.
AHP	13.4 bn. $	1.4 bn. $	43%	—	56.2%	n.s.
Pfizer Inc* (Health Care)	10.0 bn. $	1.4 bn. $	49.0%	83.9%	83.9%	n.s.
Eli Lilly	7.35 bn. $	1.2 bn. $	41.9%	100%	n.s.	100%
Takeda Chem. Industries	7.37 bn. $	0.63 bn. $	13%	100%	66%	n.s.
Fujisawa Pharm. Co.	2.45 bn. $	0.33 bn. $	23%	100%	91%	100%
Bayer AG* (Health)	7.74 bn. $	1.05 bn. $	47.4%	27.9%	24.9%	46%
Boehringer Ingelheim*	3.77 bn. $	0.65 bn. $	79.4%	83.9%	83.9%	85.5%
Glaxo Wellcome*	11.99 bn. $	2.06 bn. $	96%	100%	n.s.	100%
Pharmacia & Upjohn	7.12 bn. $	1.27 bn. $	68%	90.8%	90.8%	n.s.
Hoffmann-LaRoche*	7.83 bn. $	1.66 bn. $	98%	62.8%	62.8%	85.7%
Rhône-Poulenc Rorer	5.42 bn. $	0.88 bn. $	70%	c. 30%	36.3%	46%
Hoechst M. Roussel	8.66 bn. $	1.49 bn. $	90%	25.6%	23.9%	57.7%
E. Merck (Pharma)	4.62 bn. $	0.44 bn. $	79.1%	56.2%	56.2%	80.7%
Schering AG*	3.24 bn. $	0.59 bn. $DM	85%	100%	65.8%	n.s.
Solvay SA (Health)	1.50 bn. $	0.23 bn. $	94%	16.4%	14%	60%

*1995

Source: company reports. Own calculations on the basis of average foreign currency rates

1. A patent analysis was carried out for the 16 enterprises selected for the three periods 1983-86, 1987-90 and 1991-94.

2. In twelve of the sixteen enterprises, senior managing and managing directors of R&D were interviewed. The interviews were held in the R&D laboratories in Germany.

3. In addition, publicly accessible materials on the firms selected such as articles in specialist journals, company reports and brochures were analyzed as background material.

6.3.2   Global Distribution of Patents for Selected Firms

An attempt will now be made, using patent analysis for the selected enterprises, to describe the internationalization of R&D activities in relation to firms. The database for this analysis is provided by patent applications to the European Patent Office on the basis of priority years. The patent applications of the 16 enterprises were evaluated for the three periods 1983-86, 1987-90 and 1991-94. For these three periods, the patent applications to the European Patent Office were worked out on the basis of the priority years registered by each enterprise in pharmaceuticals. In addition, a subdivision was made into four subsectors: (1) Vitamins, antibiotics, alkaloids, (2) Hormones, (3) Enzymes, microorganisms, serums, vaccines and (4) Other therapeutic/diagnostic aids. The patent applications were identified for twelve countries of the European Union, for Switzerland, the US and Japan.

The methodological problem in this enterprise-related analysis is that the enterprise or corporation involved in each case has to be defined by an appropriate set of applicants' names. Due to highly dynamic developments in the acquisition, fusion and reorganization of enterprises, particularly in the fields of pharmaceuticals under review here, it is this defining of the "boundaries" of the firm or corporation which is the greatest source of methodological uncertainty.

In the field of pharmaceuticals the 16 enterprises analyzed represent c. 14 % of patent applications to the European Patent Office worldwide, in the period 1991-94. The distribution of the patents of the 16 firms selected corresponds roughly to the distribution by countries of the patent applications as a whole, although Germany, with 18 %, is definitely over-weighted with regard to patent applications within the 16 firms (cf. figure 6.9). When considering the patents of the 16 selected enterprises, it is remarkable that the proportion of patents lodged in Germany by firms from other countries, at 9 %, lies far below the share of patents of foreign firms in France (31 %) or Great Britain (45 %). In comparison with these countries, Germany seems to be less attractive as a location for the R&D activities of foreign firms. Within Europe, Great Britain obviously occupies the forefront. The

Pharma	EU	FRA	GER	GB	NL	I	CH	CAN	USA	JPN	Rest of World	Total
Total number of patents	5731	946	1520	1392	276	484	280	347	8217	2028	921	17523
Distribution acc. to countries	32.7%	5.4%	8.7%	7.9%	1.6%	2.8%	1.6%	2.0%	46.9%	11.6%	5.3%	100%
Number of regd. comp. patents	983	178	448	186	17	39	33	32	1131	287	25	2491
Distribution acc. to countries	39.5%	7.1%	18.0%	7.5%	0.7%	1.6%	1.3%	1.3%	45.4%	11.5%	1.0%	100%
Number of patents of foreign enterprises 1)	181	55	40	83	17	39	3	32	316	97		630
Distribution acc. to countries	28.8%	8.8%	6.4%	13.2%	2.7%	6.2%	0.5%	5.1%	50.2%	15.5%		100%
Patent share of foreign enterprises	18.4%	31.0%	9.0%	44.9%	100%	100%	9.6%	100%	27.9%	34.0%		25.3%
Number of patents originating in home country 2)	802	123	408	103			30		815	189		1836
Share of patents originating in home country	74.8%	75.4%	58.5%	62.3%			14.5%		79.9%	97.4%		73.7%
Number of patents originating abroad 3)	271	40	290	62			175		205	5		655
Share of patents origin. abroad	25.2%	24.6%	41.5%	37.7%			85.5%		20.1%	2.6%		26.3%
Number of patents of enterprises4)	1073	163	698	165			204		1020	194		2491
Distribution acc. to countries	43.1%	6.5%	28.0%	6.6%			8.2%		40.9%	7.8%		100%

Examples:

1) In France foreign firms have 55 patents registered.

2) German firms have 408 patents of German origin registered.

3) British firms have 62 patents of foreign origin registered.

4) US firms have world-wide altogether 1020 patents registered with EPA.

FIGURE 6.9. Global distribution of patents for 16 selected enterprises in pharmaceuticals

share of patents of foreign firms in the US (28 %) and in Japan (34 %) is also higher than in Germany.

If one considers the origins of the patents for the selected enterprises, it emerges that the share of patents originating abroad (i.e. not from the enterprise's home country) is higher for German enterprises (41.5 %) than for French (25 %) or British enterprises (38 %) (cf. figure 6.9). Obviously the German companies in the investigation have a stronger foreign orientation, which is also clearly above the average for other countries in the European Union. The US firms investigated, on the other hand, with a 20 % share of patents originating abroad, are considerably less internationalized. The really low proportion of patents originating outside the firms' own country of origin in the Japanese firms investigated (less than 3 %) underlines the very low degree of internationalization of R&D. If the subsector of biotechnology only (enzymes, microorganisms, serums, vaccines) is considered, the attractiveness of the US goes up substantially again: 35 % of patents in this field are applied for by foreign enterprises. Due to the low numbers of patents applications involved, i.e. for only 16 selected enterprises, these data should be interpreted with caution. However, they would at least seem to indicate that the US, Japan and Great Britain are highly attractive as locations for the R&D of enterprises from other countries.

Conclusions should only be drawn with caution on the basis of these data because of the small numbers of patents of the firms included in the investigation. However, it clearly emerges that the internationalization of R&D in pharmaceuticals as a whole is far advanced. In this field, in the light of the firms considered here, Germany holds the lowest attraction as a location for R&D. The German producers of medicines investigated have a marked foreign orientation compared with the investigated enterprises from other countries. All in all, Japanese firms exhibit the lowest degree of internationalization.

6.3.3   Increasing R&D Internationalization in the 1980s and Partly Re-centralization in the 1990s

Compared to manufacturing industry as a whole, the pharmaceutical industry shows an above-average degree of internationalization of R&D. Figure 6.10 should show the relationship between R&D abroad and turnover abroad. It can be generally stated that the degree of internationalization of R&D goes up when the share of enterprises' turnover abroad increases and their home market is limited. Three categories can be distinguished here (cf. figure 6.10):

1. Within the Triad, the enterprises from western Europe (B, CH, D, F, UK) are most highly internationalized with regard to their R&D. In enterprises from small countries - such as Solvay, which has its headquarters in Belgium, and Hoffmann-LaRoche with its HQ in Switzerland - a very high proportion of R&D is performed abroad.

2. The US producers of medicines, on the other hand, still perform much more of their R&D in their country of origin and their share of turnover abroad does not exceed 50%.

3. In Japanese firms, research and development is carried out mainly in the country of origin; the proportion of R&D carried out abroad is under 10 %. With the exception of a few pharmaceutical enterprises - such as Eisai, for instance - internationalization of R&D in the Japanese firms is only just beginning. However, within Japan, pharmaceutical enterprises belong to the sector which - after automobiles and electronics - is the second most advanced in its internationalization of R&D (cf. Odagiri/Yasuda, 1996, p. 1062 ff.).

The percentage of turnover abroad and the limits of the domestic market are important factors influencing the internationalization of R&D. However, they cannot be considered as the only determinants. Thus Japanese enterprises have an R&D strategy that is more predominantly home-centered than pharmaceutical enterprises from the US, despite the fact that Japan's domestic market is clearly smaller than the US home market. Moreover, the proportion of R&D performed abroad by German pharmaceutical firms - e.g. Hoechst Marion Roussel or Bayer's pharmaceuticals group - is about as high as for the pharmaceuticals group of the Swiss corporation Hoffmann-LaRoche. Obviously one important group of determinants in the internationalization of R&D is the enterprise's philosophy, history and strategy

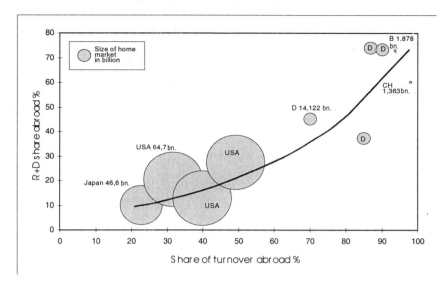

FIGURE 6.10. Internationalization of R&D increases with high foreign turnover and limited domestic market

and - deriving from these - its acquisition and R&D strategy (for a longer account of the determinants that shape the international organization of R&D, cf. Reger, 1997, p. 72 ff.).

The interviews with enterprises reveal that R&D abroad is often located at an already existing location of the corporation. This may be an existing marketing or sales unit, a regional headquarters or an acquired firm. One Japanese producer of medicines, for instance, bought itself into a German family firm at the beginning of the 1980s and successively expanded its participation. The existing R&D competence of the German firm did not play any role in the acquisition; rather, it was the existence of marketing know-how and national sales structures that was important. Today, this location is the site of the enterprise's German regional headquarter and of a clinical research unit with c. 90 employees, responsible for performing clinical research in Germany and Europe.

What results are obtained if the regional origin of the patents of an enterprise is taken as an indicator for the internationalization of R&D? The country given in the inventor's address has proved to be quite a reliable criterion for the origin of the patent, since geographical proximity between research laboratory and inventor can generally be assumed. Enterprises such as LaRoche (86.5 %) and Solvay (77.2 %) with small home markets in their countries of origin registered a very high share of their patents as originating abroad (cf. table 6.2). It can be assumed that in these enterprises, applied research is performed to a great extent outside the country of origin.

TABLE 6.2. Proportion of patents originating abroad for selected pharmaceutical companies

Enterprise	Share of patentes originating abroad in %			Growth rate of share of patents originating abroad	
	83-87	87-90	91-94	83-87 to 91-94	87-90 to 91-94
Hoffmann-LaRoche (CH)	78.9	79.3	85.5	8.2	7.9
Solvay (BE)	91.7	87.8	77.2	-17.0	-12.0
Pharmacia & Upjohn (US)	48.9	59.4	69.4	42.7	16.9
Boehringer Ingelheim (DE)	28.8	41.1	60.9	106.8	48.1
Hoechst (DE)	28.1	43.9	46.6	65.4	6.1
Bayer (DE)	42.5	51.8	45.4	7.1	-12.4
Glaxo Wellcome (UK)	34.1	45.7	37.7	10.5	-17.5
Pfizer (US)	18.5	24.1	25.4	42.9	5.7
Rhone Poulenc Rorer (FR)	77.3	73.3	24.6	-68.0	-66.5
Schering (DE)	4.3	10.2	19.3	350.5	89.5
E. Merck (DE)	6.3	14.7	17.6	181.3	19.5
Merck & Co. (US)	9.9	12.9	13.2	28.7	2.5
Eli Lilly (US)	4.0	8.5	7.9	86.6	-6.6
AHP (US)	0.9	6.3	5.1	242.4	-18.9
Fujisawa Pharmaceutical (JP)	0.0	2.8	4.9	∞	73.0
Takeda Chemical Industries (JP)	0.0	1.7	1.2	221.5	-29.1

Enterprises with their headquarters in the larger European countries also perform a significant proportion of their applied research abroad, with percentages of 61 % (Boehringer-Ingelheim), 47 % (Hoechst), 45 % (Bayer) and 38 % (Glaxo Wellcome) for patents originating abroad. At the lower end of the scale, on the other hand, the predominating enterprises are from the US with a small proportion - and Japanese enterprises (Takeda, Fujisawa) with the smallest proportion - of patents originating abroad.

Two American firms, the Swedish-US merger Pharmacia & Upjohn and Pfizer, as well as the German firms Schering and E. Merck, constitute exceptions to this rule. Merck is a special case as only those patents could be identified which were applied for by the Merck Patent GmbH in Germany and consequently its share of patents originating abroad is small. The other three enterprises provide confirmation for the thesis that the degree of internationalization of R&D is highly dependent on business strategy and company culture. Pfizer internationalized its R&D as early as the begin-

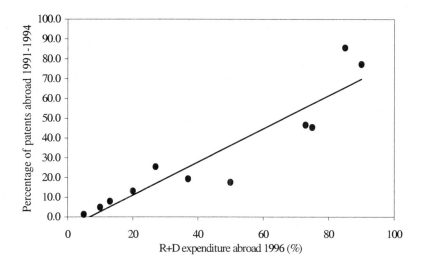

FIGURE 6.11. Comparison of the two indicators "percentage of patents abroad" and "R&D expenditure abroad"

ning of the 1980s. Pharmacia & Upjohn is an enterprise that resulted from the merging of pharmaceuticals firms in Italy, the US and Sweden. More than 20 firms joined forces to form one of the largest pharmaceutical enterprise worldwide. Today, it is hard to say whether the headquarters of the enterprise is in Sweden or the US. Pharmacia and Kabi are Swedish enterprises and make up a large part of the merger, the Corporate Management Center is in London. However, the registered head office of Pharmacia & Upjohn is in Delaware, US. If one were to consider Sweden as the headquarters of Pharmacia & Upjohn, one would reach the conclusion that the internationalization of its R&D has gone down: in 1983-86, 75 % of patents were registered as originating outside Sweden, compared to only 58 % in the period 1991-94.

Among other aspects, patent applications abroad as well as R&D expenditure abroad can be used as indicators for the internationalization of R&D. Patents are an output indicator, for the R&D activities of enterprises, and R&D expenditure an input indicator. To what extent do both indicators concur on the degree of internationalization of R&D? In figure 6.11 both indicators (patents: 1991-94, percentage of R&D abroad: 1995/96) are compared. With the exception of two values (for Hoffmann-LaRoche and Pfizer) it can be ascertained that in the selected firms the share of R&D expenditure abroad is higher - sometimes substantially higher - than the share of patent applications abroad. For Schering and Fujisawa, for instance, the share of R&D expenditure abroad is twice as high as the percentage of patents originating abroad.

Figure 6.11 clearly shows that the extent of internationalization of R&D is sometimes considerably underestimated using the indicator of "percentage of patents abroad".[3] One possible explanation for this is that the patents essentially give a picture of applied research, and that neither basic research nor development tend to appear in patents. The development itself, i.e. mainly clinical research, accounts for approximately two-thirds of all R&D expenditure and plays a very big part in the costs and time needed for the whole innovation process in the pharmaceutical industry. The differences between R&D expenditure and percentages of patents abroad also indicate that more development work is performed abroad compared with the home country (conducting clinical studies on-the-spot).

How has the extent of internationalization of R&D changed over time? Since no data are available regarding the time horizon for R&D expenditure abroad, the proportion of patents abroad in 1983-86 was compared with patents in 1991-94. With the exception of two enterprises, the share of patent applications abroad went up over this time (cf. table 6.2). Comparing the period 1987-90 with 1991-94, it can be ascertained that half the enterprises show a slight decrease in the growth rate for their share of patents abroad. This is true both for enterprises with high and low levels of internationalization of their R&D. Obviously there are phases in which the internationalization of R&D, brought on by "chaotic" growth, is then cut back and re-centralized. Following consolidation, the internationalization of R&D subsequently follows a more even course.

Although the results need to be interpreted with caution due to the small numbers of firms examined, various types of behavior can be identified (cf. figure 6.12):

1. Enterprises whose R&D was highly internationalized at the beginning of the 1980s, such as e.g. Solvay or Rhône-Poulenc Rohrer, reduced their R&D activities abroad at the beginning of the 1990s.

2. Other enterprises which also had very highly internationalized R&D at the beginning of the 1980s, e.g. Hoffmann-LaRoche and Glaxo Wellcome, allowed their R&D activities abroad to increase only slightly up to the early 1990s.

3. Enterprises with a medium level of internationalization of their R&D at the beginning of the 1980s such as Hoechst, Boehringer Ingelheim and Pfizer, substantially expanded their R&D activities abroad by growth rates between 43 % to over 100 %, with another internationalization "push" taking place at the end of the 1980s.

---

[3] This result, which due to the small number of cases can only be considered provisional, needs to be further tested with a larger number of enterprises.

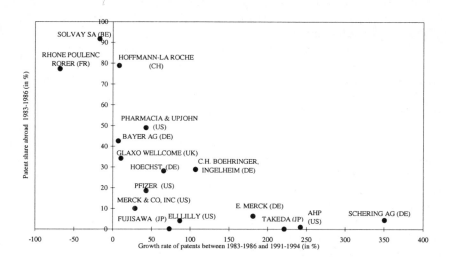

FIGURE 6.12. Patent share abroad 1983-86 and growth rate of patents between 1983-86 and 1991-94

4. Enterprises with a low level of internationalization of R&D, such as Fujisawa Pharmaceutical, American Home Products and Schering, are now showing an extremely high growth rate of their R&D activities abroad.

In the 16 pharmaceutical enterprises investigated, there was clearly a considerable "push" in the direction of internationalization of R&D at the end of the 1980s, whereas the growth curve of R&D activities abroad flattened out at the beginning of the 1990s. Once R&D commitments abroad have reached a certain level, further internationalization of R&D stagnates at a high level, or a process of re-centralization of R&D in the home country takes place. Stronger dynamics of the internationalization of R&D are shown by enterprises with a previously low level of R&D activities abroad. These enterprises are clearly in a sectorally specific "catching-up" process.

Analysis of these pharmaceutical enterprises shows that the internationalization of R&D is a slow process that takes a lot of time and is pursued with various instruments. The firms use a set of instruments such as setting up R&D laboratories ("Greenfield R&D"), mergers and acquisitions, the establishing of alliances and joint ventures, but also R&D cooperations, e.g. performing a precompetitive research project with a university or enterprise abroad, financing research teams at a foreign university or taking part in an affiliation program of a university.[4] The establishing of a research center or a team to perform clinical studies generally takes place at the location of a daughter company abroad.

The role played by takeovers and mergers in the internationalization of R&D may vary greatly. Firstly, an enterprise abroad may be taken over without regard to its existing R&D competence. In this case, market and distribution aspects play a central role in the takeover. The acquired enterprise may also - and this is frequently the case - serve as a location for the new R&D unit when expanding R&D activities abroad. Secondly, the takeover or merger may be technologically motivated, but need not necessarily advance the internationalization of R&D. One example of this is Pharmacia & Upjohn where, following the mergers of recent years, a re-organization of global R&D activities took place, resulting in a de-internationalization and re-centralization of R&D. Thirdly, the takeover or merger of enterprises with R&D activities at various different locations may lead to a growing internationalization of R&D. One example of this is the merger of Hoechst, Marion and Roussel. From the viewpoint of the German "home" country, the re-organization of R&D led in this case to an expansion of R&D activities abroad.

6.3.4   The Formation of Centers of Excellence in Selected Enterprises

The pharmaceutical enterprises in the survey with a medium to high level of internationalization of R&D have gone over to the strategy of concentrating certain competencies and responsibilities in exploratory research worldwide in one location (cf. figure 6.13). Thus, for instance, in the US Hoechst Marion Roussel has concentrated the therapeutic areas of the central nervous system, oncology and the respiratory system in Bridgewater and of biotechnology in Boston. In France, this company conducts research in the field of infectious diseases and diseases of the bone. In Frankfurt, research deals with the therapeutic areas of cardiovascular treatment, metabolism and rheumatism/immunology. Overlapping is avoided as far as possible between these research fields based on therapeutic areas and situated in different locations. When forming these global competencies at different R&D locations, the following structures can be distinguished:

---

[4] Some companies are continuously monitoring networks. For instance, Schering has set up Offices of Technology at its largest research sites in Berlin, Richmond and Osaka whose task it is to scan the research scene in both acaedmia and start-ups for new technologies in an international perspective. In this respect, Schering has transferred its research and development organization into a research, search and development organization (see Stock 1998a, 2)

Enterprise	US	EUROPE			JAPAN
		FR	DE	UK	
Bayer Pharma, Germany	*Berkeley* • Biotechnology center *West Haven* • Cancer • Bone diseases • Diabetes		*Wuppertal Elberfeld* • Cardiovascular • Anti-infective agents • Central nervous system (CNS) • Anti-viral agents	*Stoke Court* • Respiratory system • Depression	*Kansai Science City* • Allergies • Rheumatism
Hoechst Marion Roussel, Germany	*Bridgewater Drug Development Center* • Central nervous system • Oncology • Respiratory system *Boston* • Biotechnology	*Roussel Uclaf SA* • Infections • Bone diseases	*Frankfurt* • Cardiovascular • Metabolism • Rheumatism/ immunology		*HMR Kawagoe* • Bone diseases
Fujisawa, Japan				*Fujisawa Institute of Neuroscience* • Neuro sciences • Neuro pharmacology	*R&D-Centers in Tsukuba, Osaka, Nagoya:* • Immunology • Thrombosis/ cardiology • Infectious illnesses • Bone diseases • Metabolism
Rhône Poulenc Rorer, France	*Collegeville* • Bone metabolism • Thrombosis/cardiology • Rheumatism *Santa Clara* • Gene therapy	*Vitry-Alfortville* • Infections • Oncology CNS		*Dagenham* • Respiratory system	

Enterprise	US/CANADA	EUROPE				JAPAN
		IT	DE	AT	SE	
Boehringer Ingelheim, Germany	*US* • Immunology • Inflammatory diseases *Canada* • Viral diseases	*Milan* • Central nervous system (CNS)	*Biberach* • Oncology • Cardiovascular *Ingelheim* • Respiratory system • CNS	*Vienna* • Oncology		

Schering AG, Germany	*Berlex Bioscience, Richmond, California*
	• Biotechnological approaches in the fields of
	  • Oncology
	  • Thrombosis
	  • Multiple sclerosis
			Berlin
			• Endocrinology
			• Diagnostics
			• Dermatology
			• Alzheimer
			• Oncology
			• Cardiovascular
						Nihon Schering, Osaka
						• Diagnostics
						• Geriatric diseases

Pharmacia & Upjohn, US	*Pharma Product Center US, Kalamazoo, Michigan* • Central nervous system • Infectious diseases • Inflammatory diseases • Gynaecology	*Pharma Product Center Italy, Milan* • Oncology			*Pharma Product Center Sweden, Stockholm* • Urology • Thrombosis • Ophthalmology • Metabolic diseases	

	US	B	D	NL	JAPAN
Solvay SA (health care), Belgium			*Hanover* • Cardiovascular • Gastro-enterology	*Weesp* • Psychiatry • Gynaecology • Immunology • Dermatology	

FIGURE 6.13. Competencies in research centers of selected pharmaceutical enterprises, by therapeutic areas

1. Specialization or focusing at one location is undertaken primarily according to therapeutic areas or - at an aggregated level - according to "disease groups". Ideally, the division of tasks between the locations is completely free from overlaps.

2. Cross-cutting the specialization according to areas of therapy or "disease groups", responsibilities for specific technologies or methods (e.g. biotechnology, combinatorial chemistry, gene therapy) are defined and also concentrated as far as possible in one location.

3. The control of biotechnology worldwide was mainly delegated, by the interviewees from the European enterprises questioned, to the most important research location of the corporation in the US.

In addition to forming these competencies in research (pre-clinical) according to therapeutic areas, the interviewed pharmaceutical enterprises with highly internationalized R&D are also moving towards focusing the following responsibilities globally at one location:

1. Certain tasks in the innovation process such as pharmacology, toxicology and "drug safety".

2. Global product development: this means that the pre-clinical stages I and II, the clinical studies and the marketing are controlled globally from one location. In the past, "global drug development" was carried out from the home country. The qualitatively new change in highly internationalized pharmaceutical enterprises today is that global product development is controlled from one location. This strategic decision center is positioned at a site where worldwide standards can be set by the national regulatory authorities, where there is an innovative supply push from the scientific side and the market for medicines is highly dynamic and sophisticated demand is articulated.

The assigning of competencies to one location may involve research only. There is usually global specialization in exploratory research activities according to therapeutic areas or "disease groups". However, the formation of competencies may also include the entire innovation process, again with the therapeutic area as the structuring element. Pharmacia & Upjohn, for instance, has organized its worldwide pharmaceuticals business into three Pharma Product Centers (PPCs) and three market regions. These "market companies" cover three regions - America, Europe and Asia-Pacific - and are responsible at an operatiional level for sales and customer contacts within their region. The three Pharma Product Centers are situated in Stockholm, Milan and Kalamazoo (Michigan, US) (cf. figure 6.13). Each center is responsible for research and development in one or more fields of therapy, and has responsibility worldwide for production and strategic marketing in this field. Other firms such as Hoechst Marion Roussel establish Drug Development Centers (like the company's center at Bridgewater), from which product development is carried out worldwide. Mastery of this process of "global drug development" from one or more locations has great significance for the competitiveness of the pharmaceutical enterprise and was described by some firms as a core competence.

No consistent overall tendency can be recognized for exploratory research in specific therapeutic areas to be allocated to particular countries. The German and European enterprises which maintain a research center in Germany have at least been consistent in establishing the cardiovascular therapeutic area in this country. This also agrees with statements made in interviews to the effect that very high competence is to be found in Germany because of the advanced methods of therapy for heart attacks there. European pharmaceutical enterprises which have research centers in Great Britain have focused their competencies in the respiratory system/asthma field there. In the interviews, research competence in this field in Great Britain was also emphasized.

A clear pattern relating competencies at the level of enterprises or corporations with countries or regions is obviously very difficult to distinguish, because the formation of competencies within the enterprise builds up over the course of time, i.e. historically. In the interviews it was pointed out that these competencies have developed over time and "grown" historically. Consequently a re-structuring of research or product development competencies within the corporation is not made only with a view to the competence in the enterprise's environment, but also in consideration of its existing internal competence. Re-structuring is usually accomplished by a process of internal benchmarking. If a new investment is being made, however, the "environment" ranks higher in importance when selecting a location. Therefore it is not surprising that new R&D investments take place abroad in therapeutic areas or technologies that are new to the enterprise.

In the case of biotechnology or genetic engineering, on the other hand, there is a definite focusing of competencies in research centers in the US. Rhône-Poulenc Rorer, for instance, has positioned its competence in gene therapy in Santa Clara, Hoechst Marion Roussel has a biotechnology center in Boston and Bayer has one in Berkeley (cf. figure 6.13), Hoffmann-LaRoche is also active in this field in Nutley, and has transferred its decision-making to this location.[5]

---

[5] The case of Hoffmann-LaRoche shows how consistent highly internationalized corporations follow this strategy of competence center building. After having acquired Boehringer-Mannheim in early 1998, LaRoche began to establish its sixth research center in the south of Germany. This center will be charged with the competencies in cancer reseach that until now are located at Nutley, NJ, and about 500 people in Nutley, Kamakura and Mannheim will be relocated.

In the US, three main regional clusters have formed in the field of biotechnology: the cluster on the West Coast is the region around San Francisco/Silicon Valley, and on the East Coast the regions involved are the Greater Boston area and the corridor around Philadelphia, Baltimore and New York ("Mid-Atlantic"). These regional biotechnology clusters in the US are also extremely attractive to internationally active pharmaceutical companies and attract the research activities of foreign firms. In the interviews with enterprises it became clear that in the US the right sort of "climate" and "environment" prevail for performing excellent research in the area of biotechnology, and also for transferring its results into innovative medicines. Interviewed firms stated that they did not associate Germany with this type of innovative climate and environment, at least not so far. Thus in the area of biotechnology - unlike the therapeutic areas - congruence can be observed between the formation and establishing of enterprises' internal competencies, and external competence at the level of the national - or better, regional - innovation system. This is certainly a factor in the strong dynamics of these regional innovation clusters in the US.

One could expect the attractiveness of the US in biotechnology to find expression in increasing numbers of patents and growing patent shares in the US. Using patent analysis, an attempt was made to gather information about the investigated firms' distribution of competence in the US in the field of biotechnology (enzymes, microorganisms, serums, vaccines); this analysis yielded mixed results (cf. table 6.3).

Of the US firms, two (Pfizer and Eli Lilly) have concentrated their activities in this field very strongly in the US (cf. table 6.3). The other two (American Home Products and Merck & Co) continue to be strongly concentrated in their home country but are also clearly active in Great Britain. Pharmacia & Upjohn, on the other hand, following the mergers and acquisitions, has strengthened its research location in Sweden since the end of the 1980s. Glaxo Wellcome is clearly focusing its research activities more strongly in its home country of Great Britain. In view of the commitments of American Home Products and Merck & Co in Great Britain, it would appear that Britain is beginning to acquire more importance in this field of technology. Hoffmann-LaRoche has definitely focused its biotechnology in the US ever since the 1980s. Up till now Fujisawa Pharmaceutical and Takeda have concentrated their research activities in biotechnology - as in other fields - in their own country.

For the German enterprises of Schering and Boehringer Ingelheim a (low-level) increase in the US patent share in the area of biotechnology can be observed (cf. table 6.3). Bayer has been active in the US since the 1970s, following its takeovers of the two pharmaceutical firms Cutter (1974) and Miles Laboratories (1978); at the beginning of 1992, all US activities were grouped together under the name Miles Inc. Following the acquisition of Miles, the research center in West Haven was expanded and since the mid-

TABLE 6.3. Shares of patents in the US in the fields of biotechnology for selected companies

Company	Share of patents in the field of biotechnology (%)			Comments
	83-86	87-90	91-94	
Pfizer (US)	67	100	100	Re-centralization from UK to US in mid-1980s
Eli Lilly (US)	100	99	97	Concentrated in US
AHP (US)	100	97	87	Concentration in US, but slow expansion in UK
Merck & Co. (US)	97	99	84	Concentration in US, but slow expansion in UK
Hoffmann-LaRoche (CH)	81	75	82	Strong concentration in US
Schering (DE)	0	6	61	Expansion in US, but small number of patents (10) in investigation field
Pharmacia & Upjohn (US)	54	58	45	Expansion of location in SE following fusions/acquisitions
Bayer (DE)	71	68	44	Decrease in absolute numbers of patents submitted to EPO from 69 to 50 is indicative of change of registration strategy
Solvay (BE)	33	3	23	More patent applications in BE
Boehringer Ingelheim (DE)	9	8	15	Slow expansion of US location
Glaxo Wellcome (UK)	16	26	14	Re-centralization from US to UK, more patents in CH
Hoechst (DE)	4	2	5	Small number of patents indicate external generation of knowledge/ co-operations and "catching-up"
E. Merck (DE)	11	8	4	Only patent applications of Merck Patent GMBH are registered in DE
Rhône Poulenc Rorer (FR)	0	0	3	Strong concentration in FR, CA gains importance in 1990s
Takeda Chemical Industries (JP)	0	1	3	Strong concentration in JP
Fujisawa Pharmaceutical (JP)	0	0	0	Strong concentration in JP

1980s has become the corporation's second largest research center, concentrating on Bayer's molecular biology and genetic engineering activities in the US. The decrease in the percentage of Bayer's patents in the US and in the absolute numbers of patent applications is not interpreted as a sign of the dwindling importance of Bayer's American research, but taken as an indication of a change in Bayer's patenting strategy. Hoechst's research activities were focused largely in Germany and France in the 1980s (Roussel-Uclaf was taken over in 1974), Hoechst's commitment in the US was confined mainly to the fields of chemistry (Celanese was taken over in 1986). Hoechst's activities in the US and in biotechnology are typified by numerous cooperations with research institutions and biotech start-up firms - i.e. the external acquisition of biotechnological knowledge; the small share of Hoechst's US patents also point to this. The decisions to expand Hoechst's US commitments in the field of pharmaceuticals (takeover of Merrell Dow Pharmaceuticals, 1995) and to control its biotechnological research worldwide from the US were only taken from the mid 90s on. Hoechst's intensified commitments in pharmaceuticals in the US can be interpreted as a development of "catching-up".

6.3.5   Factors Affecting the Selection of Locations for R&D

When considering the allocation determinants for the R&D of large research-performing producers of medical drugs, a distinction has to be made between exploratory research (pre-clinical) and clinical research (development) in pharmaceuticals industry. Since the subdivision of the whole development process into a pre-clinical and a clinical phase is very fundamental to this sector, and since different factors influence the choice of location in each phase, these parts of the innovation process should be briefly called to mind (for more details, see chapter 4).

By definition, pre-clinical activities are classified as being part of research, and the clinical phases (phases I to III) as belonging to the development of a medicine. In order to be able to commence a research project, certain processes of molecular biology in the course of an illness need to be understood, since only in this way is it possible to investigate appropriate new therapies. The acquisition of this basic knowledge and the screening of substances take place in exploratory research. Once enough basic knowledge has been gained, the new substances can be tested out on cells and other lower organisms (in-vitro study) and then on animals (in-vivo study). The pre-clinical phase includes all research activities carried out before trials are performed with human subjects.

Clinical research is understood as development of the drug and comprises phases I, II and III. All the studies in these three phases take place in a wide variety of clinics; they are supported by the "clinical research" department of the pharmaceutical enterprise concerned and financed by the enterprise. Clinical research is the most expensive and time-consuming, and also the most cost-intensive phase of the innovation process. Following the clinical research comes the approval procedure phase: before a new medicine can be finally introduced and sold, it must be approved by the public authorities.

In exploratory (pre-clinical) research the following central factors are decisive in the choice of a location for the pharmaceutical enterprise performing the research:

- There must be a positive attitude of the general public towards biotechnology and genetic engineering. This positive public attitude is a central frame condition for industrial research activities in this field. The core question is: "Can the research be performed out and also exploited in situ?".

- Generating new drugs requires a strong innovation push. In biotechnology this comes both from science (universities and associated clinics) and from numerous scientifically excellent "start-up companies".

- The "start-up companies" and the scientific players need to have highly-developed cooperation and management skills.

- The market has to be important, both qualitatively and quantitatively, for the drug in question. Thus the great attractiveness of the US for the research activities of foreign pharmaceutical enterprises is also explained by the size of the market. In an interview it was stated that presence in the US is a necessity for research-performing pharmaceutical enterprises, as the US represents one-third of the global pharmaceuticals market. Further, customers have to be "sophisticated" and require innovative drugs.

In the research centers of the enterprises the innovation process is usually brought up to the end of Phase I - i.e., up to the stage where clinical work can begin. Even if the research results come from a laboratory in Germany, for example, this does not necessarily mean that the clinical studies will also be carried out in Germany, or that the drug will first be introduced there. Rather, a decision will be made centrally within the corporation about the sites where the studies will be conducted. The corporation's "clinical research" units are internally in global competition with one another. Clinical studies are awarded in internal competitions within the corporation. They are not assigned on the basis of specialization in certain therapeutic areas, but according to criteria in the triangle of costs - quality - time. In fact, a professional project management to conduct these often international clinical trials is decisive and absolutely necessary (see Stock, 1998). If there are problems at one location with starting the study on time or assembling the required number of test persons, other units will try to acquire the contract. Difficulties in Phase III are especially critical, as by this stage a great deal of money has been invested and market entry is approaching.

In addition, the globally distributed locations are subjected to a process of corporate "benchmarking", carried out at regular intervals. If a country or region becomes less attractive, it follows that the location comes under considerable pressure from the corporation. The consequence is that its contracts for studies decline, its workforce decreases, it is organizationally merged with other locations or is given up altogether. In clinical research (development), a combination of the following factors is important when selecting a location:

- A market of great qualitative and quantitative importance for the drug or product in question.

- High willingness and ability to cooperate on the part of clinics and doctors, and a high degree of professionalism in conducting clinical studies. This also includes availability of the necessary infrastructure in the clinics where studies are carried out, the existence of a highly developed "clinical study culture" and the performance of studies according to "good clinical practices" (GCP).

- Other necessary requirements are good cooperation at an operational level with the national approval authorities, a high degree of transparency in the approval criteria and a limited, foreseeable duration of the approval process.

- The types of problems that occur e.g. in relation to the ethics commissions involved, the speed and consistency of their decisions (for instance, when several ethics commissions need to be addressed).

- Lastly, distribution of contracts for clinical studies within the corporation is subject to the "performance triangle" of costs, quality and time.

Among producers of medical drugs, the organization of production is relatively independent of R&D. Proximity of research and development to production plays a small role in allocation decisions, since a close geographical link between these functions is not required. However, results of some interviews indicate that this might change with the growing significance of biotechnology.

6.3.6   The Formation of Regional Innovation Clusters in the US

In the mid-1980s, regional leading-edge clusters at the interface between pharmaceuticals and biotechnology/genetic engineering formed in certain regions of the US:

- *San Francisco/Silicon Valley* is considered as the up-and-coming cluster for biotechnology, microelectronics and venture capital. In the initial phase, a close relationship was expected between the content of the two technologies, and this expectation has also been confirmed by recent developments. Examples of interactions between biotechnology and microelectronics are particularly evident, for instance, in the field of genome research, where information handling, miniaturization and automation play an important role. In addition, independent groups and firms have developed in both key technologies.

- The *Greater Boston Area* is also an ambitiously growing cluster for biotechnology and venture capital, but also for software. Many old industrial buildings in Cambridge, Massachusetts, which previously housed automobile, clothing or candy factories are today used by biotechnology firms. The "culture medium" for the development of start-ups since the beginning of 1980s has been provided by the renowned universities (MIT, Harvard Medical School) and clinics (e.g. Massachusetts General Hospital, Brigham & Women's Hospital) and by investment companies specializing in biotechnology. The market value of the biotechnology firms in and around Boston is estimated at approximately 10 billion US dollars.

- The *corridor around Philadelphia, Baltimore and New York (Mid-Atlantic)* is traditionally regarded as the "cradle" of the pharmaceutical industry in the US, since numerous companies manufacturing medicines were set up here in the early 19th century, some of them by German immigrants (cf. Feldmann/Schreuder, 1996). The corporate headquarters of ten of the 25 biggest pharmaceutical enterprises worldwide are situated here, as are renowned universities/clinics well-known for their work in the area of pharmaceuticals (e.g. Yale University, University of Philadelphia, Rochester University).

The regions described above have become the most important biotechnology centers in the world and also exert a strong magnetic force on the R&D and innovation activities of foreign pharmaceutical enterprises. Since the mid-1980s, numerous research-performing producers of medical drugs have begun to make new investments in exploratory and pre-clinical research particularly in the above mentioned regions on the West and East Coast of the US. On the German side the enterprises Bayer, Hoechst Marion Roussel, BASF/Knoll, Schering, Boehringer Ingelheim and the Behringwerke (since 1997: Centeon) are represented by exploratory and pre-clinical research of their pharmaceutical groups. Other foreign enterprises performing research and development in these regions are producers of medical drugs such as Hoffmann- LaRoche, Novartis, Solvay, Zeneca, Rhône Poulenc Rorer, Takeda and Eisaj.

According to statements made in interviews, these regional innovation clusters on the East and West Coast of the US continue to represent the first choice of location for research-performing pharmaceutical enterprises with regard to biotechnology and genetic engineering. The high magnetism and uniqueness of these regional "centers of excellence" can be characterized by a concentration of the following core elements in one place:

- An extremely high quality of research,

- Access to a great number of young, talented scientists with a well-developed business sense,

- A high degree of professionalism in the universities and clinics in research cooperations with industry and in conducting clinical studies,

- Access to an unparalleled number and range of "start-up companies" in the field of biotechnology, which take the offensive in bringing their most recent research to the notice of the traditionally rooted pharmaceutical enterprises,

- The existence of business capital investment companies /venture capital funds willing to take risks,

- The fact that the R&D centers of numerous globally active pharmaceutical enterprises from the US and other countries have been established in these regions.

The combination of excellent universities and clinics and research performing "start-up companies" in a region gives rise to an unusually strong innovation push. The research head of one German corporation in the US described this phenomenon by saying that "the universities and biotechnology start-up companies drive the established pharmaceutical enterprises before them". Within the framework set by their risk minimization strategy, the established firms are the decisive buyers-up of promising future-oriented research results, and in this way they support the further development of the start-up firms.

This innovation push from the regional clusters can only be understood against the general background conditions in which the pharmaceutical industry operates in the US. The first factor is the size of the market: the US constitutes one-third of the world market in pharmaceuticals, making it virtually compulsory for internationally active medical drug manufacturers to maintain a presence there. Moreover the costs and time needed for approval are reported to be smaller in comparison with Germany, because - apart from any other reason - in the US a higher number of potential customers can be reached through one single approval by the Food and Drug Agency (FDA). Moreover, the American FDA is described as having a higher degree of transparency and professionalism at an operative level.

One other frame condition of central importance is the attitude of society to biotechnology and genetic engineering, which in the past has already exerted a considerable influence on decisions about long-term investments.

6.3.7 Attractiveness of Germany and the US as Locations for Research and Technology

In the view of the enterprises questioned, Germany can no longer be designated as the "chemistry shop of the world".[6] By contrast, in the US regional innovation clusters have formed at the interface between biotechnology and pharmaceuticals; these exercise a very strong magnetic pull on the research activities of pharmaceutical enterprises from other countries. The analysis of R&D input and output indicators in this chapter confirms the negative development in Germany. The technological situation in Germany is unfavorable in the pharmaceuticals industry, particularly with regard to biotechnology. The US has been able to gain a special lead here, and its share of worldwide patent applications grew from 42 % in 1983-86 to 50 % in 1991-94, whereas Germany's share of patent applications went down in the same period from 10 % to 6.7 %.

The change towards the development of the US as the most important global location for biotechnology/pharmaceuticals began at the end of the 1970s. An important part was played in this change by public discussion on the chances and risks associated with biotechnology and genetic engineering. In connection with this public debate, a location where research in this field could be carried out, and the results of this research could also be exploited in new medicines, became progressively more attractive to pharmaceutical enterprises. This sometimes self-destructive public debate went on not only in Germany and western Europe, but also in the US, and had a lasting influence on the investment decisions of research-performing pharmaceutical enterprises.

At the end of the 1970s, fear of the dangers of biotechnology and genetic engineering was also very great in the US. Thus a moratorium was voted by the city council of Cambridge, Boston, in 1976 forbidding research in genetic engineering at Harvard University; the genetic engineering laboratories of the Harvard Medical School came to a standstill. It is almost a historic irony

---

[6] Other studies confirm our results (see Sharp, Patel and Pavitt 1996, p. 24): "Whereas many countries have experienced declines in their shares of patenting and R&D, the US held its own. Europe, by contrast, has seen its share of both patenting and R&D fall, and variations in costs/prices from market to market indicate that although potentially a larger market than the US, it is still fragmented. The one success story among European countries is the UK which has seen a relative increase in its R&D expenditures in this sector and has been especially successful in developing products amongst the top selling drugs. (...) By contrast, Germany and Switzerland, the former dominant players in this sector, record a relatively disappointing performance."

that as a result several US researchers "emigrated" to California, or even to Switzerland, in order to pursue their research in this field. One of the most successful biotechnology "start-up" companies, Biogen, was founded in Switzerland in 1978 for this reason. After a moratorium of nine months, the genetic engineering laboratories in Boston and Cambridge were able to resume their research. Following the change of attitude in Switzerland and Europe, Biogen once more established a laboratory in Cambridge, Boston, in 1982 and re-transferred its activities back to the firm's original location in America. Clearly the public debate was much more heated and controversial in the US, but was then solved - unlike western Europe and Germany - pragmatically, and within a relatively short time.

As a location for pre-clinical research, Germany is not only in fierce competition with the US but also competes, within western Europe, with Great Britain, Denmark and Sweden. Patent analysis reveals that particularly Great Britain, but also the Netherlands, have "caught up" a great deal in biotechnology compared to their position in the 1980s (cf. figure 6.8). In western Europe the region around London and Cambridge, situated close to the seat of the European regulatory authorities, can be described as offering excellent research in biotechnology and being highly attractive to foreign R&D as a regional center of competence.

However, compared with other countries in the European Union, Germany is also under considerable pressure as a location for clinical research (development). From the viewpoint of enterprises, Great Britain, Sweden and the Netherlands are regarded as models of transparency in their authorization procedures and exemplary cooperation and management from hospitals in performing clinical studies. London gains additional importance as a location for clinical research from its proximity to the European regulatory authorities (EMEA, European Medicines Evaluation Agency). Proximity to the regulatory authorities is an important factor in conducting clinical studies fast and efficiently. This argument is also given by the firms with regard to the American FDA. It can thus be expected that in future, there will increasingly be a build-up in London of the departments or offices of enterprises which have the responsibility for obtaining approval. From the viewpoint of costs, selected eastern European countries such as Poland and Hungary are also beginning to come under consideration by firms as locations for performing clinical studies.

After the US (84.8 billion US $) and Japan (61.1 billion US $), Germany is the third largest world market for pharmaceutical products, with a volume of 18.5 billion US $ (cf. EFPIA, 1996, p. 5). Market size is an important factor for a producer of medical drugs when selecting a location for R&D. Thus in this respect Germany is highly attractive as a location but, due to certain limitations, it is not nearly as attractive as it could be. In the interviews the following were named as important disadvantages in Germany from the viewpoint of pre-clinical research:

- The negative attitude of the general public to biotechnology and genetic engineering in the past has had a lasting influence on the long-term R&D investment decisions of enterprises. Even if the "climate" in Germany has improved today, the decisions that were made will not be simply reversed.

- From the viewpoint of the enterprises, missed opportunities in the past have caused Germany's present scientific capability to fall behind.

- Cooperation in research between industry and science is inadequate or absent. The cooperation ability of the universities is often described by firms as unsatisfactory.

- The process of obtaining permission for experiments with animals is too long-drawn-out, complex. and costly. Moreover, applications are generally examined by lawyers and not by experts in the relevant field. The bureaucracy of the procedure complicates research in the field of experimental medicine. France and particularly Great Britain are given as positive examples within Europe.

The following points emerged in the interviews as the main drawbacks when performing clinical research in Germany:

- Substantial deficits at an operational level on the part of the German approval authorities and a duration of the approval procedure which is de facto too long. For instance, there were complaints that it was not possible to reach preliminary agreements between the enterprise and the Bundesinstitut für Arzneimittel und Medizinprodukte (BfArM) before the start of a clinical study. After submitting the documents for examination amendments were regularly requested (notices of deficits), which took up a lot of time. The US Food and Drug Agency (FDA) was ranked first as a positive example.

- Delays of up to a year can also be ascribed to the number of ethics commissions involved in Germany. If clinical studies (Phase III) are to be carried out in different German Laender or different university clinics, a go-ahead has to be obtained from all the ethics commissions involved. For studies covering the whole of Germany, this may be as many as 30 to 50 different commissions. If only one of these comes to a negative decision on the request to perform the clinical study, a complicated process of consensus involving all the commissions has to be organized. It was not the principle of the ethics commission per se that was criticized by the enterprises, but the large number of commissions involved and the divergent decisions they reached.

- According to statements by firms, the time needed to arrange and conduct a clinical study in Germany is between 20 % and 500 % longer than in competing countries such as Great Britain or the US.

- Lack of interest on the part of doctors and deficits in cooperation and management skills in clinics when carrying out clinical studies: here the predominant opinion of firms is that the university clinics are not at all oriented towards clinical tests; drug manufacturers often tend to be regarded as a nuisance. There is a lack of doctors specialized in testing and a lack of "study nurses" to ensure prompt and qualified realization of the studies. Moreover, the career of "study nurse", which is commonly found in other countries, does not exist in Germany.

- Since the authorization procedures at the level of the European Union are decentralized, Germany will obviously not be much in demand as a reference country. As a rule, however, a medical drug is released first in the countries where studies are carried out. Germany is in danger of becoming a "second class country " with regard to innovative medicines in Europe.

From the viewpoint of the enterprises, the main advantages of Germany as a location are the following:

- The attractiveness of a location is largely a function of the size of its market. Germany is the third largest market for pharmaceutical products worldwide, and the largest in Europe.

- High qualification and motivation of researchers and technicians, a great degree of readiness on the part of researchers to work abroad.

- Germany's central position within Europe, including its proximity to the eastern European markets.

- A very good transport infrastructure.

6.4 Conclusions

The internationalization of enterprises is more advanced in some industrial sectors than in others. Pharmaceuticals is one of the sectors with highly internationalized R&D. Differences between sectors regarding the degree of liberalization of international trade, the regulation of streams of direct investments, specific features of regional demand, economies of scale in production and the internationalization of technological knowledge, result in different levels of internationalization. The internationalization of R&D is mainly influenced by three factors, namely:

- early linkage of R&D activity to leading, innovative clients ("lead users") or to the "lead market",

- early coordination of the enterprises' own R&D with scientific excellence and the research system,

- close links between production and R&D.

The importance of lead markets in anchoring existing industrial R&D activities and attracting new activities has increased. A set of the following elements generally characterizes a lead market (cf. Gerybadze/Meyer-Krahmer/Reger, 1997, p. 209):

1. a demand situation characterized by high income elasticity, low price elasticity and a high per capita income,

2. a demand featuring high quality requirements, a ready acceptance of innovations, innovative curiosity and high acceptance of technology,

3. good frame conditions for rapid learning processes by suppliers,

4. approval standards that point the way to approval in other countries (e.g. pharmaceuticals in the US),

5. a functioning system of exploratory marketing ("lead user" principles),

6. specific pressure from problems spurring innovation,

7. "open-minded" regulations appropriate for innovation.

The market's function as a "lead market" is decisive for innovations which only fully mature when they come into close contact with demanding, innovative customers. In fields of technology or industrial sectors that are strongly science-based, it is the results of scientific research that constitute a driving force in the internationalization of innovation processes. In both cases, regional proximity to external partners such as customers, competitors and scientific institutions is an advantage. If there is a close interlinking of production and R&D activities, internationalization of R&D follows internationalization of production. The internationalization of production is then the main driving force behind the internationalization of R&D.

It emerges from this study that decisive factors for the internationalization of R&D are different within pharmaceuticals. A clear distinction has to be made between pre-clinical and clinical research, the innovation dynamics in pre-clinical research are driven by scientific development, whereas in clinical research it is the lead market that is the driving force (cf. table 6.4). In the pre-clinical phase (exploratory research and chemical development)

TABLE 6.4. Determinants of the internationalization of technological competences in pharmaceuticals

Importance of R&D link with	Pharmaceuticals	
	Pre-clinical research	Clinical research
Lead market	low	very high
Science and research system	very high	high
Production	low to high	low

the generating of new medicines is driven by scientific excellence and the most recent research results. Innovation dynamics at the interface of pharmaceuticals/biotechnology are influenced by excellent universities, research institutions and biotechnology start-up firms. It is important here that all the players should command highly developed cooperation and management skills and that there should be no barriers between the various institutions, since otherwise no transfer of scientific knowledge or technology can take place. The excellence of regional research in the form of innovative, research-performing start-up firms, universities, clinics and other research establishments offers very strong incentives for R&D investment of large companies in such a region.

In clinical research (including pharmaceutical development, clinical studies) a close link with the lead market is the decisive factor when selecting a location. The quantitative and qualitative significance of the market for the product concerned is important, as well as satisfactory cooperation with approval authorities, a high degree of transparency in approval criteria and an appropriate infrastructure in the clinics which can ensure professionalism in conducting the clinical studies.

A close link between R&D activities and production is a less important determinant for research-performing producers of medical drugs when selecting a location for R&D; production is organized relatively independently from R&D. Hints are given in the interviews that this is changing for biotechnology: closer links between R&D and production may be necessary, and of higher significance.

Highly internationalized pharmaceutical corporations with their headquarters in Germany or western Europe pursue a concept of "Triadization" of their locations, which also includes R&D activities (cf. figure 6.14). Following the phases of the innovation process a decision must again be made between exploratory research and chemical/pharmaceutical development (including clinical research). Exploratory research is mainly organized on a "matrix" principle: here competencies are distributed by therapeutic areas among a few (2-5) excellent research centers. To do this, transdisciplinary areas such as biotechnology, combinatorial chemistry and others are defined, which are controlled centrally and worldwide for the corporation from one location.

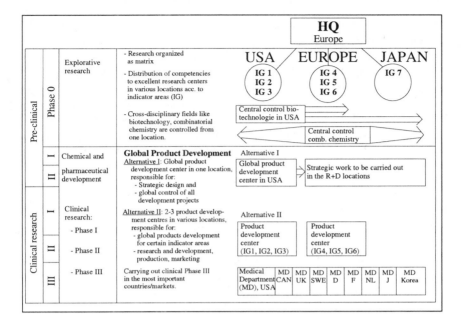

FIGURE 6.14. "Stylized facts": organization of research and development in a highly internationalized pharmaceutical enterprise

Product development is no longer controlled from the home country but from the leading center. There are two organizational alternatives here (cf. figure 6.14): firstly, a global product development center may be set up at one location, assuming worldwide responsibility for the strategic orientation and global control of all development projects. Secondly, 2-3 product development centers may be established in various locations worldwide, each having global responsibility for product development in specific therapeutic areas. In both alternatives, clinical studies in Phase II are carried out in situ in the most important countries or markets at an operational level.

From the viewpoint of a country or region and from a policy viewpoint, the establishing of a research center or global product development center is highly significant, because it is here that the relatively non-transferable "performance alliances" are created. These alliances become much less easily transferable if research and product development centers both coincide within the same region or location. This is the case, for instance, with foreign pharmaceutical firms in the mentioned regional innovation clusters in the US. With the exception of Pharmacia & Upjohn, the investigated US and Japanese pharma companies have to a minor extent internationalized their R&D activities and can be regarded as strongly home-base-oriented corporations. Research is still conducted and innovation still generated in the country of origin.

Regarding Germany and the US as location for R&D activities, the analysis of R&D input and output data show that the US has maintained and even improved their position, especially in biotechnology, since the 1980s. In contrast, Germany as one of the dominant players records a disappointing performance. The reasons for this negative development are twofold: on the one side, the environment regarded biotechnology for years wth huge distrust. On the other side, the large pharma companies were unable to recognize the great potentials of the new discoveries and were weakened by organizational inertia. In a still ongoing process German pharma companies are catching up and have heavily invested in R&D activities abroad, mainly in the US. However, R&D investment abroad of German firms was not compensated by R&D investment of foreign firms in Germany, which led in turn to the relatively low R&D expenditure in pharmaceuticals in Germany compared with other OECD countries. In contrast, the attractiveness of the US with its regional clusters at the forefront is very great, especially at the interface between pharmaceuticals and biotechnology. A report of the OECD (1997a, p. 10) shows that 47 % of R&D in pharmaceuticals in 1994 was spent by foreign companies. More recent data from Serapio and Dalton (1999, p. 308) show that R&D expenditure of US affiliates of foreign companies in drugs and medicines (including biotechnology) amounted in 1996 to nearly 60 % of private R&D funding in this sector.

7
Case Study on New Therapies for Selected Autoimmune Diseases

Sybille Hinze, Thomas Reiss

7.1 Introduction

Autoimmune diseases are disorders caused by a phenomenon called autoimmunity. Under normal conditions the immune systems is able to distinguish between self and non-self components of the body and the immune response is directed to foreign antigens only. Autoimmunity, however, causes the immune system to respond against the body itself.

Autoimmune diseases can be classified into two (however overlapping) groups:

- Organ-specific autoimmune diseases (e. g. Hashimoto's thyroiditis (thyroid gland), pernicious anemia (stomach), Addison's disease (adrenal glands), and insulin-dependent diabetes mellitus (pancreas).

- Non-organ specific (systemic) autoimmune diseases (e. g. rheumatoid arthritis, systemic lupus erythematosus (SLE or lupus), and dermatomyositis.

In the first group, autoantibodies cause local injury, inflammation or dysfunction. In the second group (systemic autoimmune diseases), tissue injury and inflammation occur in multiple sites in organs and are usually initiated by vascular leakage and tissue deposition or circulation of autologous immune complexes. Some examples of autoimmune diseases and respective targets of the disease are summarized in table 7.1.

According to Steinmann (1993), about 5 % of the adult population of Europe and North America suffer from autoimmune diseases. This number may increase, partly because autoimmunity is also suspected to play a role in diseases, which at present are not classified as being caused by autoimmunity. For example, arteriosclerosis, the cause of half the deaths in the western world, could be a candidate, where autoimmune phenomena might play a secondary role. In general, the field of autoimmune diseases and in consequence its definition is developing rapidly, so a strict classifi-

TABLE 7.1. Selection of autoimmune diseases

Diseases	Target
Addison's disease	Adrenal gland
Autoimmune hemolytic anemia	Red blood cell membrane proteins
Crohn's disease	Gut
Goodpasture's syndrome	Kidney and lungs
Graves' disease	Thyroid
Hashimoto's thyroiditis	Thyroid
Idiopathic thrombocytogenic purpura	Platelets
Insulin-dependent diabetes mellitus	Pancreatic beta cells
Multiple sclerosis	Brain and spinal cord
Myasthenia gravis	Nerve/muscle synapses
Pemphigus vulgaris	Skin
Pernicious anemia	Gastric parietal cells
Poststreptococcal glomerulonephritis	Kidney
Psoriasis	Skin
Rheumatoid arthritis	Connective tissue
Scleroderma	Heart, lungs, gut, kidney
Sjögren's syndrome	Liver, kidney, brain, thyroid, salivary gland
Spontaneous infertility	Sperm
Systematic lupus erythematosus	DNA, platelets, other tissues

Source: Steinmann (1993)

cation of diseases as belonging to the autoimmune group is not useful at the moment.[1]

The estimation of the proportion of the population suffering autoimmune diseases could also rise because autoimmune diseases are often difficult to diagnose, and thus a considerable number of people is still unaware of the underlying nature of their illnesses.

The American Autoimmune Related Disease Association (AARDA), for instance, assumes that "autoimmune related diseases affect one in every five persons and are a major cause of chronic illnesses" (AARDA, 1998). According to AARDA, "approximately 50 million Americans suffer from an autoimmune disease. Of these, the majority are women; some estimates say that 75 percent of those affected - well over 30 million people - are women" (AARDA, 1998). For example, according to the National Multiple Sclerosis Society (NMSS) about 200,000 to 350,000 people in the US (NMSS, 1998), about 115 people per 100,000 in the UK, or about 3 million people world-

---

[1] In the present study we also included Parkinson's disease even though we are aware that there are different experts' opinions about classifying Parkinson's disease as one of the autoimmune diseases. Parkinson's disease is one of the most complex of the neurological disorders. So far, the cause of the disease is not known.

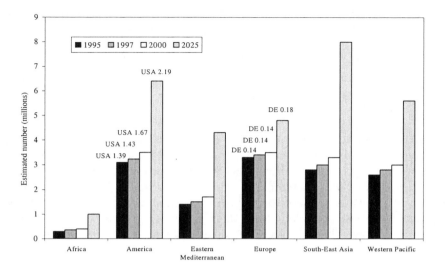

FIGURE 7.1. Distribution of insulin-dependent diabetes mellitus cases by region

wide (Houlton, 1998) suffer from multiple sclerosis. The AARDA estimates
about 65,000 to 70,000 children with juvenile rheumatoid arthritis, and
approximately 500,000 lupus patients (AARDA, 1998).

One of the most widespread autoimmune diseases is insulin-dependent
diabetes mellitus (IDDM). Although this form of diabetes accounts only for
about 5 % to 10 % of all diabetes cases (c. 90 % are non-insulin dependent
diabetes cases) (WHO[2] 1998, IDF[3] 1998) in 1995 world-wide about 7 to 13
million people suffered from IDDM and the trend is increasing.[4] According
to the WHO (1998), by the year 2025 about 300 million people will be
affected by diabetes. Assuming that the proportional distribution between
IDDM and the non-insulin dependent form of diabetes remains constant,
this would lead to 15 to 30 million IDDM patients in 2025. The majority
of all diabetes patients (~80 %) may be living in developing countries by
then, since for these countries an especially high rise in patient numbers is
predicted (see figure 7.1[5]). But the US will remain third among all countries in the number of people suffering from diabetes - following India and

---

[2] WHO = World Health Organisation.

[3] IDF = International Diabetes Federation.

[4] In 1995 according to the WHO (1998) approximately 135 million adults suffered
from diabetes. The number for IDDM was than estimated based on the assumption that
IDDM accounts for about 5 to 10 % of the cases.

[5] Estimates calculated by FhG ISI based on the regional WHO estimates for diabetes
mellitus and the assumption that insulin-dependent diabetes mellitus accounts for about
10 % of the overall diabetes mellitus cases (WHO, 1998).

China (WHO, 1998). Within Europe, Germany takes the sixth position and, according to the WHO forecast, will remain there with constant case numbers. Other countries most heavily affected by diabetes in Europe are Russia, Ukraine, Italy, Spain, and Turkey. Although the largest number of potential patients was predicted for developing countries, it is most likely that economic problems in these countries will lead to an inadequate provision with the necessary drugs. Thus, the developed industrial countries will remain the most important markets.

Autoimmune diseases cover a very diverse range. Organ- and non-organ specific forms have been mentioned above and these are spread across a number of medical specialties e. g. rheumatology, endocrinology, neurology, cardiology, gastroenterology, or dermatology. Up till now, medicine is basically organized according to these specialties, which in general focus primarily on diseases belonging to them. Thus, for a rather long time different autoimmune diseases have been dealt with rather separately. The main focus of research was on dealing with symptoms of the diseases instead of focussing on the autoimmunity itself which forms the relationship between the different autoimmune diseases and is their common cause. Two categories of factors are seen as being involved in causing autoimmune diseases: genetics and environment (Rose, 1997).

Despite the increased basic immunological knowledge and the advances made in understanding autoimmunity, this knowledge until recently had little impact on the treatment of autoimmune diseases (Kuemmerle-Descher et al., 1998). Therapies for autoimmune diseases relied completely on nonspecific immunosuppressors such as corticosteroids, which are only of limited therapeutic benefit and on the other side may themselves cause side effects. The growing understanding of the pathogenesis of autoimmune diseases has enabled the development of more selective therapies, which intervene at different points in the autoimmune process. These include immunosuppressors like cyclosporine A, azathioprine, or different therapeutic monoclonal antibodies and immunomodulators like interleukine, interferones, and cytokines. A recent example of the latter class is betainterferon for the treatment of multiple sclerosis.

The market for immunosuppressors is estimated to about 1,650 million US$ (Hüsing et al., 1998). It includes not only autoimmune diseases (about 10 % to 15 % of the total immunosuppressor market (Hüsing et al., 1998)) but also organ transplantation, where these drugs are used for lowering nonintended immune responses to transplanted organs. The market is largely dominated by "Sandimmune" of Novartis, which is a cyclosporine A formulation. In 1994 worldwide sales of Sandimmune amounted to 1,173 million US$. In 1995 a second cyclosporine A-based product, "Neorale", has been introduced by Novartis (then Sandoz) mainly because of the expiration of patent protection for Sandimmune in 1997. Combined worldwide sales for Sandimmune/Neoral were 1,255 US$ in 1997, market forecasts are 1,300 million US$ in the year 2000 and 1,400 million US$ in the year 2005 (Hüsing et al., 1998; Datamonitor, 1995).

In Germany, starting in the 1980s, autoimmunity and thus autoimmune diseases became of interest also for the pharmaceutical industry because, for some of the concerned diseases, a potentially large market had been expected (for instance for rheumatoid arthritis). Only recently, a number of products has successfully been introduced into the market, as for instance "Betaferon" against multiple sclerosis by Schering (1993: US, 1996: Europe).[6] The turnover for "Betaferon" increased from about 327 million US$ in the first half in 1997 to about 362 million US$ in the same period in 1998 (Schering 1998). Another interferon based MS drug "Avonex" was introduced into the market by Biogen (1996: US, 1997: Europe).

Therapy approaches to autoimmune diseases also include gene therapy strategies, which have been applied to the treatment of autoimmune diseases, e. g. in multiple sclerosis and rheumatoid arthritis, recently. Two concepts are being followed: "Cells targeted for autoimmune attack may be genetically modified to express therapeutic transgenes capable of modulating autoimmune inflammation or repairing damaged tissue. In a complementary strategy, autoreactive T cells may be genetically altered to deliver similar therapeutic transgene factors to the autoimmune inflammatory milieu." (Mathisen/Tuohy, 1998, p.104).

Autoimmunity is, or is assumed to be, the underlying cause for about 80 different diseases. In particular the fact that the majority of these diseases are chronic diseases, and thus require ongoing medication leads to the conclusion that this area in total may be seen as bearing a huge market potential for the pharmaceutical industry.

Because of the diverse and complex character of autoimmune diseases, the field is seen as being difficult to engage in for small and medium-sized biopharmaceutical companies. This does not mean that biopharmaceutical SMEs cannot do research on autoimmune diseases, in the contrary, as will be shown by the statistical analysis in chapter 7.2, they are very well active in this particular field. But in particular because long lasting and therefore expensive clinical trials are required, which often exceed the financial capabilities of SMEs, big pharmaceutical firms are looked for as potential partners. In certain cases where a rather focused market with well defined patient groups can be expected (like e. g. for lupus) it is easier for a biotech SME to enter the clinical stage on its own, because the required financial resources for clinics and marketing are lower under these conditions compared to less structured markets.

---

[6] In the US it has been introduced under the name "Betaseron".

7.2 Statistical Analysis

7.2.1 Methodology

In order to identify trends in research and development focused on autoimmune diseases, a statistical analysis using bibliometric and patent data was carried out. It is assumed that bibliometric data and respective indicators can be used to reflect the activities in basic and applied research while patent data can be taken to analyze applied research as well as the activities oriented on experimental development.

Bibliometric Analysis

The bibliometric analysis was carried out using on-line databases. First it was necessary to select the appropriate database requiring test searches in different databases. As a result, the bibliographic database "MEDLINE" was chosen, which is produced by the U.S. National Library of Medicine and covers world-wide biomedical literature. In total, more than 3,900 journals published in over 70 countries are included. The MEDLINE data were used for analyzing general as well as country-specific trends.

Search strategies based on keywords have been developed. Data indicating the long-term development (1970 to 1994) of the scientific field as a whole were gathered. Country-specific trends were analyzed beginning in 1987 only, because in the earlier period the information about the country of origin of the publication is not available from a sufficient number of documents.

It was also intended to analyze patterns of collaboration in autoimmune disease research. Multiple-authorship was used as an indicator. The underlying assumption is that the authors involved carried out the research leading to the paper in collaboration. While this indicator is frequently used for the analysis of research collaboration, results should nevertheless be interpreted with caution. Katz and Martin argue "the assessment of collaboration using co-authorship is by no means perfect, it nevertheless has certain advantages" (Katz/Martin, 1997, p.3). According to their argument, multiple-authorship should only be used as a "partial indicator" for analyzing research collaboration because only those activities, which eventually lead to a jointly authored scientific publication are taken into account and included in the investigation. Not all collaborations, however, result in publications and, conversely, a joint paper does not always mean that the results presented in the paper are based on research collaboration. For a more comprehensive discussion of the pros and cons of the use of multiple-authorship as an indicator for collaboration see Katz/Martin (1997).

In most databases the author affiliation is given only for the first author of the publication. One of the few exceptions, offering the affiliation of all authors participating in a publication, is the Science Citation Index (SCI), which was used for this analysis. The bibliometric analysis of collaborative activities was limited to European actors only.[7]

Information on co-authored papers and the affiliation of the different authors has been gathered from the CD-ROM Version of the SCI. This analysis was carried out using a sample of the total set of documents retrieved. Only those documents included into the database in 1995 and with at least one European author.

Furthermore, using the on-line version of the SCI, analyses concerning the contributing disciplines during knowledge generation in autoimmune research were carried out. Three different time periods (1983-1986; 1987-1990; 1991-1994) were taken into account. For this purpose the SCI was used because of the relatively fine classification differentiating between the medical disciplines offered by the database. For all documents the assigned classification was retrieved and the proportion of the single disciplines was then calculated in order to get an impression of the relative importance of single disciplines for autoimmune disease research.

Patent Analysis

Patent analyses were carried out using the on-line versions of the databases WPIL, EPAT and PCTPAT. Analyses are based on patent applications at the European Patent Office (EPO) only, because the EPO has the advantage (for international comparisons) that all countries face the same access conditions.

Country-wise activities were analyzed for the years 1980 to 1995, including a calculation of the patents according to the Patent Cooperation Treaty (PCT) for 1995 on the basis of the increase in applications contained in the database of international applications (PCTPAT). In order to get an impression of the relative importance of the research activities compared to the overall research activities, the specialization indicator RPS (Relative Patent Share), as described in chapter 6, was calculated for the most recent period of time (1991-1994).

In order to analyze relationships between science and technology, in particular the science base of the technologies, the NPL indicator (non-patent literature) was applied. The NPL indicator was constructed using citations of scientific articles in the official search reports of patents. These search reports document the state-of-the-art related to the legal claims of the patent application. The patent office examiners generally prefer to cite other patents, because technical features are more clearly described in patents than in scientific articles. But if they cannot find relevant patents, they also refer to publications. These "non-patent literature (NPL)" references are more frequent in science-based technologies, so that this characteristic can be used for their quantitative definition. Various studies have

---

[7] In particular data on Germany, France, Italy, UK, Sweden, Finland was used.

demonstrated that the average level of references to non-patent literature (NPL) is an appropriate indicator for describing the relation of a technology field to science (see for instance Carpenter/Narin, 1983; Grupp/Schmoch, 1992a; Narin/Olivastro, 1992). Thus, it is possible to operationalize the notion of science-based technologies in a quantitative way. The NPL index is calculated in the following way:[8]

$$NPLM_j = \frac{\sum_i NPL(P_{ij})}{\sum_i P_{ij}}.$$

Therein P_{ij} represents the ith patents within the technology area j and NPL the respective NPL references. For the visualization of the results, the index NPLM can be transferred into a relative form:

$$RNPL_j = \left(\frac{\sum_i NPL(P_{ij})}{\sum_i P_{ij}}\right) \bigg/ \left(\frac{\sum_i \sum_j NPL(P_{ij})}{\sum_i \sum_j P_{ij}}\right)$$

This means, the relative index $RNPL$ for a specific area j relates $NLPM_j$ to the average level for all technologies.

7.2.2 Results

Bibliometric Analysis

Between 1987 and 1994 the total number of scientific publications on autoimmune diseases in the database MEDLINE steadily increased from about 11,000 publications per year to more than 13,000 publications per year (figure 7.2). The most active producers of publications are located in Europe, which contributes roughly 25 % of all publications in 1994. The publication activity of the United States is considerably lower compared to Europe. In addition, there seems to be a relative stagnation of the publication rate in the United States between 1988 and 1994. For Japan, a small but steady increase of yearly publications can be observed which leads to a relative improvement of Japan's position within the Triad in 1994 compared to the end of the 80s.

Within Europe (figure 7.3) Great Britain is clearly the most active player in autoimmune disease research in terms of producing scientific publications. This holds true even if we assume some English language bias of the database favoring Great Britain and the United States. If we consider the different sizes of the compared countries, most remarkable is the performance of Finland, Sweden, and Italy. On the other hand, the publication

---

[8] For a more detailed discussion of the NPL-index see also Schmoch et al. (1993) or Schmoch (1997).

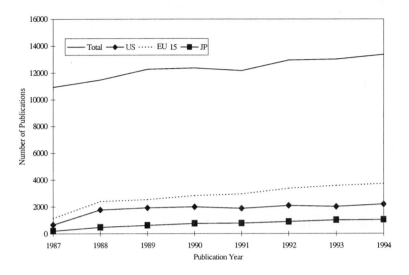

FIGURE 7.2. Scientific publications on autoimmune diseases in the Triad as covered by the database MEDLINE

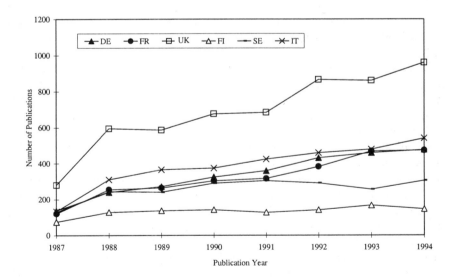

FIGURE 7.3. Scientific publications on autoimmune diseases in European countries (MEDLINE)

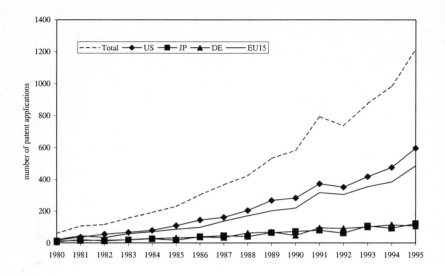

FIGURE 7.4. Patent applications at the EPO

activities in Germany and to a lesser degree in France seem to be relatively low compared to the sizes of these countries.

Patent Analysis

Patent applications concerning autoimmune diseases are starting to leap upwards at the beginning of the 80s leading to a continuous increase until 1995 (figure 7.4). The number of total patent applications at the EPO increased from 1980 to 1995 by a factor of about ten. Compared to the dynamics of patent applications for all technological areas at the EPO, which increased a little more than twofold within the same period, the growth rate for autoimmune diseases patents is extremely high, pointing to a very dynamic development.

From the point of view of the Triad, the most active contributors to patent applications are the United States and Europe (EU 15). While both regions had about the same level of patent applications, during the early days of autoimmune diseases (1980-1984), the United States gained a small advantage from the middle of the 80s until present. Similar dynamics as in the United States or Europe cannot be observed for Japan. Rather, patent applications are staying at the same level throughout the period investigated, which is comparable to the German patenting intensity.

If we concentrate on Europe, the main sites of knowledge utilization as indicated by patent applications are Germany and Great Britain (figure 7.5). For both of these countries patent applications on autoimmune diseases are increasing since 1980 almost in parallel. But while the number of German patent applications in 1995 decreases slightly, Great Britain's

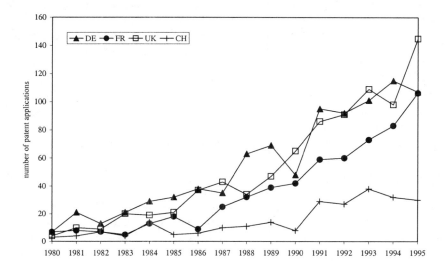

FIGURE 7.5. Patent applications at the EPO (European Countries only)

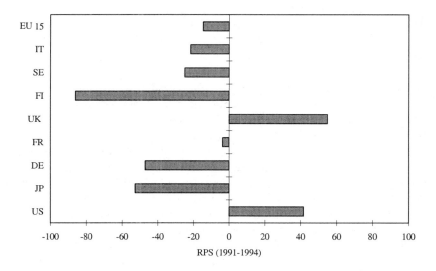

FIGURE 7.6. Relative patent specialization in the field of autoimmune diseases

activities are rising significantly. At the same time the number of French patent applications, which was increasing steadily since 1987 reached the German level. For Switzerland, after increasing activities between 1990 and 1993 a slight decrease was found. In general, Swiss activities are at a lower level compared to the other European countries described above.

Great Britain can draw on a strong knowledge base as indicated by the high publication rate of scientific papers (figure 7.3). This is not necessarily the case for Germany, which showed below-average publication behavior. From this comparison the question arises whether these disparities would lead to a more international knowledge-based network in the case of Germany compared to Great Britain, due to a not fully developed research base in Germany.

The patent specialization indicator RPS shows that Great Britain and the United States have obtained a strong position in autoimmune disease R&D (figure 7.6). France is around average while all other nations, including Europe (EU 15) as a whole, are not specialized in this area. In particular, Finland, Japan, and Germany show a relative weakness here.

7.2.3   Major Players

In order to analyze the major players in autoimmune disease R&D, the lists of patent applicants ranked according to their patent frequencies within two different periods of time (1984 to 1987 and 1992 to 1995) were elaborated. The main focus is on the US and Germany, in addition Japan, Great Britain, France, and Switzerland are included.

In the US, large pharmaceutical companies like Merck & Co., Smith Kline Beecham, Pfizer, Schering Corp., and Eli Lilly were the most active players in 1984 to 1987 (table 7.2). These pharmaceutical firms are still dominating the field in the second period (table 7.3) with changes in the rank order - now lead by SmithKline Beecham, Eli Lilly, and Pfizer. Already in the second half of the 80s a few biotechnological companies - Syntex, Cetus, Genentech and T-Cell Sciences - were found among the top 30 patent applicants. In addition, with the Dana Farber Cancer Institute, the Scripps Research Institute, the University of California and Stanford University, non-industrial research institutions were found among the most active players. Although, large pharmaceutical enterprises remain the most active patent applicants in 1992 to 1995 (table 7.3), academic institutions and biotechnological enterprises moved up in the ranking. The University of California ranks now on the fourth place, Human Genome Sciences on eighth and Genentech on eleventh.

An interesting fact is that Syntex and Genentech, biotech firms that were very active in both periods, have been taken over by Hoffmann-LaRoche. Cetus, another biotechnology enterprise very active in the second half of the 80s, now belongs to Chiron, which is the second largest biotech firm, and 49.9 % of Chiron belong to Novartis.

TABLE 7.2. Top 30 patent applicants for autoimmune diseases in the US between 1984 and 1987

Patent applicant	Number of patent applications
Merck	36
SmithKline Beecham	30
Pfizer	23
Schering	20
Eli Lilly	17
Abbott	14
G.D. Searle	14
Syntex	14
The Wellcome Foundation	14
Warner-Lambert	14
American Home Products	13
Allergan	12
Dana Farber Cancer Institute	12
ICI Americas	10
Ortho Pharmaceutical Corporation	10
University of California	10
F. Hoffmann-LaRoche	9
Merrell Dow Pharmaceuticals	9
E.R. Squibb & Sons	8
Hoechst-Roussel	8
Cetus	6
Genentech	6
Research Corporation Technologies	6
T Cell Sciences	6
Stanford University	6
United States of America (NIH)	6
Upjohn	6
Ciba-Geigy	5
Immunetech Pharmaceuticals	5
The General Hospital Corporation	5

TABLE 7.3. Top 30 patent applicants for autoimmune diseases in the US between 1992 and 1995

Patent applicant	Number of patent applications
SmithKline Beecham	74
Eli Lilly	71
Pfizer	57
University of California	38
Merck	37
American Home Products	36
Bristol-Myers Squibb	35
Human Genome Sciences	35
G.D. Searle	32
F. Hoffmann-LaRoche	25
Genentech	22
United States of America (NIH)	22
Sanofi	21
Bayer	20
Warner-Lambert	20
Chiron	19
Schering	18
Zeneca	18
Allergan	17
The General Hospital Corporation	15
The Wellcome Foundation	15
Glycomed	14
R.J. Reynolds Tobacco	14
The Scripps Research Institute	14
Abbott Laboratories	13
Pharmacia & Upjohn	13
Dana Farber Cancer Institute	11
Merrell Pharmaceuticals	11
Stanford University	11
Procter & Gamble	11

TABLE 7.4. Top 20 patent applicants for autoimmune diseases in Germany between 1984 and 1987

Patent applicant	Number of patent applications
Boehringer Ingelheim	21
Hoechst	18
BASF	13
Schering	9
Boehringer Mannheim	8
F. Hoffmann-LaRoche	8
Bayer	7
A. Nattermann	6
Asta Medica	5
Behringwerke	5
Bioferon	4
Dr. Karl Thomae	4
Max-Planck-Gesellschaft	4
Merck	4
Beiersdorf	3
Sandoz	3
Goedecke	3
Allnatur Bio-Produkte	2
Dolorgiet	2
Dr. Rentschler Biotechnologie	2

In general, for the US we found a broader range of companies and academic institutions engaged in autoimmune diseases in the early 90s compared to the second half of the 80s.

In Germany also the larger pharmaceutical companies like Boehringer Ingelheim, Hoechst, BASF, Schering, and Boehringer Mannheim (now belonging to Hoffman-LaRoche) dominate the autoimmune disease R&D between 1984 and 1987 (table 7.4). In particular Bayer increased its activities in the early 90s moving to the top of the German players (see table 7.5). In addition, there are some medium-sized pharmaceutical firms like Grünenthal, Dr. Rentschler, Byk-Gulden, and others increasingly filing patents in this area. An interesting case is Dr. Karl Thomae. This is a medium-sized biotechnology firm in Germany which has one of the largest biotechnology production facilities in Europe. A very strong increase of Thomae's patenting activities can be noted between the two periods analyzed. If we take into account that Thomae belongs to Boehringer Ingelheim, both together are the most important patent applicants in Germany for autoimmune diseases.

Considering German research institutions, only the Max Planck Society applied for autoimmune patents to a considerable extent. This would have been expected because there is one Max Planck Institute specializ-

TABLE 7.5. Top 30 patent applicants for autoimmune diseases in Germany between 1992 and 1995

Patent applicant	Number of patent applications
Bayer	41
Hoechst Marion Roussel	35
Boehringer Mannheim	26
Dr. Karl Thomae	25
Schering	24
Boehringer Ingelheim	23
Novartis	21
Sandoz	21
Merck	20
Beiersdorf	17
Ciba-Geigy	16
F. Hoffmann-LaRoche	11
BASF	10
Behringwerke	8
Jenapharm	8
Merrell Pharmaceuticals	8
Asta Medica	7
LTS Lohmann Therapie-Systeme	6
Max-Planck-Gesellschaft	6
B.R.A.H.M.S Diagnostica	5
Byk Gulden Lomberg Chemische Fabrik	5
Deutsches Krebsforschungszentrum	4
Hexal	4
Miles	4
Roussel-Uclaf	4
Cassella	3
Dr. Falk Pharma	3
Dr. Rentschler	3
Gruenenthal	3
Merckle	3

TABLE 7.6. Top 20 patent applicants for autoimmune diseases in Japan between 1984 and 1987

Patent applicant	Number of patent applications
Takeda Chemical Industries	13
Otsuka Pharmaceutical	9
Sumitomo Chemical Company	9
Fujisawa Pharmaceutical	7
Ajinomoto	5
Mitsui Toatsu	5
Suntory	5
Tanabe Seiyaku	5
Kanegafuchi Kagaku	4
Mitsubishi Kasei	4
Taisho Pharmaceutical	4
Teijin	4
Kishimoto, Tadamitsu	3
Kuraray	3
Mect	3
Mitsubishi Chemical Industries	3
Sankyo	3
Terumo Kabushiki Kaisha	3
Banyu Pharmaceutical	2
Fuji Yakuhin	2

ing in immunology. Unlike in the US universities do not appear in the list of patent applicants. Differences in the legal systems between the US and Germany may explain this. According to German law, "the right to exploit inventions resulting from university-based research supported by institutional base funds rests exclusively with the individual professor or inventor involved, not with the inventor's host institution" (Abramson et al., 1997 p. 19 and the literature cited there). Thus, universities would not have been expected as patent applicants. Rather professors as individual patent applicants might be active.[9]

There are a number of individual persons included in the list of patent applicants in Germany. However, it cannot be evaluated if they belong to universities. Besides the Max Planck Society, the German Cancer Center and the GSF Research Center for Environment and Health are the only other research institutions appearing as patent applicants. Other institutions working in the biomedical field like, for example, the European Molecular Biology Laboratory or some so-called "blue list institutions", however, seem not to file patents on autoimmune diseases.

---

[9] For the patenting behaviour of German universities, see Schmoch et al. (1995).

TABLE 7.7. Top 30 patent applicants for autoimmune diseases in Japan between 1992 and 1995

Patent applicant	Number of patent applications
Takeda Chemical Industries	28
Otsuka Pharmaceutical	20
Fujisawa Pharmaceutical	19
Pfizer	16
Kyowa Hakko	15
Ono Pharmaceutical	11
Senju Pharmaceutical	11
Kureha Chemical Industry	10
Ajinomoto	8
Eisai	8
Kanegafuchi Kagaku	6
Mitsubishi Chemical Corporation	6
Sankyo Company	6
Suntory	6
Taisho Pharmaceutical	6
Tanabe Seiyaku	6
Bayer	6
Nippon Zoki Pharmaceutical	6
Seikagaku	5
Shiseido Company	5
Toray Industries	5
Yamanouchi Pharmaceutical	5
Yoshitomi Pharmaceutical Industries	5
Cephalon	4
Chugai Seiyaku Kabushiki Kaisha	4
Nisshin Flour Milling	4
Sanen Pharmaceutical	4
Sumitomo Pharmaceuticals	4
Daiichi Pharmaceutical	3
Japan Tobacco	3

Also in Japan pharmaceutical companies dominate patenting activities (tables 7.6, 7.7). Takeda was found to be the most active company within both periods of time analyzed. Following are Otsuka Pharmaceutical, Sumitomo, and Fujisawa.

Pharmaceutical firms also dominated autoimmune R&D in Great Britain (tables 7.8, 7.9) in the second half of the 80s. The major players were Fisons, Beecham Group, SmithKline Beckman, Searle, Glaxo, and Lilly Industries. The list compiled for the early 90s reflects the changes in the worldwide organization of the pharmaceutical industry. Fisons the leading

TABLE 7.8. Top 20 patent applicants for autoimmune diseases in Great Britain between 1984 and 1987

Patent applicant	Number of patent applications
Fisons	15
Beecham Group	10
SmithKline Beckman	8
G.D. Searle	7
Glaxo Group	7
Lilly Industries	7
British Technology Group	6
Efamol	6
Amylin	5
National Research Development Corp.	5
Unilever	5
F. Hoffmann-LaRoche	4
Imperial Chemical Industries	4
The Wellcome Foundation	3
University College London	3
Akzo	2
Bayer	2
Bioscience International	2
May & Baker	2
Phares Pharmaceutical Research	2

player (according to patent application numbers) was acquired by Rhône-Poulenc Rorer in 1995.

The Beecham Group and SmithKline Beckman - number two and three in 1984-1987 - merged in 1989 into SmithKline Beecham, now the most active patent-filing company in autoimmune diseases in Britain. Following are Zeneca, Merck Sharp Dome. Strongly engaged in R&D in autoimmune diseases are biotechnological companies - British Biotech Pharmaceuticals and Celltech Therapeutics placed on the third and fifth position of the list. Among the top 20 the University College of London is the only academic institution appearing during both periods considered.

In France a research institution, namely the Centre International de Recherche Dermatologique, was most active in filing patents on autoimmune diseases between 1984 and 1987 (table 7.10). Following were the pharmaceutical companies Roussel-Uclaf, Adir et Companie, Synthelabo and L'Oréal (with the latter ones belonging to the same group). In the period 1992 to 1995 (table 7.11) Rhône-Poulenc Rorer significantly increased its share on patents now leading on top of the list followed by Adir et Companie, L'Oréal, Sanofi, and Merrell Pharmaceuticals.

A rather high number of patents were again filed by research institutions - the Institut National de la Santé et de la Recherche Médicale (INSERM)

TABLE 7.9. Top 30 patent applicants for autoimmune diseases in Great Britain between 1992 and 1995

Patent applicant	Number of patent applications
SmithKline Beecham	67
Zeneca	35
British Biotech Pharmaceuticals	29
Merck	27
Celltech Therapeutics	24
Roussel-Uclaf	13
Glaxo Group	12
Knoll	12
Scotia Holdings	11
Eli Lilly	10
Chiroscience	8
Lilly Industries	8
The Wellcome Foundation	8
British Technology Group	7
Zeneca	7
F. Hoffmann-LaRoche	6
Unilever	6
Rhône-Poulenc Rorer	5
University College London	5
Cancer Research Campaign Technology	4
Cortecs	4
Hoechst Marion Roussel	4
Medical Research Council	4
Novartis	4
Astra	3
Glaxo Wellcome	3
Ludwig Institute for Cancer Research	3
Pfizer	3
Stringer, Bradley Michael John	3
Warner-Lambert Company	3

TABLE 7.10. Top 16 patent applicants for autoimmune diseases in France between 1984 and 1987

Patent applicant	Number of patent applications
Centre International de Recherches Dermatologiques	12
Roussel-Uclaf	10
Adir et Compagnie	6
Synthelabo	4
L'Oréal	3
Merrell Dow Pharmaceuticals	3
Rhône-Poulenc Santé	3
Sanofi	3
Albert Rolland	2
Centre National de la Recherche Scientifique (CNRS)	2
Delalande	2
Institut Pasteur	2
Laboratoires Chauvin-Blache	2
Medibrevex	2
Unilever	2
Université Pierre et Marie Curie Paris VI	2

and the Centre International de Recherches Dermatologiques Gallderma - CIRDG Gal - which is the major research center of the international Galderma company, a joint venture between Nestlé and L'Oréal.

Swiss R&D on autoimmune disease is also dominated by the large pharmaceutical companies - lead by Sandoz, Hoffmann-LaRoche, and Ciba Geigy in 1984 to 1987 and consequently in 1992 to 1995 (tables 7.12, 7.13) Novartis took the leading position being significantly ahead of Hoffman-LaRoche. These two companies are the only Swiss players contributing significantly (in terms of patent applications) to autoimmune disease R&D. Meanwhile, Hoffmann-LaRoche acquired the German pharmaceutical firm Boehringer Mannheim, one of the most active German contributors. This acquisition could potentially also strengthen the position of Hoffmann-LaRoche in autoimmune disease R&D. However, if the merger between Ciba and Sandoz to Novartis in 1996 is taken into account, Novartis turns out to be the clearly dominant player in Switzerland.

Taken together, the analysis of patenting behavior in the four countries indicates that the types of players involved are basically the same (pharmaceutical companies, universities, research institutions and hospitals). However, there are some specificities (small and medium-sized biotechnology enterprises, small spin-off firms working on diagnosis), which are explained partly by differences in the national systems of innovation. The latter are

TABLE 7.11. Top 30 patent applicants for autoimmune diseases in France between 1992 and 1995

Patent applicant	Number of patent applications
Rhône-Poulenc Rorer	65
Adir et Compagnie	45
L'Oréal	18
Sanofi	16
Merrell Pharmaceuticals	14
Sandoz	13
Zeneca	13
Institut National de la Santé et de la Recherche Médicale (INSERM)	12
Novartis	11
Pierre Fabre Médicament	10
Centre International de Recherches Dermatologiques	8
F. Hoffmann-LaRoche	7
Bio Mérieux	6
Synthelabo	6
Ciba-Geigy	5
Elf Sanofi	5
Fournier Industrie et Santé	4
LVMH Recherche	4
Pharmacia & Upjohn	4
Centre National de la Recherche Scientifique (CNRS)	3
Hoechst Marion Roussel	3
Laboratoire Européen de Biotechnologie	3
Roussel-Uclaf	3
Schering	3
SmithKline Beecham	3
Anda Biologicals	2
Bayer	2
Goupil, Jean-Jacques	2
Institut Pasteur	2
Janssen Pharmaceutica	2

TABLE 7.12. Top 5 patent applicants for autoimmune diseases in Switzerland between 1984 and 1987

Patent applicant	Number of patent applications
Sandoz	25
F. Hoffmann-LaRoche	10
Ciba-Geigy	7
Joshi, Rajendra K., Dr.	3
Speiser, Peter Paul, Prof. Dr.	3

TABLE 7.13. Top 18 patent applicants for autoimmune diseases in Switzerland between 1992 and 1995

Patent applicant	Number of patent applications
Novartis	69
Sandoz	52
Ciba-Geigy	32
F. Hoffmann-LaRoche	18
Duvnjak, Marko	3
Glaxo Group	3
Grabarevic, Zeljko	3
Mildner, Boris	3
Mise, Stjepan Mr.Sc.	3
Petek, Marijan Mr.Sc.	3
Rotkvic, Ivo Mr.Sc.	3
Seiwerth, Sven	3
Sikiric, Predarag, Dr.Sc.	3
Suchanek, Ernest, Dr.Sc.	3
Turkovic, Branko	3
Udovicic, Ivan	3
Eprova Aktiengesellschaft	2
Marigen S.A.	2

also characterized by the existence of different types of funding organizations and procedures.

In general, medium-sized and large pharmaceutical companies are present in all countries analyzed. Small and medium-sized biotechnology firms play an important role in R&D for the development of the field. While these companies are in particular located in the US and Great Britain and were found among the most active patent applicants there, this is obviously not the case to the same extent in the other countries analyzed. Taking into consideration results coming out of the analysis of scientific publications, and thus focusing more on basic research activities, it was found that public research centers, universities, and hospitals belong to the group of contributors working on autoimmune diseases in all countries.

7.3   Core Success Factors for Companies in this Field

Autoimmune diseases embody the challenge the pharmaceutical sector faces now and in the near future. Diversity, complexity and the often chronic character of autoimmune diseases lead to increasingly complex and expensive pharmaceutical R&D (Thayer 1998, p.37) requiring changes in the way pharmaceutical R&D has been organized.

So far, large pharmaceutical companies tend to focus their activities mainly on non-specific immunosuppressants, which are currently the most common treatment for autoimmune diseases. Unfortunately, these treatments are often not very effective and may cause severe side effects. Now developments of more specific therapies are on the way.

For biopharmaceutical SMEs the hesitation of big pharmaceutical enterprises to engage in R&D on more specific treatments for autoimmune diseases opens new business opportunities. The lack of specific drugs and thus, an unmet clinical need, leaves a niche to focus on. The potential market size appears to be large, not least because of high treatment costs as such per case.

According to the interviews carried out, for small and medium-sized biopharmaceutical firms markets of 100 to 200 million US$ are in principle interesting. An additional important factor is the market structure. Preferable is a very focussed market with high treatment costs per case. Under these conditions, even with low patient numbers the market would be attractive for biotech SMEs.

An example for such a niche market in particular dealt with by biopharmaceutical SMEs is lupus. Not only concentrating on one single organ but capable of potentially affecting nearly all organs, lupus is a particularly devastating autoimmune disease. Like many other autoimmune diseases it is so far mainly treated using non-specific immunosuppressants, which are often not very effective and may cause severe side effects. According to interviews carried out, big pharmaceutical companies are hardly active in the area. One reason for this restraint may be related to the difficulties expected to appear in handling this therapeutic target due to the potential complexity of the disease. The market, however, is assumed to be large. Patient numbers are estimated at about 500,000 for the US (AARD, 1998) and another approximately 500,000 for Europe (LJP, 1998). La Jolla Pharmaceuticals (LJP), founded in 1989 and based in San Diego, is an example for a biopharmaceutical firm heavily engaged in lupus R&D. In 1996 LJP formed a strategic alliance with Abbott Laboratories on the joint development of the lupus drug. This common effort meanwhile brought the project to the Phase II/III clinical trials (LJP, 1998; RECAP, 1998).

Finding a partner interested in the R&D activities and willing to engage in the project is a critical point for biopharmaceutical SMEs working on autoimmune diseases. Most of these small firms do not have the financial resources to perform clinical trials on their own, and are heavily dependent on cooperations with larger pharmaceutical firms. If they cannot find a partner at the right time and decide to go for the clinical trials on their own, this decision bears a high risk for the firm if the results are not satisfying. Financial resources often do not allow for a second attempt, and at that point finding a partner interested in collaboration becomes even harder if not impossible.

From its partnership with Abbott Laboratories LJP not only received financial support, 4 million US$ in 1996 and about 9.9 million US$ in 1997, to pursue the lupus project. LJP also benefited from the experience Abbott has accumulated with clinical trials and FDA approval procedures as well as with manufacturing and marketing processes (LJP, 1998). The limited or missing experience in handling clinical trials as well as regulatory approval procedures, and in particular marketing and sales of the potential products was mentioned during the interviews as an additional reason for getting involved into partnerships with pharmaceutical companies. The use of Clinical Research Organizations (CROs) for realizing clinical trials, regulatory consulting services for handling approval procedures, and contract manufacturing for actually producing the drugs developed were mentioned as possibilities to externalize parts of the innovation process that are not considered as core competencies of the company. Important in this context is that internally the expertise is maintained to manage all the external relationships and to guarantee a critical control inside the company.

Time is a very important factor for the success of a biopharmaceutical firm. In order to be faster than other competitors in drug discovery and development, biopharmaceutical firms improve their R&D processes. For instance, Vertex Pharmaceuticals, a biotech company based at Cambridge/MA, engaged in autoimmune disease R&D, introduced the structure-based drug design approach. This multidisciplinary approach integrates advanced biological, biophysical, and chemical methods in a coordinated and simultaneous mode (Vertex, 1998). According to the interviews, this approach may reduce the time needed for drug development processes by half and also increases the chance for the discovery of multiple lead compounds for selected targets. This new approach makes intensive use of modern information technologies and requires extensive expertise in this area. Structure-based drug design used for R&D of drugs to treat autoimmune diseases is applicable to therapeutic targets in a broad range of other diseases, too.

In addition, in order to be successful, a biopharmaceutical firm, which is engaged in autoimmune diseases R&D, has to meet the requirements described in chapter 6 in more detail for the pharmaceutical area in general.

In summary, the following success factors turned out to be critical for biotechnology firms in the autoimmune diseases area:

- It is important to focus on niche markets which are not tackled by big pharmaceutical companies. More important than the size of these markets is their structure. Focused markets with well defined patient populations are especially suited for medium-sized biotechnology firms.

- Partnerships with large pharmaceutical companies are important not only for financial reasons. Through such cooperations also access to specific know-how in manufacturing, conducting clinical trials, dealing with approval procedures, and marketing can be accessed.

- Building up a technology platform which helps to cut down the times to market of autoimmune diseases drugs is an asset which makes the biotechnology firm interesting for cooperations with large pharmaceutical corporations.

7.4   Internationalization and Cooperation

As already described in chapter 6, internationalization and globalization are important features of the innovation process in the whole pharmaceutical area. This is not only the case for collaboration focussing on applied research and development, but it already starts at an earlier stage.

Basic research on autoimmune diseases outside pharmaceutical firms, which is in particular carried out at universities, is to a significant extent done in international collaboration, too. Based on the analysis of co-authorship in scientific publications on autoimmune diseases (using the SCI), it was found that in total about 94 % of all publications are based on collaborative interaction. The majority (approximately 75 %) relies on national collaboration but 25 %, i. e. a significant proportion, are publications based on international collaboration.

TABLE 7.14. Collaboration in autoimmune disease research. Based on SCI data for 1995

	Country					
	UK	DE	FR	IT	SE	FI
Total number of publications	1430	922	758	705	375	191
single authored publications in %[a]	9.0	6.0	5.3	1.1	5.3	3.7
collaborative publications in %[b]	91.0	94.0	94.7	98.9	94.7	96.3
international publications in %[c]	22.1	27.2	24.8	22.6	32.8	32.5
national publications in %[d]	77.9	72.8	75.2	77.4	67.2	67.5

[a] all publications with only one author

[b] all publications with multiple authors

[c] all publications with at least two countries of origin of the authors

[d] all publications with only one country of origin of author(s)

The proportion of international collaboration varies between different countries (table 7.14). Small countries like Sweden and Finland seem to focus more intensively on international collaboration than bigger countries like Germany, France, or the UK. This finding can also lead to the conclusion that researchers in smaller countries seem to depend more heavily on international partners, because in their own countries it is much more difficult to find potential partners for collaboration. In total, international collaboration was found in about one-quarter to one-third of all publications in the single countries. Consequently, international collaboration is highly relevant for research on autoimmune diseases.

According to the patent analysis carried out the major players engaged in autoimmune diseases are large pharmaceutical companies. The majority of these companies are seen as global players having also established R&D activities in the most important markets world-wide, with consequences for their internal organization and management procedures (see also chapters 5 and 6). Appendix B lists alliances installed in autoimmune diseases as retrieved from the biotech alliance database provided by Recombinant Capital (ReCap) via the Internet (http://www.recap.com/).

Biotech firms, beginning in the second half of the 80s, become increasingly visible in the patent data presented in chapter 7.2.3 but mainly in the United States. If collaborations between pharmaceutical firms and biotech firms are concerned, international partnerships are well established. Collaborations among biotech firms, however, seem to focus more heavily on the US. A reason for this is the availability of a wide range of biotech firms here. But, according to the interviews, international collaboration becomes in particular relevant the closer a product comes to its market introduction. To carry out clinical trials, in particular phase IV trials, in international markets an important measure is to establish knowledge and familiarity of the physicians in a particular market with the firm's products

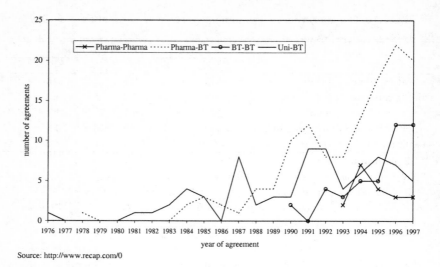

Source: http://www.recap.com/0

FIGURE 7.7. Alliances in autoimmune diseases by partners involved

was mentioned. Biotech firms in particular rely on firms with established international infrastructures for marketing and sales.

In general, different types of alliances or collaborations, concerning the partners involved and the phases of the innovation process covered, appeared in the area of autoimmune diseases over the last 20 years. An analysis of all the alliances in the area of autoimmune diseases, which were included in the ReCap database, indicates that first research collaborations started as early as in 1976 between the University of California in San Francisco and Genentech.

The database allows retrieval of alliances by disease areas. Autoimmune diseases are covered as autoimmune diabetes, autoimmune immunosuppressants and autoimmune immunomodulators. In total, 283 alliances were found (see appendix B). Partners involved in an agreement may be pharmaceutical firms, biotech firms, and research institutions, which are mainly universities but also include e. g. NIH institutes and others. As already pointed out by the example given, collaborations started first in the second half of the 70s. Slightly after the first agreements between universities and biotech firms, pharmaceutical firms started collaborating with biotech firms. Until the mid 80s the number of collaborations seemed to be rather low, but towards the end of the 1980s first the university-biotech agreements widened, and then in particular the number of relationships between pharmaceutical firms and biotech firms increased. First alliances among biotech firms appeared only in the early 90s, and collaborations including different pharmaceutical firms can be found even later. Cooperations between phar-

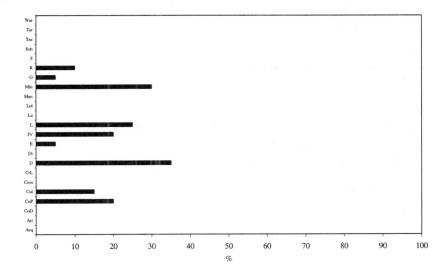

FIGURE 7.8. Types of agreements between pharmaceutical companies only (N=20)

maceutical firms and universities are not shown by the Recap database (see figure 7.7).

Taken together, this analysis of cooperations in autoimmune diseases illustrates the changing role of biotech firms during their evolution. In the early stages there were close links mainly to academic research which persist until present. Some pharmaceutical firms started already during those early days, cooperating with the new biotech scene. However, only with the beginning of the 90s the strongly increasing cooperation intensity between biotech firms and the pharmaceutical industry points to a growing awareness of the significance of biotechnology among pharmaceutical firms. Also during the 90s biotech firms seem to start a kind of horizontal integration indicated by the growing significance of biotech-biotech cooperations. In the following a more detailed analysis of the type of agreements will be presented.

Agreements between collaborating partners cover different types of activities. In figures 7.8 to 7.11 the relevance of the types of collaboration is displayed depending on the partners involved.[10] Obviously, the emphasis laid on particular types of collaboration varies. Relations between pharma-

---

[10] The types of alliances are denoted by the following abbreviations: Acq=Acquisition; Ast=Asset Purchase; CoD=Co-Development; CoM=Co-Market; CoP=Co-Promotion; Col=Collaboration;   Com=Commercialisation;   Cred=Credit;   CrL=Cross-License; D=Development; Di=Distribution; E=Equity; JV=Joint Venture; L=License; Lo=Loan; Lol=Letter of Intent; Man=Manufacturing; Mkt=Marketing; Mrg=Merger; O=Option;

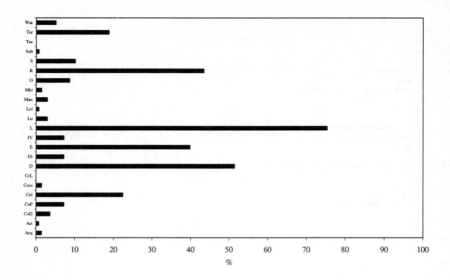

FIGURE 7.9. Types of agreements between pharmaceutical companies and biotech firms (N=138)

ceutical firms are focussing mainly on two types of activities. First, there are market-related agreements like marketing activities (30 % of all agreements) and co-promotion (20 %). Second, there are cooperations related to know-how and technology transfer indicated by development (35 %) and licensing (about 25 %) agreements.

A different picture emerges when analyzing agreements between pharmaceutical companies and biotech firms (figure 7.9). There is a strong focus on know-how and technology transfer indicated by research (43 %), development (51 %), and licensing (75 %) agreements. In addition, obtaining equity is an important means of pharmaceutical companies to participate in the activities of biotech firms.

Agreements between different biotech companies (figure 7.10) are strongly oriented towards licensing (56 %) and to a lesser extent towards development, research, and equity. This pattern confirms observations made during the interviews that licensing of new technologies is an important way for broadening the technology portfolio of biotech firms. The same observation holds true also for relations between research institutions and biotech companies. Licensing and research are by far the most common types of agreements. This clearly indicates that an important flow of knowledge and technology from research institutions to biotech firms exists. In addition,

---

R=Research; S=Supply; Sec=Security; Set=Settlement; Sub=sublicense; Swp=Swap; Tec=technology; Ter=Termination; W=Warranty.

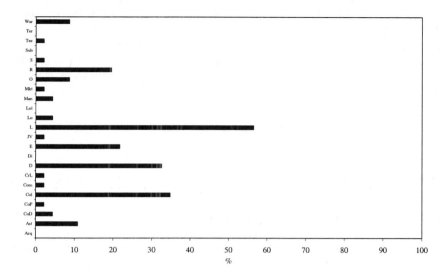

FIGURE 7.10. Types of agreements between biotech companies only (N=46)

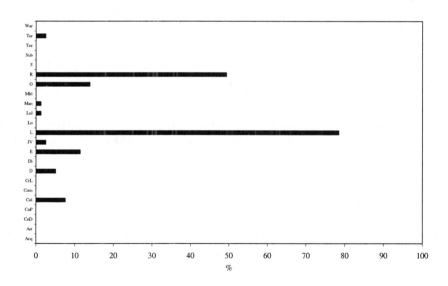

FIGURE 7.11. Types of agreements between research institutions and biotech companies (N=79)

these data also reflect the active licensing policies of some of the leading universities in the United States like, for example, Stanford, University of California, and MIT.

This statistical analysis of agreements between different actors in the autoimmune diseases arena will be complemented by an in-depth elaboration of corporations based on case study interviews in the following chapter. This analysis aims to track the path of knowledge flow between the different players in autoimmune diseases.

7.5   New Distribution of Roles in the R&D Process

Starting from the 1950s, it became possible to create autoimmunity artificially in animals by vigorous immunizing. In the following years experiments showed that autoimmunity could occur in humans spontaneously and by the 1960s it was found that autoimmunity could cause a number of diseases. Today, this period is seen as the very beginning of R&D on autoimmunity. Biochemistry is considered as the pioneer discipline within the development of research on autoimmune diseases. Later on, new approaches have been followed, increasingly based on molecular biology. Also cellular immunology developed rapidly and led e. g. to the identification of cytokines and interleukines. In particular, advances in biology and molecular biology led to a knowledge increase within the field of autoimmune diseases.

Universities were the first to concentrate on basic research on autoimmunity, despite the fact that there was "remarkable reluctance by medical scientists to accept the view that mammalian, and more particularly the human, body is capable of reacting immunologically to its own antigens" (Glynn and Holborow, 1965). Application orientation and in particular patenting were not an issue for this research community. Thus, not surprisingly, for a rather long time, "pure" basic knowledge generation took place.

In the interviews with research institutions and enterprises, which focus on autoimmune R&D, it was pointed out that the emergence of biotechnology led to a rethinking within the biology community. As in other areas, also in autoimmune disease research scientists increasingly considered the potential for further applications of research results.

Up to now, the autoimmune causes have been confirmed scientifically only for a very limited number of diseases. For the majority of diseases, autoimmunity is still one hypothesis to consider. For a period of time, it was typical to associate a wide range of diseases, for which the causes of their appearance were still unclear (idiopathic diseases) to autoimmunity. For most of these diseases, autoimmune causes are still to be approved.

These still open cases require further basic research but within the context of the indication concerned.

Limited knowledge about the mechanisms leading to autoimmune diseases resulted in industrial activities, in particular performed by large pharmaceutical firms that focused rather on non-specific therapies, which, for instance, reduce inflammatory activity. Provided that the pathogenesis of autoimmune diseases is understood, the next generation of therapies will aim at the underlying mechanisms causing the disease (the genes involved, immunological specificity, etc.). Recently, in particular small and medium-sized biotech companies became actively engaged in these topics.

In industry, autoimmune disease research is organized in research teams and it seems to be quite rare that university researchers participate directly in these teams. Academic research inputs are integrated in a more indirect fashion during the initial (basic) phase of knowledge production. As pointed out in the previous part, the knowledge flows between the different actors are very complex and diverse. This knowledge concerns scientific theory ("know-why"), property studies, technical information (testing, screening), research skills ("know-how": exchange of researchers, of PhD students), knowledge on networking ("know-who": personal contacts in a specific field), etc.

R&D on autoimmune diseases is characterized by the involvement of different kinds of players, who are the same in all countries considered, even if the relevance of specific actor groups differs between the countries. These actor groups are pharmaceutical companies, universities, research institutions, hospitals as well as small and medium-sized biotechnology enterprises. Between these actor groups relations exist at the national as well as at the international level. Three types of links can be distinguished:

- between industrial companies (pharmaceutical companies and biotech SMEs) and public research institutions, universities and hospitals

- between industrial partners only

- between public research actors.

As the interviews with actors in the autoimmune diseases arena showed, links between industrial companies and public research centers, universities, and hospitals are often realized through research contracts and/or collaborative agreements and focus on clinical studies, on molecules screening, on testing and analyzing the potential effectiveness, and the properties of the products or the molecules. These contracts may be formal with money transfers when they concern testing and other routine services, or formal non-disclosure contracts without any money transfers when they concern more fundamental work. These research contracts or collaborative agreements can be found in all countries and are both national and international. They concern very often the pre-clinical stage and the clinical research

TABLE 7.15. NIH research programs on autoimmune diseases in the 90s

Year	Title of the program
1995	Interdisciplinary programs in autoimmune disease
1996	Role of microbes in autoimmune and immune-mediated diseases
1996	Gender in the pathogenesis of autoimmunity: mechanisms
1997	Autoimmunity: genetics, mechanisms, and signaling
1998	Autoimmunity centers of excellence

stage, which more specifically involve (university or non-university) hospitals. Frequently, firms are mainly interested in cooperating with specific well-known institutions or scientists and are thus establishing collaborative links internationally. Exchange of researchers was identified as a practice in several countries. Industrial researchers join public research centers or universities to use their facilities and exchange information about immunology and other types of knowledge, and vice versa university researchers go to industrial laboratories. Collaboration between industry and universities is sometimes conducted in a (more or less) barter system, without formal contracts or agreements.

Another form of collaboration in autoimmune disease R&D between industry and public research institutions found was hosting PhD students and post-doctoral researchers. Most of the pharmaceutical companies in Europe use this opportunity. These kinds of links are judged important for both the academic and the industrial partners.

Co-publications, conference arrangements, seminars, and co-patenting seem also to be usual practices between industries and academic actors and are not specific to one country.

Collaborations between industry and public research institutions are also facilitated by governmental research programs such as the German program "Gesundheitsforschung 2000" or Biomed at the European level. However, industrial companies are somewhat reluctant to join programs because of the fact that research results are open to everyone. In the US the NIH just very recently established a number of research programs on autoimmune diseases (see table 7.15).[11] In particular the program initiating centers of excellence on autoimmunity takes on the task of enforcing multidisciplinary collaboration between the medical specialties concerned, and in addition requires in particular collaboration between basic and clinical research. Explicitly the collaboration of the Autoimmunity Centers of Excellence with industry is encouraged (see appendix C).

Recruitment from the academic system is another form of absorbing knowledge, in particular if contacts with university research groups are already established. Small and medium-sized biotechnology companies as

---

[11] Specific information on the programmes can be found at the NIH webpage: http://www.nih.gov/grants/guide/...

a rule perform this principle also at a higher hierarchical level. Leading university researchers are often found as members of the advisory boards of biotech SMEs. These contacts frequently lead to formal and informal research collaboration between the company and the university labs.

For industry, university research is considered as a window to the research frontier. The relations between public research centers and industry are important, especially on topics concerning symptomatic treatments. On the contrary, the relations are much more complicated and scarce on topics concerning the causes of the autoimmune diseases. This kind of research is new, very risky, and not much advanced.

The research and development on autoimmune diseases that pharmaceutical companies perform by themselves concentrate on applied research and product development. According to R&D executives, these companies are dependent on the basic research that is performed in the university system - both national and international - and the information that is produced and transmitted by academic researchers. The companies try to "tap in" the scientific development in the area. Scientific developments on autoimmune diseases are usually followed attentively by corporate researchers. As a consequence, academic contacts seem to be important for pharmaceutical companies.

But there are some problems of collaboration between industrial partners and universities that emerge because of conflicts of interests. The most important reasons for conflicts with universities concern publication and intellectual property rights because of contrasting interests between pharmaceutical firms and academic institutions. Furthermore, academic research often does not meet the requirements of industry due to the lack of application orientation. Because the time factor is seen as essential for the success of pharmaceutical R&D, research at universities often is, from the point of view of industry, characterized as lacking efficiency.

Small and medium-sized biotech firms are seen as important mediators between the academic and the industrial systems. We will focus our attention on these specific relations below.

Links between industrial companies only, include collaboration between large pharmaceutical firms and biotech or R&D firms. Small and medium-sized biotech companies, which are strongly science-based and application-oriented, play an increasingly important role in R&D on autoimmune diseases (see chapter 7.2). Most of the biotech SMEs are located in the US. This can be seen as one reason for the high relevance of international collaborations within the field - meaning also that many collaborations concerning autoimmune diseases involve American partners.

Biotech SMEs follow highly innovative and often risky approaches in particular in the early phases of the innovation process. The closer the innovation comes to the market the more intensively biotech firms are looking for collaborations with large or medium-sized pharmaceutical companies, as a rule for financial reasons, but also due to lacking experience with clinical trials, regulatory approval processes and marketing and sales activities. During the product development phase, pharmaceutical companies often depend on the large-scale collaboration with R&D firms rather than with academic institutions. At the same time, pharmaceutical companies are looking for interesting offers by biotech firms or even by actual competitors in order to complement their own product pipelines. Thus, collaborations, in particular between biotech SMEs and large pharmaceutical companies, are an increasingly important feature of the division of labor in the pharmaceutical industry. This holds particularly true for the area of autoimmune diseases because of the different directions followed so far by biotech SMEs and pharmaceutical companies, with the latter rather concentrating on non-specific approaches.

Biotech SMEs can be considered as important mediators between the academic sector and industry. It seems that the SMEs cope with academic institutions and their specific working behavior more easily because of common roots in the same environment.

Collaboration between large pharmaceutical firms and biotech firms is perceived as being less conflict-ridden than between pharmaceutical firms and public research institutions. Clearly defined contracts, based on milestone agreements, exist. Problems concern, in particular, the financing agreements.

Another important reason for collaboration between different industrial firms is linked to the costs and the difficulties to enter specific markets because of administrative and marketing barriers. Thus, experienced partners are sought who have a well-organized infrastructure in the market aimed at.

In the development of new therapies, the companies rely on their own R&D, the knowledge and technology provided by the R&D firms, and, but in a quite indirect way, the "cognitive maps" that fundamental research provides them with. The research for new drugs is often entirely financed with internal funds and firms, monitor patents, and scientific publications.

Links between public research institutions are organized in an informal way (co-publications, conferences, informal meetings, etc.). Relations mainly depend on individuals. More formally organized are collaborations based on specific governmental research programs (national or European).

As the large pharmaceutical companies organize their activities concerning autoimmune diseases within the scheme of disease areas the danger exists that too little is done to improve the knowledge of the underlying cause of the diseases and transform this into products. Small and medium-sized biotech firms are filling the gap. In the interviews it was mentioned that these firms have rather more specific research programs targeted to autoimmunity and T-cells in particular.

7.6   Conclusions

Diseases spread over a wide range of medical subfields and showing extremely diverse symptoms belong to autoimmune diseases. Common to them is the cause of the illness - autoimmunity. Shifting the focus from treating the specific symptoms of the different diseases to focusing on the cause of the diseases requires coordinated efforts of all relevant medical subfields. Industry as well as academic actors are challenged in the same way. In industry, in particular in pharmaceutical companies, where research activities have been basically organized by indication areas, the organization of R&D is challenged, because autoimmune diseases in their complexity do not fit easily in the existing departmental structure. New organizational concepts are needed, which facilitate the availability and the exchange of knowledge across these indication areas. In addition, due to the global distribution of internal research locations of pharmaceutical companies, concepts can assure thematic integration only, if at the same time the integration of the different research locations is guaranteed.

Autoimmune disease R&D is performed by large pharmaceutical firms as well as small and medium-sized biotech companies and research institutions. The importance of these actors differs between countries. But for the field as a whole each group is of importance for the further development. A thematic division of labor seems to exist between pharmaceutical companies and biotech SMEs. So far, pharmaceutical companies tend to focus on non-specific treatments of autoimmune diseases, while biotech SMEs follow more specific approaches directed to autoimmunity as such. In this sense, at present complementary approaches are followed. Direct competition between these groups is avoided. This is one reason why autoimmune diseases are seen as attractive niche markets for biotech companies. Competition is strongest among biotech SMEs themselves.

The knowledge base in autoimmune diseases of the member countries of the European Union is well developed. The European advantage in basic research (measured by scientific publications), however, disappears in the area of applied research and development (measured by patent applications). Here, the US is clearly ahead.

Autoimmune disease R&D has a strong international component. Approximately 25 % of all publications on autoimmune diseases are based on international collaboration. The collaboration between large pharmaceutical companies and biotech SMEs is also organized internationally. The presence of a large number of biotech SMEs in the US becomes obvious as American biotech firms are frequently collaborating with large multinational pharmaceutical companies, independent from the location of their headquarter.

Different reasons for collaborations between biotech SMEs and pharmaceutical companies exist. On the one hand, from the SME point of view, there is the financial interest. Biotech SMEs often do not have sufficient financial resources to realize extensive clinical trials, in particular the latter phases, which require large patient populations. In addition, clinical trials, prosecuting approval procedures, marketing, and sales do not belong to the core competencies of biotech SMEs. Lacking experience in handling these phases of the innovation process is another incentive to induce collaborations. Clinical trials are often also considered as preparing the market where a potential product will be introduced, and for this reason international clinical trials have to be performed. Partners offering a well-established international infrastructure are essential.

Alternatively to collaborating with pharmaceutical companies, clinical trials are outsourced and carried out by CROs (Clinical Research Organizations) or consultants, specialized in preparing and following drug approval procedures. These services are then only used when they are needed and it is not necessary to provide respective capacities internally.

Differences concerning the organization of collaborations exist. While links between industrial partners or with research institutions are often realized through research contracts and collaborative agreements, relations among research institutions themselves are usually less formally organized. Problems occurring due to different cultural backgrounds between the partners have to be overcome. Biotech SMEs are often seen as important mediators between the academic and the industrial world.

Important and absolutely essential for the success of a company engaged in autoimmune disease R&D is the optimal integration of the multiple partners involved in the innovation process at different phases. Internally, knowledge is required to manage these processes.

Time is a very important factor for the success of the companies. New approaches for carrying out R&D, for instance structured drug design or information based drug design are introduced. Increasingly often, these require expertise in information technologies.

In general, it became obvious that autoimmune diseases are a field, which seems to rather typically represent the developments in the pharmaceutical sector. Due to its diversity, the field is organized across the normal organizational structure of the pharmaceutical sector, which is based on therapeutic areas or "disease groups". This fact rather reinforces the implementation of the new technical and organizational paradigms described in the previous chapters.

8
Summary and Conclusions

Andre Jungmittag, Guido Reger, Thomas Reiss

8.1 Changes in the Innovation Process and Conclusions for R&D-performing Actors

The objective of this study was to analyze international changes in industrial innovation processes from the example of the pharmaceutical industry. In concrete terms, new paths in the development of active substances and medicines were to be explored. The starting point was the assumption that the innovation processes in this sector have changed considerably in the last 15 - 20 years. One-dimensional, linear single-actor type processes are being replaced by multi-dimensional, complex, multi-actor schemes. This leads to a disintegration of the innovation process in the pharmaceutical industry. A new modular interactive framework for innovation is emerging. As a consequence, new players are becoming more important, with biotechnology firms playing a key role. They can be perceived as mediators of knowledge dissemination. They are the actors who are capable of picking up the results of basic research at universities and other institutions, adding value to this know-how which leads to a transformation into forms which can be directly utilized by the pharmaceutical industry.

In order to collect empirical evidence for this type of changes, its repercussions on significant input measures and on the differing performance of the national pharmaceutical industries, the analysis ranged between different aggregation levels, in which other instruments were also applied in each case. Thus in the first part of this study the meso-economic conditions and impacts were the focus of attention: the differing environments as a result of the different innovation systems, the dynamics of the markets and changes in market structures, input factors in the innovation process such as R&D expenditure, and the concomitant performance indicators, such as patent applications. In the second part the evidence was destilled from data which were obtained at a much lower level of disaggregation: data on cooperations between companies which were picked from the RECAP database accessible via the Internet, data about scientific cooperations, which were depicted according to the number of co-publications, interviews with company representatives on the innovation strategies of multinational pharmaceutical enterprises and an in-depth case study on new therapies for autoimmune diseases.

The concept of the national innovation systems is introduced in chapter 2 and the differentiation from the technological or sectoral innovation systems discussed. Proceeding from the fairly rough characterisation of the economic constitution of the US as a liberal market economy and Germany as a coordinated market economy, it can be demonstrated that these differences are also reflected in the areas of the innovation systems which affect the pharmaceutical sector. This extends from the various profiles of the innovation strengths in both countries up to the arrangement of regulations in the public health system, which directly or indirectly concern the pharmaceutical industries. In the first case, Germany's strength lies in the "cumulative" product and process innovations in established technologies, especially in mechanical engineering and road vehicle construction, in electrical engineering and the chemical industry. The US have their particular strengths in "radical" innovations in the fields of newly emerging technologies (e.g. biotechnology, microprocessors) as well as in large-scale, complex technical systems in extraordinarily R&D-intensive sectors. In the second case in the US the public health system is financed by a high private share, while in Germany the main part is met by the social security system. Pricing policy and the (very modest) refunds for medicines are handled liberally in the US, whilst these matters are very strictly regulated in Germany by the state.

In chapter 3, a number of economic indicators (production, consumption, employment, foreign trade and direct investments abroad) for the pharmaceutical sectors were compared in nine OECD countries in the interval from 1980 to 1995. Summing up, these indicators provided a relatively clear, if also unsurprising picture of the competitiveness of the individual national pharmaceutical industries. The nine countries are categorized in three clusters. The first cluster contains the small countries Canada and Sweden, which are presently at a fairly low level but with medium and high growth rates. In terms of productivity, these two countries - with the highest growth rates - follow on the US with second place (Sweden) and third place (Canada). These two countries are clearly catching up. The second cluster consists of countries on a low or medium level (the Netherlands, France, Germany and Japan), with only low growth rates. These countries have been showing disappointing performances for years and must take care not to fall behind. The third cluster comprises the leading countries Great Britain and the United States which show medium or high levels and medium average annual growth rates.

The innovation process and observable technological-scientific dynamics in the pharmaceutical industry are the subject of the fourth chapter. Starting from the basic characteristics of the innovation process to obtain new pharmaceutical drugs, and the great significance of R&D hereby in generating innovations, the new ways of discovering and developing medicines are analysed in detail. Mainly three fundamental technological developments and achievements contributed to the changing methods of drug discovery and development which emerged during the last decade. First, a whole set of new approaches (such as genomics or functional disease models) led to an increase of the number of potential drug targets. Secondly, new systems for High Throughput Screening were developed. Thirdly, the number of chemicals with potential pharmaceutical activity could be raised via combinatorial approaches by orders of magnitude. All in all, these changes are leading to a new scheme of drug discovery and development which is characterized through higher complexity and necessitates the interaction and integration of more different disciplines.

This new path of drug discovery and development has also important implications for the industry, because it requires new types of knowledge. In particular, sequencing genomes, deriving information from genome sequences, parallel handling of large numbers of samples and large pieces of information, computation of an increasing wealth of information, high-speed screening, new synthetic chemical approaches like combinatorial chemistry, and pharmacogenomics are becoming increasingly important. Likewise the number of different scientific disciplines which are forming the basis for the development of these new types of knowledge is increasing. In addition to chemistry, pharmacology and medical research which are the traditional disciplines of drug development, molecular biology, biotechnology, bioinformatics, robotics, and combinatorial chemistry are gaining in importance. These new disciplines are emerging not only in an evolutionary manner within a broader disciplinary frame. Rather, new disciplines at the borderlines of traditional disciplines are becoming important. Bioinformatics is an example of such a new interdisciplinary field.

The new types of knowledge and the related disciplines go beyond the experience and traditional R&D capabilities of pharmaceutical firms. Therefore, strategies, scope, and organization of pharmaceutical R&D need rethinking. In principle, two strategies are obvious: Firstly, the in-house establishment of the new technologies which could be achieved, for example, through mergers and acquisitions. Secondly, the utilization of special scientific and technological expertise from external sources which would include mainly high-tech firms, research organizations or universities. Strategic cooperations would be the way of implementation. Both approaches need to take into account how the area of the new ways of drug discovery is developing. In particular, it is important to spot the new key players in the different fields. The changing paradigm of drug discovery also offers new opportunities for innovative, specialized biotech firms. Nearly all of the critical technologies are being developed by such small and medium-sized enterprises.

Against the background of the changing innovation process an analysis of alliances within the pharmaceutical industry with the help of the database RECAP, which was the subject of chapter 5, produced a number of intesting results. It was possible to derive the preferred alliances in the pharmaceutical industry and to outline differences between the structures of groups of alliances. In connection with the particular companies' structures concerning subsidiaries, it was possible to draw conclusions about the growth and innovation strategies of single companies and to highlight differences and similarities. Furthermore, conclusions about different strategies of alliances in connection with different types of partners could be drawn. It must be taken into consideration that most alliances of pharmaceutical companies with other pharmaceutical companies are alliances between competitors. The alliances are very often strategic ones and are motivated by reasons which are different from motives of purely acquiring knowledge. Very often these alliances are initiated in order to minimize risks of costly R&D and the often more cost-intensive marketing. The bias towards other than direct R&D alliances can be explained by financial and market-oriented reflections concerning the market introduction and diffusion of new drugs; new knowledge is mainly acquired by alliances with biotechnological companies. It is not surprising that more than half of the analyzed biotechnological companies can be defined as start-ups; this large share is a strong expression of the great importance of basic scientific knowledge of biotechnology in the pharmaceutical industry - and the alliances are very often a consequence of industry-university contacts.

Chapter 6 deals with the internationalization of R&D in the field of pharmaceuticals and biotechnology. Against the background of the changing innovation process the development of the fundamental input factor (R&D expenditure) and an innovation output indicator (the patent aplications at the European Patent Office) are compared and analysed for a number of OECD countries. In absolute figures there is a strong concurrence between the input and output indicators. The two countries with the highest R&D expenditures (US and Japan) show in the period from 1991 to 1994 the greatest number of patent applications in the area of pharmaceuticals. In midfield, Germany seems to be somewhat more efficient in generating innovations. It applied for rather more patents than Great Britain, with considerably less expenditure on R&D. France on the other hand shows the same R&D expenditure as Germany, but with considerably less patent applications, not only as compared with Germany, but also as against Great Britain. For the other countries, the ranking for the R&D expenditure and the patent applications agrees again. If the growth of R&D expenditure since the beginning of the 90s is considered, then the US, Great Britain, Sweden and Canada are conspicuous. These countries are the only ones which clearly positively specialized in patent applications in the pharmaceutical area, whereby Sweden is subsumed here under the group of other countries. The same applies for the subsector of enzymes and microorganisms, i. e. of biotechnology. Therefore the picture obtained from the analysis of the market structures and market dynamics concurs well with the model of innovative strengths. Excellent research and the strong technology base of the US and Great Britain and Sweden in Europe obviously attract foreign R&D investment. The enterprises' strategies are the main focus of interest in chapter6. The analysis showed that internationalization of enterprises is more advanced in European companies than in US or Japanese pharma firms. Internationalization of R&D is mainly influenced by three factors: first, an early linkage of R&D activity to leading, innovative clients ("lead users") or to the "lead market", secondly, an early coordination of the enterprises' own R&D with scientific excellence and the research system, and thirdly, close links between production and R&D. Furthermore, the analysis provides evidence that internationally active enterprises think in terms of value-added chains and process chains. Consequently, the criteria for selecting a location for R&D include not only factors of supply, such as a well-developed research infrastructure, but also demand factors, which are increasingly playing a more important part in the decisions of enterprises. Only by linking various value-added chains (relatively) non-transferable "performance alliances" in a region can be created.

It emerges from the study that a clear distinction has to be made between pre-clinical and clinical research; the innovation dynamics in pre-clinical research are driven by scientific development, whereas in clinical research it is the lead market that is the driving force. In the pre-clinical phase (exploratory research and chemical development), the generating of new medicines is driven by scientific excellence and the most recent research results. Innovation dynamics at the interface of pharmaceuticals/biotechnology are influenced by excellent universities, research institutions and biotechnology start-up firms. It is important here that all the players should command highly developed cooperation and management skills and that there should be no barriers between the various institutions, since otherwise no transfer of scientific knowledge or technology can take place. The excellence of regional research in the form of innovative, research-performing start-up firms, universities, clinics and other research establishments offers strong incentives to attract the research activities of multinational enterprises to a region. In clinical research (including pharmaceutical development, clinical studies), a close link with the lead market is the decisive factor when selecting a location. The quantitative and qualitative significance of the market for the product concerned is important, as well as satisfactory cooperation with approval authorities, a high degree of transparency in approval criteria and an appropriate infrastructure in the clinics which can ensure professionalism in conducting the clinical studies.

A close link between R&D activities and production is a minor determinant for research-performing producers of medical drugs when selecting a location for R&D. Production is organized relatively independently from R&D, however, this is changing with the growing importance of biotechnology-based production processes. Highly internationalized pharmaceutical enterprises generally pursue a concept of "Triadization" of their locations, which also includes R&D activities. Following the phases of the innovation process a decision must again be made between exploratory research and chemical/ pharmaceutical development (including clinical research). Exploratory research is mainly organized on a "matrix" principle: here competencies are distributed by therapeutic areas among a few excellent research centers. To do this, transdisciplinary areas such as biotechnology, combinatorial chemistry and others are defined, which are controlled centrally and worldwide for the corporation from one location. Product development is no longer controlled from the home country, but globally. There are two organizational alternatives here: first, a global product development center may be set up at one location, assuming worldwide responsibility for the strategic orientation and global control of all development projects. Secondly, 2 - 3 product development centers may be established in various locations worldwide, each having global responsibility for product development in specific therapeutic areas. In both alternatives, clinical studies in Phases II and III are carried out in the most important countries or markets at an operational level.

Our analysis was complemented by an in-depth case study of new therapies for selected autoimmune diseases. R&D in this area is performed by large pharmaceutical firms as well as small and medium-sized biotech companies and research institutions. The importance of these actors differs between countries. But for the field as a whole, each group is of importance for the further development. A thematic division of labor seems to exist between pharmaceutical companies and biotech SMEs. So far, pharmaceutical companies tend to focus on non-specific treatments of autoimmune diseases, while biotech SMEs follow more specific approaches directed to autoimmunity as such. In this sense, at present complementary approaches are being followed. Direct competition between these groups is avoided. This is one reason why autoimmune diseases are seen as attractive niche markets for biotech companies. Competition is strongest among the biotech SMEs themselves.

Based on bibliometric data, it can be shown that the science base in the field of autoimmune diseases in European countries is superior to that of the United States. On the other hand, exploitation of research is more efficient in the United States. As indicated by patenting behavior and also cooperation patterns, this advantage in exploitation is due to the existence and activities of mediating biotechnology firms. Thereby, the case study points to the key role of biotech firms in the disintegrating pharmaceutical innovation system. This depends to a great extent on the traditional organization of research in the large pharmaceutical companies. Research activities have been basically organized by indication areas, but autoimmune diseases in their complexity do not fit easily into the existing departmental structure. Because of the different focuses of the cooperation partners, significant synergies can occur and pharmaceutical companies can acquire new knowledge that they could only generate themselves with difficulty or at any rate at great expense. The mediator role played by biotech SMEs is to build bridges between academic and industrial research, which often have different "cultural" backgrounds and working methods.

Naturally the biotech SMEs profit from the cooperations with pharmaceutical big businesses. The financial interest is often important. Biotech SMEs often do not have sufficient financial resources to realize extensive clinical trials, in particular the later phases, which require large patient populations. In addition, clinical trials, pursuing approval procedures, marketing, and sales do not belong to the core competencies of biotech SMEs. The lack of experience in handling these phases of the innovation process is another incentive to collaborate. Clinical trials are often also considered as preparing the market where a potential product will be introduced, and for this reason international clinical trials have to be performed. Partners offering a well-established international infrastructure are essential.

If the results from the general cooperation analysis in chapter 5 and the in-depth analysis of the cooperations on the development of new therapies against autoimmune diseases are brought together, then the evolution of the role of biotechnology firms since 1980 can be traced pretty well. Here, three stages can be observed. Links between biotech firms and universities emerged already in the early stage. These were later complemented by additional links between pharmaceutical firms and biotech firms. A very recent development is the growing cooperation intensity between different biotech firms. Biotech firms seem to respond to the problem of becoming increasingly a commodity supplier instead of a unique technology specialist (compare chapter 4). Via horizontal integration services, products of biotech firms could be enriched with additional properties and information, thereby strengthening the position of biotech firms. Also the role of the pharmaceutical industry seems to have changed recently. They developed from being a customer of biotechnological knowledge to a producer of such knowledge.

8.2 Conclusions for Research and Technology Policy

In conclusion, the question arises which implications for research and technology policy emerge from the results of the study. In the empirical part of the study the comparison between Germany and the US predominates. Continuing from here, our conclusions regarding technology policy concentrate on these two countries, whereby we must admit that the need for action is indubitably higher in Germany.

The great quantitative importance of the German market for pharmaceuticals - it is the third largest market in the world after the US and Japan, and the largest market in Europe - contrasts strongly with Germany 's lack of attractiveness as a location from the viewpoint of R&D-performing pharmaceutical companies. The analyses of patents, OECD data on production and R&D, and interviews with enterprises all indicate that Germany as a location for the pharmaceutical industry is unfavorable. This development has worsened over the last few years and can probably not be reversed within a short time. The position of Germany as a location for pharmaceuticals is especially inadequate in biotechnology. In this important area the United States occupies a dominant position worldwide and Great Britain in Europe.

The US is regarded worldwide as a highly dynamic and innovative market in pharmaceuticals, the American Food and Drug Agency (FDA) is the trendsetter and sets the standards in clinical testing procedures and approval. Particularly the three regional innovation clusters in the Greater Boston area, San Francisco/ Silicon Valley and the Mid-Atlantic region can be described as unique clusters at the interface of pharmaceuticals and biotechnology, which are extremely attractive to foreign R&D-performing pharma companies. Particularly at this interface, the US can be described as the lead market, and firmly-anchored performance alliances have formed there within the regional innovation clusters. This lead market, and the regional innovation clusters that have established themselves in this environment, are characterized by:

1. A high demand associated with high income: the US, with a per capita consumption of medicines of ca. 235 US $ (manufacturers' selling prices) is second only to France, with a per capita consumption of ca. 265 US $ (Germany: 217 US $).

2. Readiness to accept new drugs and a high acceptance of biotechnology and genetic engineering.

3. Good framework conditions for rapid learning processes between science, start-up firms and large pharmaceutical enterprises.

4. Trendsetting in clinical test procedures and approval procedures by the American FDA, which set the standards for other countries.

5. A strong innovation push from scientific excellence in universities/ clinics, other research institutions and the numerous biotechnology start-up firms.

6. Open-minded regulation that favors innovation.

7. Intensive ("innovation stimulating") competition within the regional innovation cluster.

When aiming to improve the situation in Germany, research and technology policy also has to bear in mind the particularities of pre-clinical and clinical research. In the pre-clinical research phase it is the pharmaceuticals/biotechnology interface that has to be considered. It is not sufficient, however, for policy to be oriented exclusively towards improving the research infrastructure. Rather, attention should be focused on the presence and interplay of various players within a region. The following aspects are important for building up regional innovation clusters in pharma/Biotechnology:

- A great innovation potential comes from regional "start-ups", which deserve special attention as they are an effective means of technology transfer.

- Excellent universities/clinics represent the scientific "culture medium" for biotechnology firm founders; readiness to cooperate with industry and appropriate attitudes of professionalism in public R&D institutes are an important prerequisite.

- For financing and management consulting, specialized business capital investment companies/ venture capital funds are needed - if possible on the spot.

- Only a few biotechnology firm founders can succeed in expanding from "research boutiques" to research-performing producers of medical drugs, because of the large amount of time and financial resources this requires. Large enterprises are the biotechnology firms' most important customers and they are in a position to support the further growth of these firms by purchasing licenses or supporting research projects. Therefore the business strategy of biotechnology start-up firms needs to be oriented particularly towards these customers.

- R&D centers, or the R&D of foreign corporations in the region, strengthen innovation potential and facilitate contacts with biotechnology firms.

- It is generally true to say that the cooperation between industry and science needs to be improved. Moreover, in the pharmaceutical industry, as a science-based sector, basic research is very important for the generating of innovative medicines and therapies. Gaps that have arisen need to be identified and closed.

With the exception of the last point, the suggestions made here relate to the interface between biotechnology and pharmaceuticals. Because of the great importance of biotechnology as a key technology for the development of new therapeutic drugs and the strong magnetism exerted by the US, particularly by the three regional innovation clusters, this particular orientation in Germany is necessary. In summary, it can be stated that it is the promotion of the interaction between different players within a region which is decisive for establishing regional innovation clusters. Beside the "scientific culture medium" provided by excellent universities and clinics, this requires effective technology transfer through the establishment of regional start-up firms and the formation of specialized business capital investment companies for financing and management consulting.

Regarding the attractiveness of a location, clinical research has great significance for market entry: during testing procedures doctors and clinics come into direct contact with new medicines for the first time and become aware of the new product. The enterprises in the survey perform clinical research in almost all western European countries, as well as in the US, Canada and Japan. In accordance with the European approval procedure, it is not essential for clinical tests to be carried out in Germany. Clinical research in Germany (particularly Phases II and III) comes under great pressure from the positive examples set by countries such as Great Britain, the Netherlands and Sweden, and from the practice of corporate benchmarking. Points of application for policy in order to improve this situation are:

- Improvement of cooperative relations between industry and clinics is very important.

- Basic management in the clinical area (e.g. good clinical practice) as a part of study courses.

- Formation of centers of excellence for clinical studies with the necessary infrastructure (doctors specialized in testing and trained "study nurses") In this context, the development of a recognized career structure for suitable nurses would be a good idea.

- Cooperation should be improved between industry and approval authorities. One possibility to reduce reservations at an operational level would be, for instance, a temporary exchange of personnel between enterprises and approval authorities.

All in all, a need is seen for action on the part of research and technology policy in the area of pharmaceuticals, in order to improve Germany's competitive situation. The most recent policy approaches, such as the "BioRegio" competition were welcomed by the enterprises in the survey as a "step in the right direction". Improving Germany's situation as a location for pharmaceuticals has to be undertaken with a medium- to long-term perspective, as the investment decisions of companies are long-term and cannot be reversed ad hoc. From the viewpoint of the enterprises, the "self-destructive" debate about Germany as a location, and about the chances and risks associated with biotechnology, has tended to produce negative impacts and has not caused the situation in Germany to make positive progress.

References

AARD (1998), http://www.aarda.org.

Abramson, H. N.; Encarnação, J.; Reid, P. P.; Schmoch, U. (eds.) (1997), Technology Transfer Systems in the United States and Germany, Washington D.C.

Andrade, M. A.; Sander, C. (1997), Bioinformatics: from genome data to biological knowledge, in: Current Opinion in Biotechnology 8, 675-683.

Arrow, Kenneth J. (1983), Innovation in Large and Small Firms, in: J. Ronen (ed.), Entrepreneurship, Lexington.

Banerjee, P.; Rosofsky, M. (1997), Re-inventing Drug Discovery: The Quest for Innovation and Productivity. Synopsis of an article in Scrip Magazine (November 1997), accessed via http://ac.com/services/pharma/phar_dd.html.

Behrmann, N. B.; Fischer, W. A. (1980), Overseas R and D Activities of Transnational Companies, Cambridge/MA.

Bellot, E.; Bondaryk, R., Luther, A.L. (1997), Closing the loop in combinatorial chemistry, in: European BioPharmaceutical Review Sept., 52-57.

Bevan, P.; Ryder, H., Shaw, I. (1995), Identifying small-molecule lead compounds: the screening approach to drug discovery, in: TIBTECH 13, 115-121.

Bogner, W. (1996), Drugs to market, Oxford.

Breschi, S.; Malerba, F. (1996), Technological regimes, Schumpeterian dynamics, and spatial boundaries, in: Edquist, C. (ed.) (1997), Systems of Innovation: Technologies, Institutions and Organizations, London/Washington, 130-156.

Cantwell, J. (1994), Transnational Corporations and Innovatory Activities, in: The United Nations' Library on Transnational Corporations, Vol. VIII, London.

Carlsson, B. (ed.) (1997), Technological Systems and Industrial Dynamics, Boston/Dordrecht/London.

Carlsson, B.; Stankiewicz, R. (1995), On the nature, function and composition of technological systems, in: Carlsson, B. (ed.), Technological Systems and Economic Performance: The Case of Factory Automation, Boston/Dordrecht/London, 21-56.

Carpenter, M. P.; Cooper, M., Narin, F. (1980), Linkage between Basic Research Literature and Patents, in: Research Management 13, 30-35.

Casper, S. (1998), National institutional frameworks and high-technology innovation in Germany: the case of biotechnology, mimeo, Berlin.

Casper, S.; Matraves, K. (1997), Corporate governance and firm strategy in the pharmaceutical industry, WZB Working Paper, FS IV 97-20.

Chiesa, V. (1996), Managing the Internationalization of R&D Activities, in: IEEE Transactions on Engineering Management, 43, 7-23.

Christoffersen, R. E. (1997), Translating genomics information into therapeutics: A key role for oligonucleotides, in: Nature Biotechnology 15, 483-484.

Commission of the European Communities (CEC) (ed.) (1998), Internationalisation of Research and Technology: Trends, Issues and Implications for S&T Policies in Europe, ETAN Working Paper Prepared by an Independent Expert Working Group for the European Commission, Directorate General XII, Brussels, Luxembourg.

Datamonitor (1995), Global pharmaceutical forecasts, London.

Davenport, Thomas H.; Prusak, Laurence (1998), Working Knowledge. How Organizations Manage What They Know, Boston.

Die Woche (1997), "Uns fehlt Wissen". Der Pharma-Forscher James Niedel über Probleme und Fortschritte bei der Entwicklung neuer Medikamente (25 July 1997), in: Die Woche No. 31, 25.

Dodgson, M. (1993), Technological Collaborations in Industry, London/ New York.

Drews, J. (1995), Der Einfluß der Arzneimittelforschung auf das Krankheitsverständnis in der klinischen Medizin, in: Herzog. R. (ed.), F&E-Management in der Pharma-Industrie, Aulendorf, 14-23.

Drews, J. (1995a), Innovationsmanagement in der pharmazeutischen Industrie, in: Lonsert, M.; Preuß, K.-J; Kucher; E. (eds.), Handbuch Pharma-Management, Wiesbaden, 766-784.

Drews, J. (1995b), The Impact of Cost Containment on Pharmaceutical Research and Development, Tenth CMR Annual Lecture.

Drews, J. (1996), Genomic sciences and the medicine of tomorrow, in: Nature Biotechnology 14, 1516-1518.

Drews, J., Ryser, S. (1997), The role of innovation in drug development, in: Nature Biotechnology 15, 1318-1319.

Edquist, C. (ed.) (1997), Systems of Innovation: Technologies, Institutions and Organizations, London/Washington.

Edquist, C. et al. (1998), The ISE Policy Statement: The Innovation Policy Implications of the 'Innovation Systems and European Integration' (ISE) Research Project, Linköping (available on CD).

Erbsland, M.; Mehnert, A. (1992), Regulierung der nationalen Pharma- märkte in der Europäischen Gemeinschaft, ZEW Discussion Paper, Industrial Economics and International Management Series No. 92- 13.

Erbsland, M.; Wille, E. (1994), Zu den Effekten von Gesundheitsreform- und Gesundheitsstrukturgesetz auf den Arzneimittelmarkt. Auf den Weg von der korporativen zur staatlichen Regulierung?, ZEW Dis- cussion Paper, Industrial Economics and International Management Series No. 94-11.

European Federation of Pharmaceutical Industries' Associations (EFPIA) (1996), The Pharmaceutical Industry in Figures. Key Data, Update 1996, Brussels.

Feldmann, M.; Schreuder, Y. (1996), Initial Advantage: the Origin of the Geographic Concentration of the Pharmaceutical Industry in the Mid-Atlantic Region, in: Industrial and Corporate Change 5, 839-862.

Florida, R. (1997), The Globalization of R&D: Results of a Survey of Foreign-affiliated R&D Laboratories in the USA, in: Research Policy 26, 85-103.

Freeman, C. (1988), Japan: a new national system of innovation, in: Dosi, G. et al. (eds.), Technical Change and Economic Theory, Lon- don/New York.

Friedrich, G. (1996), Moving beyond the genome projects, in: Nature Biotechnology 14, 1234-1237.

Gambardella, A. (1995), Science and Innovation. The US Pharmaceutical Industry during the 1980s, Cambridge.

Gehrke, B.; Grupp, H. (1994), Innovationspotential und Hochtechnologie - Technologische Position Deutschlands im internationalen Wettbe- werb, Heidelberg.

Gelbert, L. M.; Gregg, R. E. (1997), Will genetics really revolutionize the drug discovery process?, in: Current Opinion in Biotechnology 8, 669-674.

Gerybadze, A.; Meyer-Krahmer, F.; Reger, G. (1997), Globales Management von Forschung und Innovation, Stuttgart.

Gerybadze, A.; Reger, G. (1998), Managing Globally-Distributed Competence Centers within Multinational Corporations. A Resource-Based View, in: Scandura, T. A.; Serapio, M. G. (eds.), Research in International Business and International Relations. Leadership and Innovation in Emerging Markets, Vol. 7, Stamford/ London, 183-217.

Glynn, L. E.; Holborow, E. J. (1965), Autoimmunity and Disease, Oxford.

Gold, L.; Alper, J. (1997), Keeping pace with genomics through combinatorial chemistry, in: Nature Biotechnology 15, 297.

Gregersen, B.; Johnson, B. (1997), Learning economies, innovation systems and European integration, in: Regional Studies 31, 479-490.

Grupp, H. (1997), Messung und Erklärung des Technischen Wandels. Grundzüge einer empirischen Innovationsökonomik, Berlin, Heidelberg, New York.

Grupp, H.; Schmoch, U. (1992a), At the crossroads in laser medicine and polyimide chemistry - Patent assessment of the expansion of knowledge, in: Grupp, H.(ed.), Dynamics of Science-Based Innovation, Berlin, 269-301.

Herzog, R. (ed.) (1995), F&E-Management in der Pharmazeutischen Industrie, Aulendorf.

Hodgson, J. (1998), Genomics: the next generation?, in: Nature Biotechnology Europroduct Focus, Spring, 5-6.

Hogan Jr.; J. C. (1997), Combinatorial chemistry in drug discovery, in: Nature Biotechnology 15, 328-330.

Houlton, S. (1998), Tackling the MS mystery, in: Manufacturing Chemist, January, accessed via: http://www.dotfinechem.com/manchem/sections/-manfeat/sxms/index.htm.

Houston, J. G.; Banks, M. (1997), The chemical-biological interface: developments in automated and miniaturised screening technology, in: Current Opinion in Biotechnology 8, 734-740.

Hubbard, R. E. (1997), Can drugs be designed?, in: Current Opinion in Biotechnology 8, 696-700.

Hüsing, B.; Engels, E.-M.; Frick, T.; Menrad, K.; Reiss, T. (1998), Xeno-transplantation, Bern.

IDF (1998), http://www.idf.org/.

Jean, T. J. (1997), Drug Discovery CROs, in: European BioPharmaceutical Review, Sept., 36-41.

Kaltwasser, A. (1994), Wissenserwerb für Forschung und Entwicklung. Eine Make-or-Buy-Entscheidung, Wiesbaden.

Katz, J. S.; Martin, B. R. (1997), What is research collaboration?, in: Research Policy 26, 1-18.

Kenney, M. (1986), Biotechnology: The University - Industry Complex, New Haven.

Kuemmerle, W. (1997), Building Effective R&D Capabilities Abroad, in: Harvard Business Review 74, 61-70.

Kuemmerle-Descher, J. B.; Hoffmann, M. K.; Niethammer, D.; Dannecker, G. E. (1998), Pediatric rheumatology: autoimmune mechanisms and therapeutic strategies, in: Trends in Immunology Today 19(6), 250-253.

Leschleg, J. (1996), Innovation in the healthcare industry and the importance of patenting human genes, in: Genetic Engineering News, 1st March, 4 and 39.

Lichter, J. B.; Kurth, J. H. (1997), The impact of pharmacogenetics on the future of healthcare, in: Current Opinion in Biotechnology 8, 692-695.

LJPC (1998), http://www.ljpc.com/TrgDsTxt.html.

Lundvall, B. A. (ed.) (1992), National Systems of Innovation: Towards a Theory of Innovation and Interactive Learning, London/New York.

Lyall, A. (1996), Bioinformatics in the pharmaceutical industry, in: TIBTECH 14, 308-317.

Malerba, F.; Orsenigo, L. (1990), Technological regimes and patterns of innovation: A theoretical and empirical investigation of the Italian case, in: Heertje, A./Perlman, M. (eds.), Evolving Technology and Market Structure, Ann Arbor, 283-305.

Malerba, F.; Orsenigo, L. (1993), Technological regimes and firm behaviour, in: Industrial and Corporate Change 2, 45-71.

Malerba, F.; Orsenigo, L. (1995), Schumpeterian Patterns of Innovation, in: Cambridge Journal of Economics 19, 47-66.

Mansfield, E.; Teece, D.; Romeo, A. (1979), Overseas Research and Development by US-based Firms, in: Economica 46, 187-196.

Marshall, E. (1998), NIH to produce a 'working draft' of the genome by 2001, in: Science 281, 1774-1775.

Mathisen, P. M.; Tuohy, V. K. (1998), Gene therapy in the treatment of autoimmune disease, in: Trends in Immunology Today 19(3), 103-105.

Münt, G.; Grupp, H. (1995), Konkordanz zwischen der internationalen Patent- und Warenklassifikation, Bericht an das BMBF, Karlsruhe.

Myers, P. L. (1997), Will combinatorial chemistry deliver real medicines?, in: Current Opinion in Biotechnology 8, 701-707.

Narin, F.; Olivastro, D. (1992), Status report: Linkage between technology and science, in: Research Policy 21, 237-249.

National Science Foundation (1996), Science and Engineering Indicators 1996, NSB 96-21, Washington D.C.

National Science Foundation (1998), Science and Engineering Indicators 1998, NSB 98-1, Arlington.

Nelson, R. R. (1987), Understanding Technical Change as an Evolutionary Process, Amsterdam.

Nelson, R. R.; Rosenberg, N. (1993), Technical innovation and national systems, in: Nelson, R. R. (ed.), National Systems of Innovation: A Comparative Study, Oxford, 3-21.

NIH (1998), http://www.nih.gov/grants/guide/rfa-files/RFA-AI-98-010. html.

Nisbet, L. J.; Moore, M. (1997), Will natural products remain an important source of drug research for the future?, in: Current Opinion in Biotechnology 8, 708-712.

NMSS (1998), http://www.nmss.org/infoframe.html.

Nonaka, I.; Takeuchi, H. (1995), The Knowledge Creating Company: How Japanese Companies Create the Dynamics of Innovation, New York/ Oxford.

Nosi, J. (1999), The Internationalization of Industrial R&D: From Technology Transfer to the Learning Organization, in: Research Policy 28, 107-118.

Odagiri, Yasuda H. (1996), The Determinants of Overseas R&D by Japanese Firms: An Empirical Study at the Industry and Company Levels, in: Research Policy 16, 1059-1079.

OECD (1994), Using Patent Data as Technology Indicators: Patent Manual 1994. The Measurement of Scientific and Technological Activities, Paris.

OECD (1996), Globalisation of Industry - Overview and Sector Reports, Paris.

OECD (1997), STAN Database, Paris (available on diskettes).

OECD (1997a), Session on Globalisation. Internationalisation of Industrial R&D: Patterns and Trends, Paris, October 1997.

Patel, P.; Pavitt, K. (1994), Technological Competencies in the World's Largest Firms: Characteristica, Constraints and Scope for Managerial Choice. Paper presented at the Prince Bertil Symposium, Stockholm School of Economics in June 1994.

Patel, P.; Vega, M. (1999), Patterns of Internationalisation of Corporate Technology: Location vs. Home Country Advantages, in: Research Policy 28, 107-118.

Pavitt, K. (1984), Sectoral patterns of technical change: Towards a taxonomy and a theory, in: Research Policy 13, 343-373.

Persidis, A. (1997), Combinatorial chemistry, in: Nature Biotechnology 15, 391-292.

Persidis, A. (1998), Lead validation platforms, in: Nature Biotechnology 16, 100-101.

Polanyi, Michael (1967), The Tacit Dimension, Garden City.

Porter, A. L.; Roessner, J. D. (1991), Indicators of National Competitiveness in High Technology Industries. Final Report to the National Science Foundation, Atlanta.

Porter, M. E.; Stern, S. (1999), The New Challenge to America's Prosperity: Findings from the Innovation Index (edited by the Council on Competitiveness), Washington D.C.

ReCap homepage: www.recap.com.

Reger, G. (1997), Koordination und strategisches Management internationaler Innovationsprozesse, Heidelberg.

Reger, G.; Beise, M.; Belitz, H. (1999), Innovationsstandorte multinationaler Unternehmen. Internationalisierung technologischer Kompetenzen in der Pharmazeutik, Halbleiter- und Telekommunikationstechnik, Heidelberg.

Roberts, E.B. (1995), Benchmarking the Strategic Management of Technology (I), in: Research Technology Management 38, 44-56.

Roberts, E.B. (1995a), Benchmarking the Strategic Management of Technology (II), in: Research Technology Management 38, 18-26.

Roessner, J. D. (1993), Patterns of Industry Interaction with Federal Laboratories, Atlanta: School of Public Policy, Georgia Institute of Technology.

Ronstadt, R.C. (1977), Research and Development Abroad by U.S. Multinationals, New York.

Rose, N. R. (1997), Autoimmunity - The common thread, in: Focus. The quarterly newsletter of the American Autoimmune Related Diseases Association, accessed via: http://www.aarda.org/common_thread_art.html.

Saxenian, A. (1994), Regional Advantage: Culture and Competition in Silicon Valley and Route 128, Cambridge, MA.

Schering (1998), Geschaeftsbericht 1. HJ. 1998, accessed via: http://www.schering.de/.

Schmoch, U. (1990), Wettbewerbsvorsprung durch Patentinformation, Köln.

Schmoch, U.; Strauss, E.; Grupp, H.; Reiss, T. (1993), Indicators of the scientific base of European patents. Report to the CEC, DG XII, Karlsruhe, FhG-ISI.

Schneider, I. (1998), Robotic systems for HTS, in: Genetic Engineering News February 15, 21.

Schneider, M. et al. (1995), Gesundheitssysteme im internationalen Vergleich, Ausgabe 1994, Augsburg.

Schwarzer, B. (1994), Prozeßorientiertes Informationsmanagement in multinationalen Unternehmen. Eine empirische Untersuchung in der Pharmaindustrie, Wiesbaden.

Sedlak, B. J. (1998), Functional genomics, in: Genetic Engineering News, 1st February, 1.

Senker, J. (1996), National systems of innovation, organizational learning and industrial biotechnology, in: Technovation, 16(5), 219-229.

Serapio, M. G.; Dalton, D. M. (1999), Globalization of Industrial R&D: An Examination of Foreign Direct Investments in R&D in the United States, in: Research Policy 28, 303-316.

Sharp, M.; Patel, P.; Pavitt, K. (1996), Europe's Pharmaceutical Industry: An Innovation Profile. Final Report Prepared for DG XIII-D-4. European Commission, Brussels, Luxembourg.

Soskice, D. (1994), Innovation strategies of companies: a comparative institutional analysis of some cross-country differences, in: Zapf, W. (ed.), Institutionsvergleich und Institutionsdynamik, Berlin, 271 - 289.

Soskice, D. (1997), Divergent production regimes, in: Kitschelt, H. et al. (eds.), Continuity and Change in Contemporary Capitalism, Cambridge.

Steinmann, L. (1993), Autoimmune diseases, in: Scientific American 269 (3), 74-83.

Stock, G. (1998), Management des Wandels ist die bestimmende Herausforderung, in: Blick durch die Wirtschaft No. 140, 4.

Stock, G. (1998a), Interaction between Industry and Academia. The Experience of a German Pharmaceutical Company, in: Industry & Higher Education, December, 1-5.

Swayzee, J, Alliances in the Pharmaceutical Industry: Extracts from a Report prepared by Andersen Consulting in conjunction with NewCap Communications. Accessed via: http://www.ac.com./services/pharma/phar_alliance.html.

Thayer, A. M. (1998), Pharmaceuticals: Redesigning R&D, in: Chemical & Engineering News, February 23, 25-41.

Vertex (1998), http://www.vpharm.com/.

Warr, W. (1998), Strategic Management of Drug Discovery. Summary, accessed via http://www.pjpbpubs.co.uk/scriprep/959.html.

Whitehead, R. S. (1998), Combinatorial chemistry at the crossroads, in: Nature Biotechnology 16, 2-3.

WHO (1998), World Diabetes No. 3. Accessed via http://www.who.ch/ncd/dia/nl_no.3.htm#GBD and http://www.who.ch/ ncd/dia/dia_est.htm.

ZEW/NIW/DIW/ISI/WSV/WZB (1999), Zur technologischen Leistungsfähigkeit Deutschlands - Zusammenfassender Endbericht (Gutachten im Auftrag des Bundesministeriums für Bildung und Forschung), Bonn.

Appendix A
Top Twenty Pharmaceutical Companies with Subsidiaries

Company	Associated Firms	Description	Type	Size
Abbott (US)	Ross	subs.	Ph	small
AHP (US)	American Cyanamid (US)	subs.	Ph	big
	Davis & Geck (US)	subs.	Ph	small
	Digital Gene Technologies (US)	subs.	Bt	small
	Fort Dodge Labs (US)	subs.	Ph	small
	Genetics Institute (US)	subs.	Bt	big
	Immunex (US)	majority	Bt	big
	Lederle Standard Products	subs.		small
	QLT Photo Therapeutics (CA)	filed by AHP	Bt	small
	Robins A.H. (US)	subs.	Ph	small
	Scientific Protein Labs (US)	subs.	Bt	small
	Storz Ophthalmics (US)	subs.	Dev	small
	Whitehall Laboratories (US)	subs.	Ph	big
	Wyeth-Ayerst (US)	subs.	Ph	big
	Wyeth-Lederle (US)	unit of W.-A.		small
Astra (SE)	Synbicom AB (SE)	subs.	Ph	small
Bayer (DE)	Cutter Labs (US)	subs.		small
Boehringer	Fermenta (SE)	acquired	Bt	small
Ingelheim (DE)	Karl Thomae (DE)	subs.	Ph	big
	Nippon Boehringer Ingelh. (JP)	subs.	Ph	small
	Pharmavene (US)		Bt	small
	Roxane Laboratories (US)	subs.	Bt	big
Bristol Myer	Apothecon (US)	subs.	Ph	small
Squibb (US)	ConvaTec (US)	subs.	Ph	small
	Linvatec (US)	subs.	Ph	small
	Mead Johnson (CA)	subs.	Ph	small
	Squibb (US)	merged	Ph	big
	Squibb Diagnostics (US)	subs.	Ph	big
	Zimmer (US)	subs.	Ph	small
Glaxo	Affymax (US)	subs.	Bt	small
Wellcome (UK)	Affymetrix (US)	subs.	Bt	small
	Burroughs Wellcome (US)	merged 1995	Ph	big
	Wellcome (US)	acq. 1995	Ph	big
Hoechst M.	Aventis (DE)	subs.	Ph	big
Roussel (DE)	Behringwerke (DE)		Ph	big

continued on next page

continued from previous page

Company	Associated Firms	Description	Type	Size
	Behring Diagnostics (DE)	subs.	Ph	big
	Biotech Australia (AU)		Bt	small
	Celanese (MX)		Ph	big
	Chiron Behring (DE)	subs.	Ph	big
	Controlled Therapeutics (UK)	51% 1993	Bt	small
	Hoechst (DE)		Ph	big
	Hoechst Japan (JP)		Ph	big
	Hoechst-Roussel (DE)	subs.	Ph	big
	MMD (US)	subs.	Ph	big
	Roussel-Uclaf (US)	subs.	Ph	big
	Selectide (US)	subs.	Bt	small
	Sumitomo (JP)		Ph	big
Hoffmann-	Autocyte (US)	subs.	Bt	small
LaRoche (CH)	Boehringer Mannheim (DE)	subs.	Ph	big
	Corange (US)	subs.	Ph	big
	DePuy (US) 84% owned	Ph	big	
	Genentech (US)	subs.	Bt	big
	Helicon Therapeutics (US)		Bt	small
	Produits Roche (US)	subs.	Bt	small
	Roche Bioscience	subs.	Bt	small
	Roche Diagnostic Systems	subs.	Bt	small
	Roche Molecular Systems (US)	subs.	Ph	small
	Syntex (US)	subs.	Ph	small
	Syva (US)	subs.	Ph	small
Johnson &	IOLAB	subs.	Ph	small
Johnson (US)	Janssen (US)	subs.	Ph	small
	McNeil Consumer Prod. (US)	subs.	Ph	big
	Ortho Pharmaceutical (US)	subs.	Ph	small
Eli Lilly (US)	Adv. Cardiovascular Syst. (US)	subs.	Ph	small
	Jenner Biotherapies (US)		Bt	small
	Pacific Biotech (US)	subs.	Ph	small
	Sphinx Pharmaceuticals (US)	subs.	Bt	small
Merck (US)	Astra-Merck (US)	JV	Ph	big
	Calgon (US)	subs.	Ph	small
	DuPont Merck (US)	partner	Ph	big
	Merck Frosst (CA)	subs.	Ph	small
Novartis (CH)	Chiron (US)	49.9%	Bt	big
	Cetus	subs.		
	Ciba Geigy (CH)	subs.	Ph	big
	EuroCetus	subs.		
	Genetic Therapy (US)	subs.	Ph	big
	Geneva Pharmaceuticals (US)	subs.	Ph	small
	Gerber Products	subs.		
	Novartis Crop Protection	subs.	Ph	small
	Sandoz (CH)	subs.	Ph	big
	SyStemix (US)		Bt	small

continued on next page

continued from previous page

Company	Associated Firms	Description	Type	Size
	Zoecon	subs.		small
	Zyma	subs.	Ph	small
Pfizer (US)	Shiley	subs.	Ph	
Pharmacia-	Adria Labs (US)	subs.	Ph	small
Upjohn (US)	Kabi Pharmacia (SE)	subs.	Bt	small
	Upjohn (US)	merged	Ph	big
Rhone Poulenc	Armour (FR)	subs.	Ph	small
Rorer (FR)	Appl. Immune Sc. (US)	subs.	Bt	small
	Connaught	subs.		
	Centeon L.L.C. (US)	subs.	Ph	big
	Dermik (US)	subs.	Ph	big
	ExVivo Therapies	subs.	Ph	small
	Fisons (US)		Ph	small
	Pasteur Merieux (FR)	subs.	Ph	big
	Rorer (UK)	merged	Ph	small
	RPR Genecell (US)	subs.	Ph	small
Schering Plough (US)	Key Pharmaceuticals	subs.	Ph	small
Smith Kline	Norden Labs	subs.	Ph	small
Beecham (UK)	SB Biologicals	subs.	Ph	small
Warner Lambert (US)	Parke-Davis (US)	subs.	Bt	small
Zeneca (GB)				

Bt = biotech firm; Ph = pharma firm; Dev = device firm; subs. = subsidiary

Appendix B
R&D Agreements in the Autoimmune Diseases Area

Agreement	Cat.[1]	Field[2]	Date	Type[3]	Size	Equity	Roy.	Subject
Abbott / Biorex	PB	D	10/97	D,L				Bimoclomol for diabetic neuropathy
Abbott / La Jolla Pharmaceutical	PB	M	12/96	D,E,L,S	$50.0	$12.0		LJP394 for Treatment of Lupus
Abbott / MediSense	PB	D	3/96	Acq	$876.0			Acq for cash of glucose monitoring co.
Abbott / Metabolex	PB	D	1/97	Col,D,E		$4.0		Insulin resistance drugs for Type 2 diabetes
Abbott / SpectRx	PB	D	10/96-12/97	D,E,L,R				Bloodless glucose monitoring
Ajinomoto / Seragen	PB	D	12/94-6/97	D,L	$2.8			In-license of IL-2 gene
Alberta Research Council / Amylin	UB	D	1/93	D,Man				AC0137 manufacture
Allergan / Allergan Specialty Therapeutics	PP	D	3/98	D,E,L,O,R	$200.0			Retinoid development corporation
Alteon / Quintiles Transnational	BB	D	8/96	R				CRO services for pimagedine
Ambalal Sarabhai Enterprises / Magainin	PB	D	1/98	Com,D,JV				Magainin peptide compounds in India
Amgen / Ontogen	BB	S	4/93	D,E,L				Immuno-suppressive drugs
Amylin / ChemDiv	BB	D	2/98	Col,R				Screening TakeOneSet library
Amylin / Trega Biosciences	BB	D	10/92	D,R				Peptide screening technology
Amylin / Tripos,Amylin / Panlabs	BB	D	8/97	Col,L				Access to Tripos' library
Anesta / TheraTech	BB	D	10/90	L,Lo				Glucose/alcohol technology
Ares-Serono / Signal Pharmaceuticals	PB	M;S	11/97	CoP,D,E,L,R	$59.0	$10.0		Nuclear factor kappa B (NF-kB) inhibitors
Ariad Pharmaceuticals / Mitotix	BB	S	7/97	Ast,L				FRAP purchase from Mitotix
ArQule / ICAgen	BB	M;S	7/96	Col,D				Screening of ion channel receptors
Astra AB / Celltech	PB	M	5/94	D,S	$1.1			MAb for immune disorders
Bausch & Lomb / Dura Pharmaceuticals	PB	S	7/85	D,L				Hu IgE pentapeptide

---

1   P: pharmaceutical firm, B: biotech firm, R: research institution

2   D: autoimmune-diabetes, M: autoimmune-immunemodulators, S: autoimmune-immune-suppressives

3   see legend figure 7-8

Bausch & Lomb / Dura Pharmaceuticals	PB	S	7/85	D,L				Hu IgE pentapeptide
Baxter / Cantab Pharmaceuticals	PB	S	8/91-5/95	L,R,Ter	$15.0		13 %	Anti-CD45 for transplant rejection
Baxter / MediSense	PB	D	1/91	D,L				Glucose monitor
Baxter / Neocrin	PB	D	6/92	JV	$9.0			JV for diabetic cell implants
Baxter / VIMRx	PB	M;S	10/97-12/97	Ast,JV	$120.0		20 %	Cell therapy JV
Becton Dickinson / Cygnus	PB	D	2/96-3/98	Di,Ter	$20.0			GlucoWatch glucose monitoring
Berlex / Pharmacopeia	PB	M	2/95-11/97	D,E,L,R	$20.0	$3.5		Combinatorial screens for MS
Beth Israel Hospital / Seragen	UB	D	8/84-6/94	L,R	$1.1			Fusion toxins
BioChem ImmunoSystems / Biomerica	BB	M	9/97	L,Mkt				Allerquant 90G marketing
Biosyn AG / Peptide Therapeutics	PB	M	3/95	Col,D,R				Allergy vaccines
Boehringer Ingelheim / ISIS Pharmaceuticals	PB	S	7/95	Col,E,Lo,R	$100.0	$19.0	50 %	ICAM-1 MAbs & antisense
Boehringer Mannheim / CellPro,Corange / CellPro	PB	S	12/93-4/95	D,E,L,Mkt,Ter	$220.0	$74.0		Stem cell selection system products
Boehringer Mannheim / Dura Pharmaceuticals,Corange / Dura Pharmaceuticals	PB	S	5/91-12/91	O				Picumast for allergy
Bristol-Myers Squibb / Celltech	PB	M	5/94	Man				Single-chain protein production
Bristol-Myers Squibb / Collagen	PB	S	7/88-9/90	D,L,Ter	$2.5			TGF-Beta2 therapy
Bristol-Myers Squibb / Genzyme Transgenics	PB	M;S	9/97	D,L				Humanised MAbs for autoimmune disorders
Bristol-Myers Squibb / Lipha SA	PP	D	4/94	Mkt				Glucophage for diabetes in US
Bristol-Myers Squibb / Molecumetics	PB	M;S	9/98	D,L,R	$45.0			Screening for inflammatory diseases
Bristol-Myers Squibb / Pharmacopeia	PB	M	11/97	Col,D,L,R	$40.0			Screening for chemokine receptors
Bristol-Myers Squibb / Procept	PB	D;S	2/90-12/94	Col,E,L,R,Ter,W	$11.3	$1.3		T Cell Antigen Receptors
Burroughs Wellcome / Cantab Pharmaceuticals	PB	M	4/90	Sub				Cell line in-license
Burroughs Wellcome / CytRx	PB	M	4/91-10/95	L,Ter	$27.0		15 %	Poloxamer 188

Company								Description
Byk Gulden / Quidel	PB	M	9/94	Di				Allergy products in Poland
Caltech / T Cell Sciences	UB	S	5/84	L,R	$0.7		6 %	T-cell antigen receptor
Cambridge University / Cortecs	UB	M,S	7/96	Col,R				Delivery of microbial antigens
Centeon / Medarex	PB	S	4/96	D,L	$32.0			H-22 MAb for autoimmune hematological diseases
Cephalon / SIBIA	BB	D	3/92-10/96	L	$1.8		4 %	IGF-1 for CNS & other uses
Charing Cross and Westminster Medical School / KS Biomedix	UB	S	12/96	L				Treatment for ageing muscle
Children's Diabetes (Denver) / Somatix Therapy	UB	D	4/84	L,R				Fetal cell research
Chiron / Procept	BB	M,S	9/94	L,O,R				Screening of Chiron peptoids
Chiron / Ribozyme Pharmaceuticals	BB	D	7/94-2/96	CoP,D,E,Man,R,W		$10.0	50 %	HIV, diabetes, cardio, cancer & ophthal. targets
Chiroscience / Trega Biosciences	BB	S	5/97	Col				Combinatorial chemistry for cell adhesion
Chugai / ImClone Systems	PB	S	1/93-12/93	L,R,Ter	$35.0		8 %	Stem Cell Receptors & T-SCF
Chugai / Vertex	PB	S	9/90	E,L,O,R	$30.0	$2.0		FK-506 mimic & immunophilins
Ciba-Geigy / Affymax	PB	S	7/91	D,E,R,Ter	$32.5	$15.0		Screening for tyrosine kinases +
Ciba-Geigy / ISIS Pharmaceuticals	PB	S	10/90	CoP,E,L,R	$100.0	$15.5	20 %	C raf kinase & PKC antisense inhibitors
Ciba-Geigy / Tanox Biosystems	PB	S	5/90	D,E,L	$30.2	$4.0	20 %	MAbs for IgE-mediated allergic reactions
Ciba-Geigy / Unigene Labs	PB	D	10/85	L,R	$3.0		5 %	Protease inhibitors
City of Hope / Cell Therapeutics	UB	D	1/98	JV,L				Cell City LLC diabetes company
Connaught / Damon Biotech	PB	D	8/84	JV	$0.5		50 %	Vivotech JV for diabetes
Cortecs / Exocell	BB	D	6/95	Col,D,L				Diagnostics for monitoring diabetes
CSIRO / Biota	UB	D	5/95-7/97	L,R	$1.4			Oral form of insulin
CV Cancer Center / Abgenix	UB	S	3/97	L				Abs for organ transplant
Dana Farber / Cell Genesys	UB	S	6/92-1/96	E,L		$0.0		L-selectin LAM-1
Dana Farber / Procept	UB	D,S	2/87-5/94	L,R	$5.1			T cell activation
Darrow Laborarories / Carrington Labs	PB	D	12/96	Di				Wound care, diabetic & radiation products in Brazil

DJ Pharma / Dura Pharmaceuticals	PB	M	7/98	CoP				Dura's Rondec product line
Duke University / Apex Bioscience	UB	M	9/94	R	$1.0			Nitric oxide biology
Duke University / Sphinx Pharmaceuticals	UB	S	10/87-11/91	E,O,R	$0.1	$0.0	0%	Ceramide therapy
Eisai / IDEC Pharmaceuticals	PB	M;S	12/95	Col,D,L	$37.5			PRIMATISED Abs to gp39 antigen
Elan / RTP Pharma	PB	S	10/97	D,JV				New formulations of ciclosporin
Eurand International / Exocell	PB	D	10/96	D,L				EXO-266 for kidney damage in diabetes
FibroGen / Medarex	PB	S	7/98	D,L	$30.0			HuMAb-Mouse tech. for anti
Fred Hutchinson / Cytel	UB	S	5/91	L				MAbs to Alpha4B1 integrins
Fujisawa / Burroughs Wellcome	PP	S	6/94	Mkt				Imuran immunosuppressant for US
Gamida / Alteon	PB	D	12/95	D,L				Pimagedine in Israel, South Africa, Jordan, Cyprus and Bulgaria
Genentech / Celtrix Pharmaceuticals	BB	M	4/93	CoD,CrL,E,O	$4.0	$4.0		TGFß & receptor
Genentech / Glycomed	PB	M;S	12/90-5/95	E,L,R,Ter,W	$26.8	$7.0		Selectin inhibitors
Genentech / Khepri	BB	S	8/92	E,L,W	$0.5	$0.5	5%	Enkephalinase (endopeptidase)
Genentech / Sensus	BB	D	7/94	E,L				hGH antagonists
Genentech / Xenova	BB	M	12/90-5/93	Col,E	$18.5	$8.5		Small molecule pharmaceuticals
Genetics Institute / Ixion Biotechnology	BB	D	6/96	L,R				Stem cells from islets
Genetics Institute / Repligen	BB	M	11/95	Ast				Purchase of immune modulation business
Genetics Institute / Repligen	BB	M	9/95	Ast,L				Acq. of Repligen's immune modulation business
Genzyme / Biogen	BB	M	9/98	Com,L				Avonex in Japan
Genzyme / LeukoSite	BB	M;S	6/97	Col				Access to Genzyme's library
Genzyme Molecular Oncology / Hexagen	BB	D	3/98	Col,D,R				Gene expression for diabetes
Glaxo / Amylin	PB	D	10/91-6/95	Com,E,JV,L,R,Ter		$2.5		Diabetes & bone metabolism
Glaxo / Eukarion	PB	S	2/97	L,R				Synthetic catalytic scavenger tech.
Glaxo / Sankyo Pharmaceutical	PP	D	9/97	CoP				Troglitazone in Europe
Glaxo / Sequana Therapeutics	PB	D	7/94-2/98	Col,L,R,Ter	$20.0			Gene discovery for Type II diabetes & obesity

Partners								Description
Grunenthal / Chiron	PB	S	6/85	D,L,R,S				Recombinant superoxide dismutase
Gull Laboratories / Shield Diagnostics	PB	S	8/96	Di				Autoimmune diagnostics
Heska / ImmuLogic	PB	M	6/98	L				Allervax diagnosis and treatment
Hoffmann-La Roche / BioFocus	PB	S	9/97	Col,R				New immunosuppressants
Hoffmann-La Roche / Genentech	PB	D	10/96	L	$28.4			NGF License Ex-US
Hoffmann-La Roche / Millennium	PB	D	3/94	CoP,D,E,L,R	$70.0	$6.0		Genomics for diabetes & obesity
Hoffmann-La Roche / Protein Design Labs	PB	D;M;S	1/89-11/92	E,L,R	$24.9	$5.2		Hu MAbs to IL-2 receptor
ICOS / Cambridge Antibody Technology	BB	S	12/97	Col,D				Antibody-based therapeutics
IDEC Pharmaceuticals / Protein Design Labs	BB	S	3/97	L	$1.0			Humanised MAb for autoimmune disease
Johns Hopkins / Celgene	UB	S	7/95	Col				Thalidomide-related drugs
Johns Hopkins / Cortech	UB	S	2/87	L,R	$0.6		10 %	ASIM Technology
Johnson & Johnson / Fujisawa	PP	S	6/95	D,Mkt				Prograf for organ transplants in Aus. & New Zeal.
Joslin Diabetes Center / AutoImmune	UB	D	10/92	L,R	$0.1		5 %	Oral tolerance to insulin
Joslin Diabetes Center / Procept	UB	D	9/92	R				Diabetes protocol
Kirin Brewery / Advanced Tissue Sciences	PB	S	3/93	Col,D,L,O,R	$39.0			Stem cell proliferation factor
Kissei Pharmaceutical / Purdue	PP	D	4/97	D,L				KAD-1229 in Americas
Kobayashi Pharmaceutical / Bioject	PB	D	9/92-9/93	Di,E,Ter	$0.8	$0.5		Biojector system 2000 in Japan
Laboratoires Servier / Kissei Pharmaceutical	PP	D	10/95	D,Mkt				KAD-1229 for diabetes in Europe
Leo Pharmaceutical / La Jolla Pharmaceutical	PB	M	9/95-5/96	CoD,L,S,Ter	$40.0			LPJ394 for lupus in Europe & Mideast
Lifescan / Amylin	PB	D	6/95-3/98	Col,D,E,L,Lo,Ter,W	$92.5	$20.0		AC137 for diabetes
Lifescan / Selfcare	PB	D	11/95-10/96	Di				Testing system for blood glucose
Lilly / AutoImmune	PB	D	12/94	Col,L,O	$20.0			Oral tolerance for diabetes
Lilly / Boehringer Mannheim,Lilly / Corange	PP	D	11/94	CoP				Accu-Check glucose monitor & Humulin

Partners	Type		Date	Codes	$1	$2	%	Description
Lilly / Boehringer Mann-heim,Lilly / Corange	PP	D	6/95	JV				Disease management for diabetes
Lilly / Boehringer Mann-heim,Lilly / Corange	PP	D	1/94	JV				Belgian JV for Humulin & Accu-trend
Lilly / Genentech	PB	D	8/78-7/80	D,L			8 %	Recombinant insulin
Lilly / Insulin Mimetics	PB	D	8/94	L,R	$2.3			Oral insulin substitute
Lilly / Ligand Pharmaceu-ticals	PB	D	11/97-5/98	Col,D,E,L,O,R,W	$174.0	$37.5		Retinoids for diabetes & metabolic
Lilly / Oclassen Pharma-ceuticals	PB	S	8/92	L,Man				Cordran topical corticosteroids
Lilly / Repligen	PB	M;S	3/92-9/95	Col,E,L,R,S,Ter	$38.0	$4.0	20 %	CD11b Abs & polypeptides
Lilly / Sphinx Pharmaceu-ticals	PB	S	10/91-5/93	E,L,R,Ter	$16.6	$4.0		Protein kinase C isozymes
Lipha SA / Shaman	PB	D	9/96	CoP,D,E,L	$29.5		50 %	Plant-derived compounds for Type II diabetes
Mass General Hospital / Diacrin	UB	D	10/89-12/93	L,R,Ter				Islet transplants for diabetes
Mass General Hospital / Ergo Science	UB	S	2/97	L				Compound for immune dysfunc-tion
Mayo Foundation / Incyte Pharmaceuticals	UB	M	1/92-1/93	Col,E,L,R	$0.3			Eosinophil, basophil & mast proteins
MedImmune / BioTrans-plant	BB	S	10/95	Col,D	$16.0			Anti-CD2 Abs & anti-T-cell receptor Abs
Meiji Milk Products / Ascent Pediatrics	PB	M	4/95	CoD,L				Immunologics for pediatrics
Merck / Biogen	PB	S	11/97	Col,D,L,R	$145.0			VLA-4 for asthma & inflammation
Merck / ImmuLogic	PB	D,S	9/89-6/92	E,L,R	$22.7	$10.3		Autoimmune therapies
Merck / Lilly	PP	D	6/96					Disease mgmt. for type I diabetes
Merck / Shaman	PB	D	8/92-6/93	O	$0.0		0 %	Screening for diabetes, pain, HBV & HCV
Meridian Diagnostics / Inova Diagnostics	BB	M	3/95	L				Autoimmune diagnostics in Italy
Miravant / Ramus Medical Technologies	BB	S	12/96	CoD,E				RAPIDGRAFT technology for vessel grafts
MIT / ImmuLogic	UB	M	4/87-10/92	E,L	$1.0	$0.0		Immune modulators
MIT / T Cell Sciences	UB	M	6/87	L	$0.1		3 %	Heterodimeric T lymphocyte rec.
MIT / T Cell Sciences	UB	M	6/87	L	$0.1		3 %	T lymphocyte receptor subunit
Mitsubishi Chemical / IDEC Pharmaceuticals	PB	S	11/93	Col,D,L	$1.5			Primatised anti-B7 Abs in Asia
MMD / Affymax	PB	M;S	5/91-7/92	D,E,R	$22.5	$7.5		Drug screens for IL-1, IL-2, MHC II

MMD / Affymax	PB	M;S	5/91-7/92	D,E,R	$22.5	$7.5		Drug screens for IL-1, IL-2, MHC II
MMD / Alteon	PB	D	12/90-6/98	CoP,D,E,L,S,Ter	$18.1	$5.0	50 %	Pimagedine for diabetes
MMD / Cortech	PB	S	6/87-12/96	E,L,R,Ter,W	$19.2	$7.6	10 %	Elastase Inhibitors
MMD / ImmuLogic	PB	S	2/92-10/96	E,L,Lo,R,Ter	$90.0	$18.0	50.1 %	Allergen-specific therapeutics
MMD / Novopharm	PP	D	8/93	Mkt				Sucralfate for ulcers & metformin for diabetes
Mylan Laboratories / VivoRx	PB	D	9/95	D,E,R		$15.0		Cell therapy for diabetes
Neocrin / CytoTherapeutics	BB	D	12/93	Ast,L,Tec	$2.0		0 %	Diabetes programme
Neoprobe / Cira Technologies	BB	S	3/96-4/98	E,L,O			6 %	Mitogenic stimulation tech for infection & inflam
New England Medical Center / Cistron,Tufts University / Cistron,MIT / Cistron,Wellesley / Cistron	UB	M	12/83	L,R	$1.1		7 %	Human IL-1 cloning
NIH / Alexion	UB	S	12/93	O,R				CRADA for graft rejection & autoimmune
Nippon Kayaku / Signal Pharmaceuticals	PB	D	2/98	CoD,Col,L,R			50 %	Nippon Kayaku's compounds for peripheral neurorathies
Novartis / BioTransplant	PB	S	10/97	Col,D,L	$36.0			Xenotransplantation
Novartis / T Cell Sciences	PB	S	10/97	E,L,O	$25.0			Option to license sCR1
Novartis / Trega Biosciences	PB	D	5/98	D,E,L,R	$39.0			Small molecules for obesity & diabetes
Novartis / Yoshitomi	PP	S	10/97	D,L				FTY720 for transplantation
Novo Nordisk / Alanex	PB	D	10/95-12/96	Col,L,R	$4.7			Small molecules for diabetes
Novo Nordisk / Anergen	PB	D;S	8/93-3/96	CoP,D,E,L,S	$25.0	$8.0		MHC II Peptides in MS & Diabetes
Novo Nordisk / Aradigm	PB	D	6/98	D,E,L		$5.0		AERx inhaler device
Novo Nordisk / Dr Reddy's Laboratories	PB	D	3/97	L,R				Compounds for diabetes and cancer
Novo Nordisk / Dyax	PB	D	1/97	Col,D,L				Phage display for diabetes
Novo Nordisk / Lifescan	PP	D	6/95	JV				Insulin products & glucose monitors
Novo Nordisk / Mayo Foundation	UB	D	7/96	Col				Management of diabetes
Novo Nordisk / Ontogen	PB	D	9/96	D,E,L	$18.0			PTPase inhibitors for diabetes and gyn
Novo Nordisk / Scios	PB	D	5/96-9/96	L,O				Insulinotropin technology

Novo Nordisk / Trega Biosciences	PB	D	2/96	L,R,S	$4.0			Screening for diabetes and osteoporosis
NTIS / Protein Design Labs	UB	M	10/88	L			5 %	Anti-Tac MAb
NTIS / T Cell Sciences	UB	M	12/85	L	$0.1		4 %	Soluble IL-2 receptor
Ono Pharmaceutical / Shaman	PB	D	5/95-12/96	D,L,R				Plant screening for Type II diabetes
Ono Pharmaceutical / Telios	PB	M;S	8/90	D,E,L,O,R	$25.3	$15.0		TGF-beta
Ontario Cancer Institute / T Cell Sciences	UB	M	4/84-4/87	L,O,R	$0.4		5 %	TCAR protein
Orphan Europe / Sparta Pharmaceuticals	PB	S	12/95	D,Di,L				Spartaject busulfan in Europe
Ortho Pharmaceutical / Xoma	PB	D;S	3/90-4/92	E,L,S,Ter	$11.0	$5.0		XomaZyme-CD5 & -CD7
Ortho-McNeil / Ergo Science	PB	D	2/98	CoD,E,L	$40.0	$10.0	50 %	Bromocriptine for diabetes and obesity
Osteometer BioTech / Cortecs	PB	D	6/96	Col,L,R				Oral insulin for diabetes
Parke-Davis / Sankyo Pharmaceutical	PP	D	9/96	CoP,JV			50 %	Troglitazone for diabetes in US
Pasteur Merieux / Sangstat	PB	S	10/93	Col,L,Man,W				Thymoglobuline & other products
Peptide Therapeutics / Biomira	BB	S	1/96	Col,D,Man				Active Allergy Vaccine product
Perseptive Biosystems / ChemGenics	BB	M	5/96-1/97	JV,L,W			50 %	ChemGenics Pharm for drug discovery
Pfizer / Alza	PP	D	10/94	CoP				Glucotrol XL for type II diabetes in US
Pfizer / Inhale Therapeutic Systems	PB	D	1/95	Col,D,E,L		$10.0		Pulmonary delivery for insulin
Pfizer / Scios	PB	D	9/88-5/96	Di,JV,Ter	$30.0			Meta Bio JV, metabolic diseases
Pfizer / T Cell Sciences	PB	D	8/86	D,L,R	$7.0		10 %	Arthritis & diabetes treatments
Picower Institute / Alteon	UB	D	9/91-2/93	L,R	$2.8			AGE-related research
Procept / VacTex	BB	M;S	1/96	Col,D				CD-1 system for immune system disorders
Procter & Gamble / Regeneron	PB	D	5/97-9/97	D,E,L,R,W	$135.0	$60.0		Right to all R&D projects
Repligen / T Cell Sciences	BB	M;S	10/97	Col,D				Screening for immunotherapeutics
Rhone-Poulenc Rorer / Applied Immune Sciences	PB	S	6/93-11/95	Acq,Col,E,JV,Lo,O,R	$285.0	$134.0	50 %	Cell Manipulation services

Roche Bioscience / Leuko-Site	PB	M,S	7/96	D,E,L,R				Eotaxin & CKR-3 for asthma & allergy
Rockefeller University / Alteon	UB	D	2/95	L				Peptidic glucagon receptor agonist
Rockefeller University / Alteon	UB	D	3/94-2/95	L,O				Glucagon amide & analogues
Ross / Metabolex	PB	D	2/97	D,L,Mkt,R				IPF for use in nutritional products
Salk Institute / Cantab Pharmaceuticals	UB	S	5/91	L				MAbs to CD45
Sandoz / Ajinomoto	PP	D	1/94	Col,D,Mkt				Oral antidiabetic A-4166
Sandoz / Allergan	PP	S	3/93	D,L				Cyclosporine A for eyes
Sandoz / Cytel	PB	D,S	9/89	D,E,R	$24.0	$9.0		Autoimmune & transplant therapy
Sandoz / Gensia Sicor	PB	D	12/91	CoP,D,R	$22.0			Purine compounds for diabetes
Sandoz / Procept	PB	S	9/93-1/95	CoP,D,L,Man,R	$27.0			Immunosuppressives from CD4 and CD2
Sangstat / Gensia Sicor	BB	S	3/97-12/97	E,L,S		$5.0		Supply of Cyclosporine
Sankyo Pharmaceutical / Glycomed	PB	M	2/94-6/97	Col,D,E,L	$17.0	$3.0		CAMs & Galardin for Far East
Sankyo Pharmaceutical / ImmuLogic	PB	M	5/98	D,L				Ceder pollen allergy
Sankyo Pharmaceutical / Metabasis Therapeutics	PB	D	4/97	Col,D,E,L,R		$7.2		Type II diabetes drugs
Sanwa Kagaku Kenkyusho / Telik	PB	D	1/97	D,E,L	$22.5			TRAP for drug discovery for diabetes
Schering AG / ImmuLogic	PB	M	3/95	Col,E,L,S	$35.5	$8.0		Immunotherapeutics for MS
Schering-Plough / Auto-Immune	PB	S	3/92	L,O,R,Ter	$57.0		15 %	Oral type II collagen for RA
Schering-Plough / Celltech	PB	D	12/92	CoP,D,L				MAbs for inflammation & MS
Scripps Research Institute / Cytel	UB	S	6/92-10/95	E,JV,L,R,Ter	$0.4	$0.0	47 %	Formation of Sequel Therapeutics
Scripps Research Institute / Cytel	UB	S	10/91	L,R				Sialyl LeX carbohydrate
Searle / Hybridon	PB	M	1/96	D,E,Lol,L,R,S	$176.0	$10.0		Antisense for cancer, inflammation & immunomodulation
Seikagaku Corp. / IDEC Pharmaceuticals	PB	M,S	12/94	Col,D,L	$26.0			Anti-CD23 MAbs for allergic rhinitis
Shaman / Access Pharmaceuticals	BB	D	3/97-4/97	L	$0.3			Masopracol analogues for diabetes
Sloan-Kettering / Xoma	UB	M	1/82	L,O,R	$1.0		6 %	Murine MAbs to HLA markers

Smith & Nephew / Advanced Tissue Sciences	PB	D	4/96-8/98	E,JV	$80.0	$20.0	50 %	Dermagraft JV for diabetic foot ulcers
SmithKline / Cortech	PB	S	11/95-3/97	D,L,Ter	$25.0			Bradycor for brain injury & stroke
SmithKline / Magainin	PB	D	2/97	D,Di,S	$32.5			Cytolex in N.A.
SmithKline / RIBI Immunochem	PB	S	4/96	L,S				Allergy vaccines
Sparta Pharmaceuticals / Horizon Pharmaceuticals	BB	D	12/97	Ast				PZG for diabetes
Stanford / Cantab Pharmaceuticals	UB	S	6/94	L,O				NGF receptor & ACT-4-L ligand on CD4+ T cells
Stanford / ImmuLogic	UB	M	12/91-7/93	L,O				Histamine as immune modulator
Stanford / Protein Design Labs	UB	M	7/90	L				Antagonist to gamma INF
Stanford / Sangstat	UB	M	10/91	L				HLA peptides
Stanford / SyStemix	UB	M	6/88-9/88	L				SCID-hu mammals
Stanford / T Cell Sciences	UB	M	3/85-2/87	L	$0.1		6 %	T cell receptor antigen
Stanford / Telik	UB	M	4/95	L,R				Inflammation, allergy and auto-immunity
State Univ of New York / Cortech	UB	S	6/87-7/94	E,L	$0.1	$0.0	4 %	Elastase inhibitors
Sumitomo Pharmaceuticals / Cytel	PB	S	10/91-2/95	D,E,L	$45.0	$5.0		Selectin adhesion molecules (LEC-CAMs)
Summit Pharmaceuticals / Exocell	PB	D	11/96	Di				Glycacor MAb for diabetes assay in Japan
Supragen / Zynaxis	BB	M	11/94	L,R				Zyn-Linkers for autoimmune drugs
Synergen / Selectide	BB	M;S	12/92	Col,E,L		$3.0	8 %	IL-1ra & TNFra screening
Syntex / GeneMedicine	PB	M;S	4/94	Col,E,JV,L	$25.0	$15.0		Gene therapy for inflammation
Syntex / Immunex	PB	M	10/84-8/89	L,R,S,Ter	$1.4			Interleukin-1
T Cell Sciences / ArQule	BB	S	3/96	Col,D				Non-peptidic small molecule arrays
Taisho Pharmaceuticals / Tularik	PB	M;S	4/95	D,L				Small molecules for immune in Asia
Takara Shuzo / Tanox Biosystems	PB	S	11/94	CoD	$13.0			MAbs for IgA nephropathy for Japan
Takeda / Novo Nordisk	PP	D	10/96	Col,R				Small molecule screening for Type II diabetes
Tanabe / Dura Pharmaceuticals	PB	S	8/88-11/91	D,E,R	$11.5	$10.0		Pentigetide & syn. peptides
Temple University / Aeson Therapeutics	UB	D	12/95	L				Fluasterone (DHEA) for cancer & T II diabetes

Temple University / Aeson Therapeutics	UB	D	12/95	L				Fluasterone (DHEA) for cancer & T II diabetes
Teva Pharmaceutical / Medi-Ject	BB	M	6/96	L				needle-free drug delivery system for Copaxone
Thomas Jefferson University / Raggio-Italgene	UB	M	11/92	D,L,R	$1.5			Computer-designed peptides
Torii Pharmaceutical / BioCryst	PB	S	5/96	D,E,L	$22.0	$1.5		PNP inhibitors in Japan
Tsumura / Phytera	PB	M;S	7/96	D,L,R				Screening of ExPAND plant cell culture
UC Berkeley / Vion Pharmaceuticals	UB	S	7/94	O,R	$0.8		5.5 %	Biomedical microcapsule
UC San Diego / Dura Pharmaceuticals	UB	M	7/81-1/87	L	$0.1		5 %	Allergy-blocking polypeptide
UC San Diego / Signal Pharmaceuticals	UB	S	2/98	E,L		$0.0		Transcription factors in p38 pathway, MKK3 and MKK4
UC San Francisco / Cell Genesys	UB	M	12/91	L				TCAR transduction
UC San Francisco / Genentech	UB	D	8/76-6/80	L,R	$0.4			Insulin, hGH & IGF-1
UC San Francisco / Procept	UB	M	1/92	R				Inhibitors of CD2-CD4
University of Alberta / Briana Bio-Tech	UB	M	5/97-10/97	LoI,L				Synthetic peptide for MS
University of Cambridge / Cantab Pharmaceuticals	UB	M	8/89-3/92	L,R				Cell lines for MAbs
University of Chicago / Centocor	UB	M	2/83	O,R	$0.1			MAbs to T & B cells
University of Florida / Ixion Biotechnology	UB	D	2/95-10/96	L				Islets of Langerhan for diabetes
University of Georgia / LXR Biotechnology	UB	S	6/93	L			5 %	Pollen proteinase
University of Kentucky / MedImmune	UB	S	6/94	D,L,R				Anti-T-cell MAb transplantation drug
University of Massachusetts / Diacrin	UB	D	10/90	L,R				Diabetes therapy
University of Massachusetts / Signal Pharmaceuticals	UB	S	10/97-12/97	E,L		$0.0		Transcription factors in p38 pathway, MKK3 and MKK4
University of Minnesota / Amylin	UB	D	11/91	E,L		$0.0		Diabetes treatment

University of Oxford / Cantab Pharmaceuticals	UB	S	3/93	O,R				T cell receptors
University of Oxford / Merck	UB	D	6/96	Col,R				Gene discovery for type I diabetes
University of Oxford / Oxford Gene Systems,University of Oxford / British Biotech	UB	M	4/87-4/89	L				Antigen presentation
University of Rhode Island / Cypros Pharmaceutical	UB	S	2/98	L				compounds to raise adenosine levels
University of Tennessee / Sertoli Technologies	UB	D	4/96	D,L				Cellular transplants for Type I diabetes
University of Texas / Neocrin	UB	D	7/96	L				Diabetes cell therapy
University of Texas / Somatix Therapy	UB	D	7/85	R				Human fetal cells
University of Washington / Cytel	UB	S	1/91	L,R	$0.8			SLeX/ELAM-1
University of Washington / Darwin Molecular	UB	S	10/95	L				T cell receptor technology
University of Washington / Sugen	UB	M	2/94	L				PTPase products
University of Western Ontario / Amylin	UB	D	10/96	R				Glucagon-like peptide (GLP-1) for diabetes
Upjohn / Emisphere Technologies	PB	D	5/90-3/95	E,L,Ter	$4.2	$1.0	7 %	Oral microsphere del of insulin
Upjohn / Tanabe	PP	S	11/94	Col,L				Cellular adhesion molecules
Utrecht University / Medarex	UB	M;S	1/97	Col,R				Human Fc receptors
Veterans Portland / Xoma	UB	S	2/90	L,R				T cell receptor peptides & Abs
Vical / Corixa	BB	M	5/96	D,L,O				LeIF gene encoding immunomodulator
Wake Forest University / Transkaryotic Therapies	UB	D	7/92	O,R				Diabetes project
Washington University / Alteon	UB	D	6/95	L				Pimegedine to inhibit nitric acid
Washington University / CytoTherapeutics	UB	D	3/89-3/92	L,R	$1.2		2 %	Islet encapsulation
Washington University / Sphinx Pharmaceuticals	UB	M	6/92	L,R	$5.0			Phospholipase A2
Wyeth-Ayerst / Affymax	PB	S	2/94	Col,D,E,L	$155.0	$10.0		Screening of drug targets

Wyeth-Ayerst / Emisphere Technologies	PB	D	10/88	L,O,R	$2.5		10 %	Heparin & insulin oral delivery
Wyeth-Ayerst / NanoSystems	BB	S	5/97	D,L				NanoCrystal for Rapamune
Wyeth-Ayerst / OSI Pharmaceuticals	PB	D;M	12/91-12/93	Col,L,R	$2.1			Transcription & cell adhesion
Xoma / Connetics	BB	M	6/94	L,Lo,W	$1.4			TCR peptide technology
Yamanouchi / Alteon	PB	D	6/89-9/92	E,L,R	$10.0	$3.0		Pimagedine technology
Yamanouchi / T Cell Sciences	PB	M	12/86	D,L	$3.9		6 %	TCAR diagnostics in Japan
Zaiya / Axiom Biotechnologies	BB	M	9/96	Col,D,R				Cell-based screening of DC40 receptor
Zeneca / Boston Life Sciences	PB	M;S	6/95	D,L,R	$8.0			MHC II gene transcription inhibitors
Zenyaku Kogyo / IDEC Pharmaceuticals	PB	D;M;S	5/91-11/95	Col,E,L,Ter	$9.5	$7.5	8 %	B-Cell & Autoimmune MAbs
ZymoGenetics / Corixa	PB	S	9/96	L,R				Autoimmune disease treatments

Appendix C
From the Call for Tender for the NIH Program "Autoimmunity Centers of Excellence" Released in May 1998 (NIH 1998)

"Since the affected organ system varies in different diseases, autoimmune diseases are treated by multiple clinical specialists. Thus, multiple sclerosis is treated by neurologists, type 1 diabetes, Graves' disease, and Hashimoto's thryoditis by endocrinologists, systemic lupus erythematosus, rheumatoid arthritis, and scleroderma by rheumtologists, idiopathic thrombocytopenia purpura by hematologists, and inflammatory bowel disease by gastroenterologists: many diseases will be increasingly approached by immunologic interventions, a cooperative group with the capability to evaluate a new agent[1] in any number of diseases offers considerable advantages. Increased interaction of clinical specialists in planning, performance, and evaluation of trials/studies should lead to a more coordinated approach to development of new immune-based therapies for all autoimmune diseases.

The major goal of this program is to support an integrated basic and clinical research program focused on tolerance induction and immune modulation to prevent or treat autoimmune diseases. The close interaction between basic researchers and clinicians will accelerate the translation of basic advances to the clinic and the utilization of patient materials for basic research. NIAID[2] is seeking multidisciplinary centers that emphasize new ideas, novel approaches, and state-of-the-art technology to increase our understanding of the basic mechanisms of autoimmunity and self tolerance and the translation of that knowledge to design and evaluate clinical interventions to prevent or treat autoimmune disease. The clinical components of the Autoimmunity Centers of Excellence will perform pilot or exploratory clinical trials or clinical studies, hereafter designated clinical trials/studies, in patients with autoimmune disease(s) to test, evaluate, develop, or determine mechanism of action of agents or interventions to prevent or treat autoimmune diseases by induction of tolerance or immune modulation. While

---

[1] Agents = "agents which block co-stimulatory signals (anti-CD40L, CTLA4-Ig) or cytokines (anti-TNF-alpha, TNFR:Fc, IL-1Ra), interrupt or alter binding of antigen to MHC (antigen peptides, MHC peptides, peptide oligomers), or modulate the appearance and activity of regulatory cells (various cytokines and anti-cytokines)" (NIH 1998).

[2] National Institute of Allergy and Infectious Diseases.

industry has supported some translational activities, industrial-supported trials have generally not focused on questions about basic mechanisms of action of these agents. Collaboration of the Autoimmunity Centers of Excellence with industry in performance of clinical trials/studies and adjunct basic mechanistic studies is encouraged." (NIH 1998)